D1481860

REALIGNING AMERICA

American Presidential Elections

MICHAEL NELSON

JOHN M. MCCARDELL, JR.

REALIGNING AMERICA

MCKINLEY, BRYAN, AND
THE REMARKABLE
ELECTION OF 1896

R. HAL WILLIAMS

UNIVERSITY PRESS OF KANSAS

Published
by the
University
Press of Kansas
(Lawrence,
Kansas 66045),
which was
organized by the
Kansas Board of
Regents and is
operated and
funded by
Emporia State
University,
Fort Hays State
University,
Kansas State
University,
Pittsburg State
University,
the University
of Kansas, and
Wichita State
University

© 2010 by the University Press of Kansas

Library of Congress Cataloging-in-Publication Data

Williams, R. Hal (Richard Hal), 1941–
Realigning America : McKinley, Bryan, and the remarkable
election of 1896 / R. Hal Williams.
        p.   cm. — (American presidential elections)
Includes bibliographical references and index.
ISBN 978-0-7006-1721-0 (cloth : alk. paper)
    1. Presidents—United States—Election—1896. 2. United
States—Politics and government—1893–1897. 3. McKinley,
William, 1843–1901. 4. Bryan, William Jennings, 1860–1925.
5. Political campaigns—United States—History—19th century.
I. Title.
E710.W485 2010
973.8'8—dc22   2009047245

British Library Cataloguing-in-Publication Data is available.

Printed in the United States of America

10 9 8 7 6 5 4 3 2 1

The paper used in this publication is recycled and
contains 30 percent postconsumer waste. It is acid free
and meets the minimum requirements of the American
National Standard for Permanence of Paper for Printed
Library Materials Z39.48-1992.

For Linda, Lise, Scott, Lori, and Ella

CONTENTS

Every election seems "critical" at the time it is held. Few seem quite so conse-
quential in the broad sweep of history. Yet most historians would agree that
of the handful of American presidential elections worthy of the designation,
that of 1896 is wholly deserving.

To make such an observation may seem to imply that there is nothing
fresh to be said about the topic. And in fact the narrative, in general at least,
is well known, often expressed as a series of "either/or" propositions: gold *or*
silver, city *or* country, farmer *or* urban worker, east *or* west, McKinley *or* Bryan. Such a formulation draws heavily on what remains the chief rhetorical
legacy of that campaign, William Jennings Bryan's famous "Cross of Gold"
speech, delivered before a rapt convention of Democratic party delegates
who hastened to award him the presidential nomination. "Burn down your
cities and leave our farms," cried Bryan, "and your cities will spring up again
as if by magic; but destroy our farms and the grass will grow in the streets of
every city in the country."

That speech also introduced a view of the competing political parties that
resonates in our own time. "There are those who believe," Bryan charged,
"that if you just legislate to make the well-to-do prosperous, that their prosperity will leak through on those below." "The Democratic idea," he continued, "has been that if you legislate to make the masses prosperous their
prosperity will find its way up and through every class that rests upon it."

Either/or. Surely a "critical" election.

The editors realized, early on, that any series on key presidential elections
must include a study of 1896. But how revisit, and reconsider, so well known
a tale? Much to our delight, R. Hal Williams, one of the preeminent scholars
of the subject, someone who has over the course of an academic lifetime ex-
amined this election closely and carefully, agreed to take on this challenging
assignment. Readers will, we hope, share our delight in the result.

For this is no mere rehash. Three interpretations stand out, and each is
likely to be a bit controversial. The first involves Bryan. This is not simply a
gifted speaker who takes the Democratic convention unexpectedly by storm.
Williams's Bryan sees an opportunity and grabs it. The nomination is a prize
he has had in view long before the convention, and by a combination of luck
(the residue of design) and calculation, he wins it, as he predicts he will.

The second involves Mark Hanna, whose "front porch" strategy, actually suggested by the candidate himself, cannily guided his candidate, McKinley, to victory. Williams actually sees Hanna as a human being rather than a caricature, as the first modern political operative who grasps how politics is changing. He is not the one-dimensional fund-raising machine so often encountered but a shrewd, insightful politician who understands what is required to get his man elected.

Finally, there is the retiring incumbent, Grover Cleveland, who fares poorly. He is no portrait in courage but rather an increasingly out-of-touch, pathetically and increasingly irrelevant chief executive, whose party repudiates him in a way no other party has ever repudiated a sitting president.

It remains a riveting story, this clash of personalities, philosophies, and campaign techniques. Recalling the election years later in a famous poem, Vachel Lindsay wrote,

There were truths eternal in the gab and tittle-tattle.
There were real heads broken in the fustian and the rattle.
There were real lines drawn.

A "critical" election, indeed.

AUTHOR'S PREFACE

The "battle of the standards," the presidential election of 1896, ranks among the most important elections in American history.[1] Political scientists and historians call it a critical election, one of a handful (1800, 1828, 1860, and 1932 were the others) that brought fundamental realignments in American politics.[2] New voting patterns replaced the old, a new majority party arose to govern the country, and national policies shifted to suit the new realities. The battle of the standards extended the decisive results of the election of 1894 and reshaped politics for decades to come. It was aptly named. Fiercely fought, the battle matched forces that drew on different traditions and pointed the nation toward alternative futures. Unfolding, it gathered a charged excitement that sparked a lifetime's memories. Those who lived through it never forgot it.[3]

This book tells the story of that election. Though it examines state and local patterns, it focuses on national events and figures, tracing the year's party battles and the development of a national party system. Conflicting parties and philosophies fought it out in the 1896 election, with the Republicans—the party of central government, national authority, sound money, and activism—defeating the Democrats—the party of states' rights, decentralization, inflation, and limited government. A third party, the People's party, added to the election's importance. Out of the decade's party battles, patterns emerged that governed the nation until the 1920s and 1930s and beyond. In that sense, the election of 1896 became a critical watershed, one of a handful of key events marking the passage between an older era and a new.

The story actually began in the late 1880s and early 1890s, when conditions affecting American farms and factories helped produce the important trends that came together in 1896. Significant elections in 1890, 1892, and 1894 set the scene as well. The story culminated in one of the most hard-fought and compelling elections in the nation's history, the stirring contest between William McKinley of Ohio and William Jennings Bryan of Nebraska. It ended, tragically, in 1901 in Buffalo, New York, with the assassination of the man who had won in 1896, himself a symbol of the transition between eras. William McKinley, in many ways a modern president, was also the last veteran of the Civil War to sit in the White House.

People who lived through the election of 1896 knew somehow it was important; something recognizable as modern America was taking shape. Industrialism, large-scale enterprise, and specialized, mechanized agriculture signaled the way of the future, yet older economic patterns still held sway. Cities grew and captured the imagination, but the majority of Americans still lived on farms and in villages. Economic expansion, fueled by enormous resources and the labor of millions of workers, established new levels of production but seemed suddenly to vanish in the decade's panic and depression, the worst depression in the nation's history until the 1930s.[4]

Despite the hardships, people clung to a sense that something called progress was afoot in the country. An onlooker only sixty years old at McKinley's first inaugural had witnessed the advent for practical purposes of steel, oil, electricity, the electric light, telephones, telegraphs, the phonograph, iron-clad warships, the use of steam in ocean travel, the vast railroad network integrating the country, and a good deal more.[5] In terms of both time and space, the world was growing smaller.[6]

It was clearly smaller in 1896. Playing a vital role in the presidential election that year, that railroad network enabled William Jennings Bryan to mount his famed cross-country campaign. It also carried some 750,000 voters to Canton, Ohio, to listen to the arguments of William McKinley. Mark Hanna, McKinley's chief adviser, and his Republican lieutenants used special telephone and telegraph lines for instant communication with the candidate and party headquarters across the country. Bryan relied on those same lines to enable newspapers to relay daily reports of his pathbreaking canvass.

The election of 1896 took place in the midst of the period's major challenges: industrial and urban growth, a crisis on America's farms, panic and depression, conflicting party philosophies, a contested financial system based on silver or gold, social turmoil, and a growing sense of the country's place in the world. Each found an outlet in the decade's politics, for politics was the period's fascination, its mass entertainment and participatory sport. Millions of Americans read party newspapers, hung on the words of party leaders, and turned out in enormous numbers for elections. In the presidential elections from 1888 through 1900, well over 70 percent of the eligible electorate voted, a figure that arouses envy today.[7] In the election of 1896, the focus of this book, the number reached nearly 80 percent. In some states that year, it stood at 95 percent.

At the start of the 1890s, men such as Grover Cleveland, William McKinley, and William Jennings Bryan little suspected what lay ahead. Filled with hardship and challenge, the coming years would try their spirits as older values gave way to new, political patterns changed and then changed again, and dissident groups swept the South and West like shadows across the landscape. Populism rose and fell and in the process questioned the country's direction, disturbed political alignments, and lent its decline to the drama of the McKinley-Bryan contest in 1896. Labor would adopt a new militancy; immigrants—4 million of them arrived during the 1890s—would demand tolerance and recognition; the issues of taxes, the tariff, silver, and gold would require attention. Through it all ran challenges that tested political parties and party leaders, who responded in meaningful ways. Most of those challenges came together in the presidential election of 1896, making it one of the most intriguing and pivotal presidential elections in our nation's history.

In researching and writing this book, I have run up many debts, above all to the extraordinary staff members at libraries and archives across the country: at the Manuscript Division of the Library of Congress, the National Archives, the Southern Methodist University (SMU) Library, the Yale University Library, the Massachusetts Historical Society, the New York Public Library, and the Harvard University Library, among many others. I also had the good fortune to have the expert assistance of Billie Katherine Stovall, in the Interlibrary Loan Department at SMU, who time and again supplied research materials I could not otherwise get.

I was pleased when John M. McCardell Jr. and Michael Nelson, the editors of this important series on American presidential elections, invited me to contribute a volume on the 1896 election, and I thank them for their careful reading and helpful suggestions. Fred Woodward of the University Press of Kansas, a legend in the field, made a significant difference from beginning to end. The office of the dean of Dedman College of Humanities and Sciences and the office of the provost at Southern Methodist University provided both time and funds to help with research and writing.

Lewis L. Gould, one of the country's leading experts in the world of American politics, read the manuscript and offered, as always, insightful suggestions. I am more grateful than I can say for his help and friendship.

Some portions of the book draw on earlier work, including "From George to George: Presidential Elections in the United States, 1788–2004," an exhibition I curated at the Bridwell Library of SMU in 2004, and *Years of Decision: American Politics in the 1890s,* first published in 1978. I am grateful to the Bridwell Library for permission to use some material from the exhibition.

Susan Harper, my research assistant and friend, gave the manuscript her hard work, efficiency, and good humor. David Lee helped with transcription.

Linda, Lise, Scott, Lori, and Ella, to whom the book is dedicated, contributed more than they can know.

R. Hal Williams
Southern Methodist University
Dallas, Texas

1

1896
THE PARTY BACKGROUND

A physician, an engineer, and a politician were once arguing about whose profession was the most important. "Mine is," the physician said. "God created Eve from Adam's rib; that meant surgery, so we physicians were there at the creation." "No, no," the engineer said. "Take one step back. God created the universe from chaos. It was the greatest engineering feat in history. We engineers had to have been there at the creation." "Fair enough," the politician replied. "But who do you think created the chaos?"[1]

Americans have long had doubts about their politicians and political system, doubts we often think of as modern but that go back in fact to the Founding Fathers and before. ("If I could not go to heaven but with a [political] party," Thomas Jefferson once said, "I would not go at all.") Yet there has also been an abiding faith in the principles of democracy, and democracy, as a number of observers have pointed out, is this country's most distinguishing characteristic and its vital contribution to modern world history.[2]

America, Jane Addams, the early twentieth-century social settlement reformer, said, was the "most daring experiment in democratic government which the world has ever seen."[3]

The idea of democracy emerged in strength in the early nineteenth century, and once it did, it spread worldwide, at least in the hopes of people everywhere. Nothing guaranteed its emergence, nor its continuance even today. "Appreciating its historically contingent nature," one scholar has noted, "allows us to recognize how breathtaking its arrival was, how extraordinary its spread has been, and how uncertain its prospects are."[4]

"Politics are much discussed," Charles Dickens, the famed British author, noted on his visit to the United States in the early 1840s. Election campaigns seemed to be going on all the time, with a common feature: as soon as the last election was over, the next one began—"which is an unspeakable comfort," Dickens remarked, "to all politicians and true lovers of their country: that is to say, to ninety-nine men and boys out of every ninety-nine and a quarter."[5]

Dickens was right. In the United States of the nineteenth century, politics almost never went away. Elections took place around the year, not just those for president or Congress but also those for a host of positions—an election of one kind or another just about every month in the calendar. New Jersey, for example, had statewide elections in March, April, May, and December. Other states did the same, and then there were district, county, city, and ward elections. Each election had its own party meetings and conventions; each had its own period of campaigning and voting. "We work through one campaign," a tired Iowa politician once complained, "take a bath, and start in on the next."[6]

"The political activity that pervades the United States must be seen in order to be understood," Alexis de Tocqueville, another famous visitor, noted. "No sooner do you set foot upon American ground than you are stunned by a kind of tumult; a confused clamor is heard on every side, and a thousand simultaneous voices demand the satisfaction of their social wants."[7]

De Tocqueville did not note it, but in the United States, politics and economics formed a peculiarly American linkage. Voting and the market were perhaps the two most important means ever devised for reaching collective decisions through individual choices.[8]

Through the first century and a half of American history, people were devoted to their political party. It gave them identity, defined social relationships, provided a way to take part in the democratic process, and offered some stake in a better future. It did something more as well. In an extraordinarily mobile society, political parties often transcended state and territorial borders, and people moving into new areas could carry with them the party slogans, rituals, and identifications they had known back home. They adjusted to the new, in short, by taking with them important parts of the old.

Belonging to a political party, people had discovered, gave them a feeling of community, "an internalized sense of history, tradition, and common values." Once perceived as divisive, as they were by Jefferson and many others, the parties became schools instead, teaching "seasonal courses in how to be Americans." Party activities became lessons in civics, their rituals visible

In "The County Election" (1852), George Caleb Bingham, a prominent nineteenth-century painter, vividly depicted the new democratic politics: the crowds packed around the polling place on the porch; the gambling, drinking, and vote trading; children playing in the dirt; and in the midst of it all, the important act of Americans voting. (Amon Carter Museum, Fort Worth, Texas)

everywhere, the language plain and understood, and they all affirmed democracy, mass participation, and the role of the people in the political process.[9]

This was all new in the nineteenth century, this popular politics, as historians have called it. It was "democratic theater," the way in which ordinary Americans took their place in the nation's political system. Torchlight parades, mass rallies, stump speeches, and election day barbecues involved and empowered them. Emotion and display—the announcement of a person's partisan loyalties and his vote—made that vote more meaningful. The politics of the street, it enabled voters and nonvoters, men and women, parents and children to take visible part in the electoral process. All told, it was almost as revolutionary as the great Revolution that gave it life.[10]

Adopting techniques that worked in this new world of popular politics, people in the last half of the nineteenth century also sang, shouted, and marched. Calling themselves the Wide Awakes—always awake against slavery—a marching group began in Hartford, Connecticut, in 1856 and spread quickly across the North, enrolling all told some 400,000 people.

In the process, they unknowingly developed the famed "military style" of campaign, in which large numbers of people carried kerosene torches and wore glazed cloth capes to fend off the dripping oil; they marched in army formations. In a riveting display, row after row of marching men, torches burning, paraded through the darkened streets of towns and cities and passed before a reviewing stand on which the candidates for election stood. Tens of thousands of people watched and cheered.[11]

"You can hardly go out after dark without encountering a torchlight procession," a visitor to Maine wrote in 1860. "In the larger places not a night passes without a demonstration of some sort." The parades, an Ohioan remarked, looked "like the waves of a river on fire." As was often the case, women found ways to take part, too, in this instance with their own Wide Awake clubs; they were clad in cambric dresses, capes of the same material, and striped aprons of red, white, and blue, "each color bearing a single letter of the word 'Abe.'"[12]

Reflecting these developments, the decades that followed the Civil War became in the eyes of historians and political scientists "the party period," the time of greatest attachment to political parties in the country's history—and no wonder: Civil War loyalties, Republican or Democratic, often lasted a lifetime.

"We love our parties as we love our churches and our families," Senator Henry Blair of New Hampshire said in 1886. "We are part of them." "What the theatre is to the French, or the bull-fight or fandango to the Spanish, the hustings and the ballot-box are to *our* people," another observer said. "We are all politicians, men, women, and children."[13]

In the antiparty atmosphere of today, this can seem strange language, but in the late nineteenth century, it rang true. Electoral politics in those years built on the deeper meanings they had acquired earlier in the century. Involving more than simply electing officials, they provided public recreation and entertainment and confirmed everyone's role in the democratic process. They linked the local with the national, as local campaigns fit into statewide results, which in turn determined the outcome in the nation at large.[14]

People actually "lived" their politics, which, in the absence of national athletic events, was their era's spectator sport. They stood in the hot sun (or driving rain) and listened to speeches of three hours or more; they read party literature; they discussed the issues at home. Campaigns enlisted whole families—fathers, mothers, and children.

Party loyalty was handed down from fathers to sons and to daughters (who in most places could not vote) as well. When a reporter from the *Springfield (Mass.) Republican* returned home after casting his vote in the 1864 presidential election, which pitted Abraham Lincoln against Democratic candidate George McClellan, he called his children into the garden and, as they watched, hung a McClellan ballot on a hook and set fire to it, while the children gave three cheers for "Old Abe." He wanted, the reporter said, to teach the children "their political duty in their youth."[15]

At election time, party workers—estimated at about 5 percent of the adult male population, the equivalent today of all the country's golfers, tennis players, and skiers—put in ten or fifteen hours a week working for their party. More than half the population attended political speeches and rallies, as many as our summer visitors to zoos, fairs, amusement parks, and outdoor sports events put together. With its devotion to politics, that was a very different time, indeed.[16]

In 1896, the year of McKinley and Bryan, another innovation reflected the country's commitment to public politics, the arrival of the celluloid pinback button, which then spread more rapidly than any other single item in the history of American politics. In the 1896 campaign alone, more than a thousand varieties of celluloid buttons promoted the presidential candidates. They were cheap (often costing less than a penny apiece), durable, and attachable to clothing. Able to display any artwork that could be printed on a paper disk, they made possible an array of designs and colors that the solid metal badges of an earlier era could not carry.[17]

Highly visible, the new buttons conveyed a wide range of candidate and party messages. Wearing them on their shirts or lapels, voters could declare their political preferences for everyone to see.[18] Buttons backing McKinley usually featured his likeness and appealing slogans such as "The Advance Agent of Prosperity" or "A Full Dinner Pail," both promising an early return to prosperity after the hardships of the early 1890s. Those for Bryan almost always drew on the silver issue, making his campaign, in the judgment of experts in campaign memorabilia, the most sharply focused since John C. Frémont's Republican campaign in 1856, a telltale sign of a pattern that in the end helped to defeat the Nebraskan. For McKinley or Bryan, buttons and images proliferated, with at least 2,000 different items for the 1896 campaign, virtually double the number produced in any previous presidential election.[19]

The buttons could reveal a voter's choice for everyone to see, but another recent innovation sought to conceal it. The Australian secret ballot, which spread across much of the United States in the 1880s and 1890s, replaced in many states the timeworn system in which political parties printed their own ballots.[20] Often of different colors and sizes, those ballots alerted partisan poll watchers, who knew exactly where that vote was going. To gain some concealment, a voter could use a "paster," a thin strip of paper pasted over the name of a particular candidate on the ballot, but the rest of the ballot counted.[21]

The Australian secret ballot laws, which did in fact emerge from Australia, revolutionized the methods and processes of voting. The idea spread quickly. Massachusetts first adopted it in 1888, and by 1892, three-fourths of the states had followed. Under the new system, the state, not the party, printed the ballots, making sure they came in a uniform format regardless of party, for voters to mark in private and place, again in private, in a ballot box. Ballot reformers, of course, were delighted, but like many reforms, the secret ballot brought unforeseen consequences. Australian laws almost always called for "blanket" ballots that listed on a single ballot the candidates of all parties instead of just those of one party, a system that discouraged split tickets and third parties. Since a candidate's name, by law, could appear only once on a single ballot, the blanket ballot made it harder to "fuse" separate tickets in a strategy that had once enabled minority parties to combine various candidates in order to win. It also made it harder for poor whites, immigrants who could not read or write, and southern blacks to vote. In unexpected ways, it helped in the long run to decrease voter turnout.[22]

An eye-catching example of the new pin-back buttons, in this case a patriotic
set of flowing ribbons in vivid red, white, and blue, making clear this voter's
support for candidate William McKinley. (Hervey A. Priddy Collection,
Bridwell Library, Southern Methodist University, Dallas, Texas)

Several other features set politics apart in these years, the final decades, as political scientists have said, of the third-party system: elections were close, the franchise expanded, and people voted in extraordinary numbers.[23]

In national elections, sixteen states, mostly in the North, consistently voted Republican; fourteen states, mostly in the South, consistently voted Democratic. Elections, therefore, turned on a handful of "doubtful" states, which could swing elections either way. These states—New York, New Jersey, Connecticut, Ohio, Indiana, and Illinois—received special attention at election time. Politicians looking to win lavished money and time on them; presidential candidates usually came from them. From 1868 to 1912, eight of the nine Republican presidential candidates and six of the seven Democratic candidates hailed from these doubtful states, especially New York and Ohio.

As a result, late nineteenth-century elections were close, the closest the country has ever experienced. In the five presidential elections between 1876 and 1892, an average differential of only 1.4 percent separated the Republican and Democratic candidates. The Republicans managed to win three of the five races, but they captured the majority of the popular vote in none of them, and they had a plurality only once, in 1880, and then it amounted to a scant 9,457 votes out of over 9.2 million cast. Republicans Rutherford B. Hayes and Benjamin Harrison won the presidency in 1876 and 1888, respectively, even though they actually trailed in the popular vote. Grover Cleveland's winning margin in 1884 over James G. Blaine came to about 29,000 out of 10 million votes cast.[24]

Building on patterns that had started early in the century, the franchise again grew. The adoption of the Fifteenth Amendment in 1870 gave the vote to most adult males, black as well as white—at least for a time. What was more, in twenty-two states, aliens could vote as well as citizens, and in much of the country, restrictions against officeholding diminished. Alabama, Missouri, Virginia, and Arkansas no longer required that their governors be born in the United States. New Hampshire, which had mandated that only Protestants could serve in state offices, dropped the provision in 1877, as did Massachusetts for its governor in 1892 and Delaware for its U.S. senators in 1897.[25]

Lastly, people turned out to vote in remarkable numbers, the highest percentage in the nation's history. Large numbers of people, it is important to remember, remained unable to vote. Women could vote in national elections only in Wyoming and Utah, in Colorado (after 1893), and in Idaho (after 1896). In recognition of their supposedly natural role as mothers, women could vote in school board elections in seventeen states, and in three states, those who owned property could vote on measures involving taxes and bonds. African Americans, Asian Americans, and other minorities were also often kept from the polls.[26]

But among those who could vote, turnout was astonishingly high, averaging just under 80 percent of eligible voters in the presidential elections between 1868 and 1892, numbers unequaled before or since. In the presidential election of 1876, turnout nationwide reached 81.8 percent, the historical high for a presidential election. In only one presidential election— 1872—did the turnout sink below 75 percent, and in 1896, almost eight voters in every ten went to the polls to vote for president.[27]

In parts of the North, the numbers were dazzling. In Indiana, turnout averaged 93 percent in the presidential elections between 1868 and 1892; in New Jersey, 89 percent. In the 1896 race for the presidency, more than 95 percent of the eligible voters cast ballots in the Midwest.[28]

To get these large turnouts, politicians in the period perfected the "army" or "military style" of campaigning, which got its start in the 1850s and then grew dramatically in the decades after the Civil War. It seemed natural enough: people of the era had lived, after all, through the massive battles of the Civil War, and there were hundreds of thousands of Union and Confederate veterans who could not wait to march.[29]

In this new military style, elections became battles, the two parties formed armies, voters were troops, and the polls were the battlefield. "Even the language of politics," as one historian has noted, "was cast in military terms." At the *opening gun* of the *campaign,* the *standard-bearer,* along with his fellow *warhorses, rallied* the *rank and file* around the party *standard.* Precinct *captains* set their *phalanxes* to *mobilize* voters; party *headquarters* used their *war chests* to *enlist* supporters; party literature *armed* men for *battle;* and, on election day, the *well-drilled* ranks overwhelmed the opponent's *camp* and claimed the *spoils* of victory.[30]

The military style lasted roughly through the late 1880s, though remnants of it could be seen many years later, including an impressive flare toward the close of William McKinley's 1896 campaign. Since virtually everyone belonged to one party (army) or the other, the party's task was not so much to convert voters to the cause as to get them out on election day. To do that, it employed badges, uniforms, parades, and mass gatherings to draw crowds to listen to party speakers. Fireworks and cannon fire simulated the battlefield.[31]

Torchlight parades were the key to it all. Young Herbert Hoover never forgot the first torchlight parade he ever saw. It was 1880, and he was six years old. "I was not only allowed out that night, but I saw the torches being filled and lighted," he recalled years later. "I was not high enough to carry one but I was permitted to walk alongside the parade."[32]

Often, the parades were huge. When the revered James G. Blaine went to Indianapolis to stump for Benjamin Harrison in 1888, there were 25,000 marchers, forty brass bands, and dozens of flag-laden floats; it took an hour and a half for the marchers to pass the reviewing stand, and something on the order of 100,000 people looked on. On October 31, 1896, well after the military style had begun to wane, over 100,000 people marched for Republican candidate William McKinley in a "sound money" parade down Broadway in New York City.[33]

Disliking stalemate, the Republicans worked hard throughout the 1880s to end it. For nearly a dozen years before 1888, the two parties had been so evenly balanced that neither dared take chances. Presidential elections were notoriously close, as were races for Congress. Less than 2 percentage points separated the total Republican and Democratic vote for congressmen in all but one election between 1878 and 1888. Such margins affected the party system, making politicians cautious and giving no one the majority needed to govern.[34]

Unlike Republicans, the Democrats found this situation rather congenial. Like all politicians, they enjoyed winning elections but usually for their symbolic value and to keep activist-minded Republicans from power. Democrats believed in states' rights, decentralization, and limited government—a trilogy as suited to stalemate as to victory. "No man," one of their leaders had once written, "has the right or duty to impose his own convictions upon others."[35] The remark measured Democratic policy, since government in almost any form meant imposing convictions on others. In the late 1880s, the tradition was kept alive by Cleveland; William E. Russell, the popular young governor of Massachusetts; William L. Wilson, a smart, up-and-coming congressman from West Virginia, and other Democrats. Wilson in particular liked to quote Albert Gallatin's early dictum: "We are never doing as well as when we are doing nothing."[36]

As a consequence, most Democratic policies took on a distinctly negative cast. In the language of party platforms, Democrats "viewed with alarm" rather than "pointed with pride." They sought to slash federal activity, cut expenditures, repeal laws, and end governmental interference in the affairs of private citizens. Even their most recent issue, tariff reform, which had a positive and constructive sound, reflected the party's traditional demand for the separation of government and business. Although a few Democrats worried about the effects of negativism, wondering whether the party might actually become incapable of governing, most preferred to follow the popular Cleveland, whose initial term in the White House (1885–1889) had lifted Democratic spirits and defined the party's vision. During that term, Cleveland had vetoed over two-thirds of the measures presented to him, more than all his predecessors combined.[37]

Whenever doubts arose, Cleveland and the Democrats had only to point to the obvious appeal of their policies. Unlike the Republicans, whose strength dwindled south of the Potomac, Democrats won adherents throughout the country. Southerners above all embraced Democratic laissez-faire and not simply for reasons of tradition. Energetic governments under Republican leadership might intervene to protect African American voters in the region's elections and disrupt segregation.[38]

Elsewhere, people weary of Reconstruction commitments, resentful of taxation, and suspicious of centralization gravitated toward Democratic ranks. In an era when religious affiliation helped mold political views, Roman Catholics, German Lutherans, and other nonmoralistic groups welcomed Democratic opposition to Prohibition, Sabbatarian legislation, and similar attempts to use government to control individual standards of behavior. From immigrants to entrepreneurs, there were many in the late nineteenth century who approved the Democratic "master-wisdom of governing little and leaving as much as possible to localities and to individuals."[39]

Democratic negativism irritated Republicans, who enjoyed governing. A party that had started by telling slaveholders to keep slavery out of the territories was seldom afraid to display its convictions to others. Since then, according to party histories, Republicans had won the Civil War, emancipated the slaves, reunited the nation, guided Reconstruction, and passed the legislation that had brought the country to its present peak of industrial and agricultural growth. The Democrats had opposed it all.[40] "Progress is of the essence of Republicanism," said Thomas B. Reed of Maine. "To have met great emergencies as they arose has been our history. To meet emergencies as they shall arise must be our daily walk and duty, or we cease to be."[41]

Republicans took immense pride in their party's record. Large differences in outlook and issues set them apart from their Democratic opponents. Whereas Democrats stressed the local and negative, Republicans pursued a national vision, in which local interests merged into nationwide patterns and government became an instrument to promote moral and material growth. Reed captured some of the distinction with his usual wit: "The Republican party does things, the Democratic party criticizes; the Republican party achieves, the Democratic party finds fault." It was a partisan judgment but one that outside observers confirmed. Beatrice Webb, the British socialist, noted that Republicans "represented a faith in centralized power, in the capacity of the few who are in authority at the centre of the state or the municipality to regulate the many and manage the affairs."[42]

In 1888, to Republican delight, that faith in the party's values seemed to be rewarded at last. Benjamin Harrison, the Republican presidential nominee, won the White House, and the Republicans captured control of both houses of Congress, a twin victory that neither party had been able to claim since Reconstruction, a dozen years before. Electing Reed as Speaker of the House, House Republicans adopted over bitter Democratic objections new and controversial parliamentary rules that expedited business and blocked Democratic obstructions. The famed Fifty-first Congress passed a flood of important legislation that measured the Republican vision.[43]

It enacted the McKinley Tariff, which raised tariff rates to new levels, but included imaginative "reciprocity" provisions that enabled the president to lower rates on specific products to stimulate overseas trade, particularly with Latin America. For the first time, too, the act also offered high duties on a handful of "infant industries," such as manufacturing tinplate, used in the growing canning business, to create an entirely new domestic industry, in this case drawing on recently discovered tin ores in South Dakota's Black Hills.

The Dependent Pensions Act granted liberal pensions to Union army veterans, their widows, and their children. Both Republicans and Democrats joined in passing the Sherman Antitrust Act, one of the first federal attempts to regulate big business. The Sherman Silver Purchase Act responded to widespread agitation for the use of more silver in the currency, directing the Treasury to purchase 4.5 million ounces of silver a month and to issue legal tender in the form of Treasury notes in payment for it. Finally, Republicans in the House courageously passed a federal elections bill, which Democrats dubbed the force bill, to protect the voting rights of African Americans in the South. Unpopular in much of an increasingly racist country, the bill showed the ongoing commitment among many Republicans to older ideals of racial progress.[44]

The Fifty-first Congress was one of the most productive congresses in the country's history. Together, the House and Senate passed a record number of laws, including significant measures dealing with the tariff, silver, pensions, and antitrust issues. One of them, the Sherman Antitrust Act, continues to shape policy today. But in an era in which large numbers of voters distrusted the power of the federal government, the session posed large risks for Republicans, which Democrats happily seized upon. "From its organization down," a Democrat immediately complained, "this Congress has been a raging sea of ravenous legislation. . . . The friends of the people have only a moment to cry out before they are swept overboard to make their moans to the winds and the waves. It is not the voice of the people. It is an instrument of tyranny."[45]

The Republicans, of course, had foreseen the risks. Parties that did things were vulnerable to attack, as Reed noted waspishly: "Human nature seems incapable of prolonged virtue. It is hard to keep people always up to the Republican program." It would be especially hard as voters went to the polls in November 1890, many of them clearly uncertain about the activism of the Fifty-first Congress. Coining a telling campaign theme, the Democrats labeled it the Billion Dollar Congress and charged that the Republicans had spent that much in appropriations, subsidies, and pension grants. "[It is] a Billion Dollar Country," Reed retorted, deflecting the charge without really answering it. Voters at least had a clear choice, for the Republican Fifty-first Congress had set the issues and outlooks for the coming decade.[46]

So, in a sense, had the Republicans in several states in the Midwest, especially in Iowa, Illinois, and Wisconsin. There, as on the national level, they had used the power of government to pursue party ideals. They had governed in ways that intruded in private affairs and offended large numbers of voters. In Iowa, Republicans fought for Prohibition, hoping to end the evils of drink as they had earlier ended the evils of slavery. In Illinois and Wisconsin, they passed public school laws, well-intentioned measures that required children to attend school a prescribed number of weeks each year.

All three states illustrated broader Republican trends, since at the same time Republicans in Boston and elsewhere were "reforming" public school laws, and Republicans in Ohio, Indiana, and Nebraska were working for temperance. In cities and states across the nation, Republicans were trying, as a prominent Iowa Republican put it, "to make a police sergeant out of the party," and now, in November 1890, they were discovering that thousands of voters recoiled from the idea.[47]

In particular, many voters did not like the way the party's measures reflected certain religious precepts. Religious views, especially the tensions between liturgicals and pietists, strongly shaped political alignments in late nineteenth-century America. Members of liturgical religions—Catholics, German Lutherans, Episcopalians, orthodox Calvinists, and others—stressed the institutions and rituals of the church, assigned the church responsibility for individual morality and salvation, and consequently restricted the role of the state in prescribing personal morality. As a rule, they tended to cast their lot with the Democratic party, which also set limits on state authority.

Members of pietist churches, by contrast, tended to prefer the Republican party, with its expansive, activist outlook. Pietists—Methodists, Congregationalists, some Presbyterians, and others—played down church ritual and believed in individual salvation, confirmed in a life of pure behavior. The state, they thought, was an appropriate instrument to achieve those ends. It should promote morality and purify society, through Prohibition, Sunday-closing laws, and other measures.[48]

In Iowa, Republican pietists took control of the state party during the 1880s and pushed Prohibition measures through the legislature. "A school house on every hill, and no saloon in the valley" became their slogan. Soon, there were also fewer Republicans in Iowa hills and valleys, as angry German Lutherans and Catholics flocked in protest to the Democratic party.[49] In Illinois, Republican pietists in 1889 passed the Edwards law, which served as the model for Wisconsin's subsequent Bennett law. Both laws mandated school attendance and defined a school in terms of teaching certain subjects "in the English language." Liturgically minded voters, including the region's German immigrants, numbering in the tens of thousands, were aghast. The Republicans were threatening church, family, and language.

Democrats skillfully exploited the opening, pointing out the larger pattern. In both nation and state—whether it was the McKinley Tariff, Prohibition, the force bill, Reed's tyrannical rules, or the Bennett law—the Republicans seemed bent on abusing power and encroaching on individual liberties. The issues were emotional and extremely effective. Roger Q. Mills, a leading Texas stump speaker, brought a Wisconsin audience to its feet. "Who has given to any State," he thundered, "the right to invade the family fireside and deprive the mother who has nursed the child, and upon whose bosom it has lain, of the right of training the child?"[50]

No one, if the region's voters had their way. In the November 1890 elections, they swept the Republicans out of office in all three states. Wisconsin Republican leaders, surveying wreckage that included a lost governorship, legislature, Senate seat, and congressional delegation, spoke of "the terrible blizzard" that had struck their party. "The worst feature of the situation," noted the state chairman, "is the almost hopeless task of getting back our

German Republicans without whose help it is impossible to carry Wisconsin." The results in Illinois were only slightly less spectacular. Republican candidates fell everywhere, as Democrats took the governorship, a Senate seat, and majorities in the legislature and Congress.[51]

Iowa, which had once seemed so safely Republican that Jonathan P. Dolliver, the state's Republican senator, predicted that "Iowa will go Democratic when Hell goes Methodist," again went Democratic, as it had the year before. In 1889, thanks largely to the temperance issue, it had elected its first Democratic governor in a third of a century. Now, with the same Prohibition-sparked influences at work, it elected Democrats to six of its eleven seats in the House of Representatives. Republicans were stunned, uncertain how to reverse the forces they had set in motion. Jubilant Democrats believed they had suddenly found the key to dominance in the Midwest. For the moment, at least, they were right, but Republicans were resourceful, and the battle was far from over. It would not really end until the exciting, crucial elections of 1894 and 1896.[52]

At the time, however, there was no hiding the devastation. Across the nation, voters in 1890 deserted the Republican party in droves. "IT IS REVOLUTION," headlined the *St. Louis Republic*. "On the face of the first returns, it is hard to see what the Republicans have left." The Republicans, in truth, had virtually nothing left. They lost 78 seats in the House, a reversal of political fortunes rarely equaled in the history of congressional elections. Instead of 166 Republican members, the next House would have 88, the Democrats 235. The totals were stunning, as was the extent of the damage. Republican candidates were overwhelmed even in areas of traditional party strength. They lost badly in New England, the Midwest, and on the plains. The force bill and other issues inflated the usual Democratic majorities in the South. Dazed, President Harrison called it "our election disaster" and hoped it indicated only the midterm reversal customary to American politics.[53]

Privately, of course, Harrison knew better. The elections ruptured party alignments that had existed since the Civil War, thirty years before. Of the tier of Republican states that had once stretched from New England to the Pacific, only California, Colorado, Maine, Vermont, and a few other outposts remained. New England Democrats, accustomed to Republican supremacy, could scarcely credit the returns. Democrat William E. Russell won the governorship of Massachusetts, and the state chose seven Democratic congressmen. For the first time in decades, the Democrats had a majority of the New England delegation in the House. In Ohio, McKinley lost as expected, though he foreshadowed the Republican future with an extraordinary pro-tariff campaign that brought him within 300 votes of victory in his gerry-mandered district. But still he lost, and he was joined in defeat by such party luminaries as John C. Spooner and Robert M. La Follette, both from Wisconsin; Joseph G. Cannon of Illinois, chairman of the House Appropriations Committee; and John J. Ingalls of Kansas, a Republican patriarch who had been in the Senate since 1873.[54]

Defeats were numerous. The Republicans lost six House seats in Wisconsin, seven in Illinois, four in Iowa, one in Indiana, six in Michigan, nine in Ohio, five in Kansas, three in Nebraska, and four in Missouri. As older faces disappeared, new politicians vaulted into sudden prominence, including a young man from Lincoln, Nebraska—William Jennings Bryan, who was swept into Congress by the Democratic landslide of 1890.

Attuned to farm problems, Bryan and others welcomed evidence that the Farmers' Alliance, a rapidly growing organization of reform-minded farmers, had scored heavily in the elections. Alliance leaders boasted that the movement had influenced or controlled 2.5 million votes, almost a quarter of the total votes cast for president in 1888. No one could confirm the figure, but it was impressive nonetheless. Leonidas L. Polk of North Carolina, the eloquent and tireless president of the alliance, claimed thirty-eight avowed alliance men elected to Congress, with at least a dozen more pledged to alliance principles. The *National Economist,* the official newspaper of the order, raised the estimate to forty-four alliance members in Congress and sympathetic senators from six states.[55]

Farmers in the South and West were fed up—with low crop prices, high railroad rates, and mortgages they could scarcely bear. In the South, they called the official history of the alliance *The Impending Revolution,* and they meant it. "The spirit of rebellion against the many evils is growing," it said. "Thousands of men who have already lost all hope of a peaceful solution to the great question of human rights are calmly waiting the issue." "The farmers of the United States are up in arms," another observer wrote. "They are the bone and sinew of the nation; they produce the largest share of its wealth; but they are getting, they say, the smallest share for themselves."[56]

Southerners were particularly angry, victims of a regional economy that lagged far behind the rest of the nation. By 1890, many of them had had their fill of its chief characteristics: crop liens, depleted lands, cheap cotton, sharecropping, and living standards comparable to those of European peasants. As a Georgia farmer wrote:

We worked through spring and summer,
    through winter and through fall;
But the mortgage worked the hardest and
    the steadiest of them all;
It worked on night and Sunday, it worked
    each holiday;
It settled down among us and it never went away.

Whatever we kept from it seemed almost
    as bad as theft;
It watched us every minute and ruled us
    right and left
The rust and blight was with us sometimes, and
    sometimes not;
The dark brown scowling mortgage was
    forever on the spot.

The weevil and the cut worm, they went as
    well as came;
The mortgage stayed forever, eating hearty
    all the same
It nailed up every window, stood guard
    at every door;
And happiness and sunshine made their
    place with us no more.[57]

Alliance growth, swift and startling, upset political patterns and dismayed politicians in the South and West. As a southern Democrat said: "I don't know how it is in the West, but in my country these blatant demagogues that the Farmers' Alliance send out have raised the very deuce." Republicans knew very well how it was in the West. Farmers were breaking away from the Republican party, with a determination that resisted the normal blandishments. "I never seen the time before but what I could soothe the boys down and make them feel good," a Dakota Republican wrote in July 1890, "but seemingly this fall they are not to be 'comforted.'"[58]

In Kansas, the alliance-related People's party, organized just a few months before, shocked the Republicans in the 1890 election. It elected four congressmen, took control of the lower house of the legislature, and deposed Senator Ingalls, "the innocent victim," he said, "of a bloodless revolution—a sort of turnip crusade, as it were." William A. Peffer, a prominent Populist attorney and newspaper editor, took Ingalls's place and gained instant national prominence. Elsewhere in the Midwest, Nebraska elected a Democratic governor for the first time in its history.[59]

Aggressive farm leaders emerged in both the South and the West. In Georgia, it was Thomas E. Watson, a talented orator and organizer, a small and active, hot-tempered man with a thin face and dark-red hair brushed back from his forehead. In 1890, fed up with the desperate conditions of Georgia farmers, he won a race for Congress as an "independent" candidate on the Democratic ticket. Across Watson's South, the alliance won a swath of victories based on "the Alliance yardstick," a demand that Democratic party candidates pledge support for alliance measures in return for the organization's endorsement. When the elections were over, alliance leaders claimed on that basis a majority in eight southern legislatures, as well as six alliance-elected governors, including those in South Carolina, Georgia, Tennessee, and Texas.[60]

In the West, Jeremiah Simpson of Kansas, one of the most able of the newcomers, won a seat in Congress in 1890. Reflective and well read, a follower of the single-tax reformer Henry George, Simpson pushed for social and economic change. "We reformers," he said, "are fighting for a mud ball as big as a boulder; what we permanently win will be no larger than a diamond, but it will be a diamond."[61]

Mary E. Lease—"Our Queen Mary," her alliance friends called her—joined Simpson on the Kansas lecture trail. Thirty-seven years old, tall and slender, she had trained herself as a lawyer and become interested in woman suffrage, temperance, and other reform issues. On the lecture platform, she sparkled, hurling sentences "as Jove hurled thunderbolts." One of those sentences, urging Kansas farmers to raise less corn and more hell, became famous nationwide, though she may never have said it. Lease made 160 speeches during that alliance summer of 1890, calling on farmers to rise against Wall Street and the manufacturing East.[62]

Annie L. Diggs, also from Kansas, attracted a sizable following in a movement remarkably open to female leadership. Farther north, in Minnesota, Ignatius Donnelly brushed aside other leaders to take charge of the burgeoning movement on the northern plains. Donnelly was restless and irascible, a nationally known social critic who wrote several utopian novels, dabbled in reform politics, and "proved" that Shakespeare had not written his own plays. In 1890, he pushed long-cherished reforms and had large political ambitions, which the alliance movement might satisfy.[63]

Expansive in victory, President Polk called in reporters. "We are here to stay," he told them. "This great reform movement will not cease until it has impressed itself indelibly in the nation's history." A few days later, he talked with reporters again. Democrats should be delighted with their sweeping victory, Polk said, but victory also brought responsibilities. They now had to enact alliance reforms, or "a third party is inevitable," in the South as well as the rest of the country. "[We] are determined to gain the ends [we] are striving for, and will smash any party that opposes them."[64]

As Harrison and other Republicans recognized, the year's devastation indicated dramatic shifts in voting patterns, perhaps even the onset of Democratic hegemony. Clearly, it thrust the Democrats far into the lead for the presidential election of 1892. Somehow, since 1888's remarkable victory, Republicans had lost touch with voters, something they would have to remedy if victory were to come again. On one level, they needed to take a close look at that "police sergeant" impulse toward moral and social reform, which seemed to alienate more people than it converted. On another, they needed to review the work of the Fifty-first Congress, its measures and outlook, and the way both had been presented to the people. And finally, they needed to evaluate the challenge in the Midwest and West of this new People's party.

Public opinion seemed clear, at least for the moment. The Republicans had gone too far, raised tariffs too high, imposed values too widely, legislated too much. The judgment galled party leaders, who believed they had acted constructively in a fashion rarely seen in the past. "The sting of the present defeat," as Henry Cabot Lodge, a promising young member of the House of Representatives from Massachusetts, said in his diary, "lies in the fact that the Republican party never since the war deserved so well." That was true, perhaps, but Lodge and his fellow Republicans needed to learn from the sting and adjust approaches for the future. That was all they could do. For now, the Democrats, it was clear, were firmly in charge, and more challenges lay ahead.[65]

Grover Cleveland, the triumphant but soon beleaguered Democratic president. (Library of Congress, Washington, D.C.)

2
THE DEMOCRATS IN POWER, 1893–1896

When I consider all that we have to do as a party charged with the control of the Government, I feel that our campaign, instead of being concluded, is just begun.
—Grover Cleveland, November 1892[1]

Inauguration Day 1893 dawned cold and blustery. Rain had turned to snow during the night. Freezing winds whipped the streets of Washington, shredding flags and ripping the inaugural bunting along the parade route. Spectators shivered in the cold. To their relief, Grover Cleveland kept his inaugural address short, taking fewer than twenty minutes to outline the course of the incoming administration. Under the Democrats, government would be limited, frugal, free from "the unwholesome progeny of paternalism" that had marred the presidency of Benjamin Harrison. "The lessons of paternalism ought to be unlearned and the better lesson taught that while the people should patriotically and cheerfully support their Government its functions do not include the support of the people." The voters' verdict was clear, Cleveland said. On this day, they turned over control of the government to a party "pledged in the most positive terms to the accomplishment of tariff reform."[2]

Building on his party's triumphs in the 1890 elections, Cleveland could celebrate an impressive victory in 1892, the most decisive victory, in fact, since the first election of Ulysses S. Grant in 1872. He won 5,555,426 votes to Harrison's 5,182,690, a margin of nearly 400,000 votes, large by the era's standards. He carried the South; many of the doubtful states, including New York, New Jersey, Connecticut, and Indiana; and part of the electoral vote of several other states, including California. He also took Wisconsin and Illinois, the first Democratic candidate to do so since the 1850s. The Democrats won control of both houses of Congress. A large share of the labor vote and increased strength in the cities gave added significance to their achievement. Gaining strikingly among immigrant, Catholic, and labor voters, they carried New York, Chicago, San Francisco, Milwaukee, Harrison's own Indianapolis, and other cities. Disgruntled Republicans complained that "the slums of Chicago, Brooklyn and New York" had decided the election, but the complaint measured envy as much as anything else. The Democrats had won votes virtually everywhere.[3]

The Democrats not only had capitalized on Republican weaknesses but also had beaten back the continued challenge of the People's party in the South. The Populists had opened the campaign with high hopes.[4] At an emotional convention in Omaha, Nebraska, in July, they adopted a spirited platform calling for the free coinage of silver, an improved banking system, a graduated income tax, government ownership of the means of transportation and communication, and other reforms. Determined to cut away from the old parties, many of them planned to nominate for president North Carolina's Leonidas L. Polk, the popular and energetic head of the National Farmers' Alliance, who was telling friends that an independent Populist ticket would carry eight southern states and at least fourteen northern ones. But Polk, to people's dismay, died suddenly in June, and the Omaha convention had to turn elsewhere—to James B. Weaver of Iowa, a former congressman, Union army general, and third-party candidate (on the Greenback Labor party ticket) for president in 1880.[5]

An experienced campaigner, Weaver immediately took the stump to make up for the Populists' lack of an extensive organization and party press, much as William Jennings Bryan would do on a far larger scale four years later. He found the going difficult, especially in the South, where Democrats did not tolerate dissent. Night riders and hired toughs jostled his audiences and intimidated Populist sympathizers. The situation deteriorated as Weaver moved farther into the South, until a mob in Macon, Georgia, hurled rotten eggs, tomatoes, and rocks at the candidate and his wife.[6]

At that, Weaver regretfully called off the rest of his southern campaign and, accompanied by the fiery Mary E. Lease—"she could recite the multiplication tables and set a crowd hooting and hurrahing at her will," an opponent once conceded—focused on the plains states and silver-mining regions of the Far West. There, audiences listened more respectfully to the Populist message. "We have a system of [financial] slavery here today as inimical to human life as that which enslaved an emancipated people," Weaver told an enthusiastic crowd in Aspen, Colorado. "We wiped that out and we are on a second crusade today."[7]

The results were only partially satisfying. Weaver won 1,029,846 votes, the first third-party candidate in American history to attract more than a million popular votes. He carried Kansas, Idaho, Nevada, and Colorado, along with portions of North Dakota and Oregon, for a total of twenty-two electoral votes. A few state and local victories, including the election of Populist governors in Kansas and North Dakota and a handful of congressmen, as well as a smashing triumph for the entire state ticket in Colorado, further brightened the picture.

But for the most part, the returns were cause for disappointment among People's party leaders. Unable to penetrate the South, Weaver had been held to less than a quarter of the vote in every southern state except one, Alabama. He lost heavily in urban areas, with the exception of some mining towns in the Far West; received little support east of the Mississippi; and failed to win over farmers in the Midwest. In Iowa, he polled barely 20,000 votes; in Wisconsin, he took less than 3 percent of the vote. In no midwestern state did he win as much as 5 percent of the vote.[8]

Local candidates did no better. The August elections in Alabama and Georgia, both thought to be Populist strongholds, overwhelmed the party's state candidates. The Democrats in both states manipulated the returns to ensure Populist defeat. Thomas E. Watson, virtually a symbol of the independent movement in the South, lost his Georgia congressional seat by a wide margin. Ignatius Donnelly ran a distant third in a race for governor in Minnesota. "Beaten! Whipped! Smashed!" Donnelly, discouraged, wrote in his diary. "Our followers scattered like dew before the rising sun."[9]

The rising sun, in truth, appeared to be Democratic that year. The nation's discontented, those fed up in one way or another with current conditions and Republican rule, had voted for the Democrats, not the Populists, a signal of the basic failure of the People's party campaign. Among the Populists, discouragement began to set in. Farmers' Alliance membership plunged dramatically in 1892, for the second year in a row. The organization, once the breeding ground of the People's party, was shattered. Still, Populist leaders rallied the forces and pointed hopefully to elections in 1894 and 1896. That was the attraction of politics: another election, another chance, always lay ahead.[10]

The Democrats now had the opportunity both parties had sought for decades. The recent election confirmed 1890's dramatic Democratic trend and indicated that a permanent change might have taken place in American politics. For the first time in nearly forty years—since, in fact, the administration of James Buchanan way back in the 1850s—the Democrats controlled the White House and both branches of Congress. Some experts thought Cleveland's victory was historic: winning a popular plurality in three consecutive elections, he had matched Andrew Jackson, his hero, the only candidate who had ever done it before.[11]

Predictions spread that the Republican party, tied to Civil War issues and unable to keep pace with the changing country, would disintegrate into bickering factions and then disappear. A new party—less activist, more attuned to current moods and interests—would take its place. "The 'performers' of the party of energy," as the perceptive *Review of Reviews* put it, the Republicans had finally lost out to the Democrats, "the 'reformers' of the party of inertia." They were finished. "There is a belief in many quarters that the Republican party is about to disappear." The sponsor of actual programs, it had suffered disastrous setbacks, in ways that would never happen to the Democrats. "The Democratic party, of course, is indestructible, because it rests on a basis of permanent principles that make [*sic*] it the natural enemy of every successive new programme of innovation that comes up demanding accomplishment through active governmental agency."[12]

Woodrow Wilson, a promising Princeton University professor of jurisprudence and political economy, agreed, predicting that the 1892 election had made the Democrats the nation's majority party: "Signs are not wanting," Wilson wrote, "that the Republican party is going . . . to pieces; and signs are fairly abundant that the Democratic party is rapidly being made over by . . . the extraordinary man who is now President."[13]

On the eve of power, Cleveland himself saw both the opportunities and the danger. At a party dinner in New York, he somberly reminded fellow Democrats of their new responsibilities: "When I consider all that we have to do as a party charged with the control of the Government, I feel that our campaign, instead of being concluded, is just begun." Cleveland was right, far more even than he knew. In the coming years, the Democratic party, amid worldwide depression and social upheaval, would face its greatest challenges.[14]

His administration under way, Cleveland went to Chicago on May 1, 1893, to open the World's Columbian Exposition, one of the focal events of the entire decade. The exposition commemorated the four-hundredth anniversary of Columbus's voyage to the New World. Even more, it celebrated modern industrial and technological progress, featuring the latest mechanical inventions in acres of white plaster buildings modeled on Greek and Roman patterns. An opening-day crowd of 200,000 wandered in awe through the White City, the "enchanted city," with its sixty buildings, shimmering lagoons, gilded statues, carved fountains, and, most important, machinery. Elaborate in its symbolism, the White City celebrated social harmony, the union of architects, craftsmen, engineers, inventors, businessmen, and laborers to create the industrial society. It fused timeless, classical forms with the hurly-burly progress of the new civilization.

The machinery went far beyond the famous Corliss steam engine that had impressed the world at the Philadelphia Centennial Exposition of 1876, only seventeen years before. It fed on a much more up-to-date wonder: the new magic of electricity. To President Cleveland, the Columbian Exposition showed "the tremendous results of American enterprise," as well as the "progress of human endeavor in the direction of a higher civilization." He touched an ivory telegraph key, and the electric current unfurled flags on the 700 flagpoles, unveiled the central statue of the American Republic, lit 10,000 electric lights, started engines, and powered fountains throughout the grounds. In Machinery Hall, the thirty-seven steam engines started at once, producing, in a reporter's words, "a sound that will thrill every observer." The exposition represented power, modern and complex. It is "a force difficult for the mind to grasp," one dazzled onlooker concluded. "It is the transformation of power into beauty."[15]

For a moment in Chicago, an era paid homage to its own material and social accomplishments. A moment, unfortunately, was all it had. Three days after Cleveland opened the exposition, the stock market in New York broke, rallied, then broke again. The American economy, so lovingly celebrated in the White City in Chicago, was in danger of collapsing.

Leaving office in 1893, President Harrison and other Republicans had pointed again and again to the prosperous conditions in the country. The Democrats, now in command in both the White House and Congress, could "reform" the tariff all they wanted, but the results of Republican stewardship were clear. "There never has been a time in our history when work was so abundant or when wages were as high," Harrison said, and he filled his final annual message with figures measuring the nation's well-being. Business journals also closed 1892, "the most prosperous year ever known," with

The famed White City of 1893, with its shimmering plaster architecture, elaborate colonnades, statuary, fountains, and plentiful machinery, all celebrating the triumph of the American way of life. (Paul V. Galvin Library, Illinois Institute of Technology, Chicago)

reports of "strongly favorable indications for the future." The reports were wrong; the figures hid developing troubles. The economy was badly over-extended, teetering on the unhappy consequences of a decade of confident expansion.[16]

Confidence dwindled perceptibly early in 1893, and investors became timid and uneasy. Uncertain currency values, an inadequate banking system, depressed agricultural prices, and declining exports sapped the economy. In mid-February, a sudden flurry of panic selling hit the stock market. In a seven-hour period, investors dumped a million shares of the Philadelphia and Reading Railroad, an industry leader, and the company promptly went under. Business investment slumped, particularly in the critical railroad and construction industries, touching off a cyclical contraction of unprecedented severity.[17]

Frightened, people hurriedly sold stocks and other assets for gold, caus-ing a crisis in the U.S. Treasury. During January and February 1893, the de-mand for gold was overwhelming, both at home and in Europe, which was also on the edge of a depression. It flowed out of the Treasury, in exchange for silver coins, greenbacks, and the Treasury notes (or silver certificates) is-sued to buy silver under the Sherman Silver Purchase Act of 1890. Eroding almost daily, the Treasury's gold reserve slumped toward the $100 million mark, an amount that over the years had become a symbolic measure of the nation's commitment to back its currency in gold.

Among those who supported the gold standard, the blame fell on the Sherman Silver Purchase Act, whose silver certificates, redeemed in gold by the Treasury, acted as a constant drain on the reserve. Before taking office, Cleveland worked privately to persuade Congress to repeal the act but with-out success. Silverites would not accept repeal without a more liberal silver law. Harrison's Treasury officials hoped just to hold the line until Inaugura-tion Day. They barely made it. On March 4, 1893, as Cleveland delivered his inaugural address, the gold reserve sank to $100,982,410.[18]

The dwindling reserve worried businessmen, who sensed disaster ahead. "I sit and wonder if you gentlemen in Washington know how very uneasy the legitimate property holders and merchants of the country are about the state of the currency," a Boston financier wrote Richard Olney, Cleveland's attorney general, in mid-April. "People are in a state to be thrown into a panic at any minute, and, if it comes, and gold is withdrawn, it will be a panic that will wake the dead." Cleveland issued reassuring statements, but there was little he could do. On April 22, for the first time since 1879, the gold reserve fell below $100 million.[19]

The news shattered business confidence. Rumors spread that another large gold shipment would leave for Europe in a matter of days, and the stock market panicked and broke. On Wednesday, May 3, railroad and industrial stocks slumped badly, followed the next day by the bankruptcy of several prominent firms. The worst was yet to come. When the exchange opened that Friday, crowds filled the galleries, anticipating a panic and a flood of selling orders. They were not disappointed. Within minutes, leading stocks plunged to record lows, amid pandemonium on the floor and in the streets outside. A brief rally at the end of the day failed to repair the damage. May 5, 1893, "Industrial Black Friday," was "a day of terrible strain," long remembered in the market.[20]

Quickly, the blows piled one on the other. Bankers called in available loans and refused to grant new loans without ample collateral. Unable to get capital, businesses failed, an average of two dozen a day during the month of May. "The papers are full of failures—banks are breaking all over the country, and there is a tremendous contraction of credits and hoarding of money going on everywhere," one observer noted on May 14. A few days later, the Northern Pacific Railroad announced bankruptcy, another shattering blow to confidence. India, a British colony, suspended free silver coinage, paralyzing the American silver market. In four days, the price of silver dropped from 81 cents an ounce to 62 cents. Mines and smelters shut down throughout the mountain states, throwing thousands out of work. Receipts on the Union Pacific Railroad, which had carried much of the ore and bullion, plummeted. On July 26, the fabled Erie Railroad, a legend in railroading history, failed and precipitated another flurry on the stock market. Desperate, officials considered closing the whole stock exchange.[21]

August was the worst month. It "will long remain memorable . . . in our industrial history," said the *Commercial and Financial Chronicle*, a leading business journal. Mills, factories, furnaces, and mines shut down everywhere. Hundreds of thousands of workers were suddenly unemployed. In Orange, New Jersey, Thomas A. Edison, the symbol of the country's ingenuity, let go 240 of his 355 employees at the Edison Phonograph Works, grumbling that "the country has resolved itself into a National lunatic asylum." On August 12, *Bradstreet's*, another prominent economic commentator, reported unemployment at 1 million people. Some economists guessed 2 million, or nearly 15 percent of the total labor force.[22]

On August 15, a fourth major railroad, the Northern Pacific, went into receivership. Other railroads followed. In mid-October, the Union Pacific— with 8,950 miles of lines and 22,000 employees—declared bankruptcy, unable to meet its payroll. In December, the Atchison, Topeka and Santa Fe did the same. Wreckage was everywhere. During 1893, some 15,000 business firms and more than 600 banks failed. At year's end, Samuel Gompers, head of the American Federation of Labor, estimated unemployment at 3 million people.[23]

"There are thousands of homeless and starving men in the streets," a young reporter wrote home from Chicago that ugly December. "I have seen more misery in this last week than I ever saw in my life before." Winter storms swept the city. Hundreds slept in City Hall and other municipal buildings, huddled in hallways and staircases, close by the Columbian Exposition's enchanted city. Charities, benevolent societies, churches, and labor unions did their best to help but could not handle the unprecedented numbers. "Famine is in our midst," said the head of the local relief committee. That December, Chicago reported 75,000 unemployed; New York City, 100,000; Boston, nearly 40,000; Philadelphia, 47,000; Pittsburgh, 16,000; San Francisco, 35,000.[24] Conditions were little better in farming areas, hit by drought and low crop prices. "The problem is how to live," one Kansas farmer said in the summer of 1893.[25]

Continuing through 1897, the depression of the 1890s was the decade's decisive domestic event. It changed lives, reshaped ideas, altered attitudes, uprooted deep-set patterns. The human costs were enormous, even among the prominent. "They were for me years of simple Hell," shattering "my whole scheme of life," said Charles Francis Adams, the heir of two American presidents. "I was sixty-three years old, and a tired man, when at last the effects of the 1893 convulsion wore themselves out." The convulsion renewed questions about the costs of industrialization; sparked labor unrest and class antagonism; and in pointing up economic interdependencies, shifted the country's focus from the local to the national. Everywhere, older assumptions gave way to newer patterns and nagging doubts.[26]

The depression, vast and unsettling, offered sudden opportunity to the Republicans and Populists, who might lure the discontented and build new coalitions. It strained sectional ties and strengthened complaints of monetary conspiracies—gold in the Northeast, silver in the South and West—to take over the land. Years of crunching hardship made tempers brittle. As a Wisconsin newspaper noted in 1896: "On every corner stands a man whose fortune in these dull times has made him an ugly critic of everything and everybody." Some were uglier than others, and there was talk of revolution and war and bloodshed. Before long, there was also sharp talk about Cleveland and the Democrats and their apparent inability to "do something" about the

In the White City, as elsewhere across the country, poverty and desperation struck quickly after the panic of 1893. (Library of Congress, Washington, D.C.)

depression. It had been their misfortune to be trapped in office as an era's assumptions collapsed. Later, Cleveland would call the 1890s the "luckless years." For the Democratic party, they were far worse than that.[27]

As he often did, Cleveland was having trouble making up his mind. Originally, he had planned to spend his first summer in office sketching out a tariff bill, to be submitted to a special session of Congress in September; he had promised Democrats he would do that, as recently, in fact, as in his inaugural address. The panic, in his thinking, killed that plan and shifted his attention to industrial failures, the shrinking gold reserve, and "the silver business," as he sourly called it. Businessmen pleaded for quick action to shore up the finances and restore confidence, especially for a special session of Congress to repeal the damaging Sherman Act. Several times, Cleveland decided to follow the advice, then pulled back at the last moment. Opponents, and some friends, later suggested the delay was intentional, to allow deepening hardship to teach the silver proponents a lesson. Delay might also weaken opposition within his own party, helping to reduce the expected damage from a fight over silver.[28]

By early summer, with panic and unemployment spreading across the country, Cleveland could put off a decision no longer. Besides, the president's doctors had just discovered that he was dangerously ill. On June 18, they found a large cancerous growth on the roof of his mouth and advised an immediate operation. Cleveland swore them to secrecy, aware that a presidential health scare would further drain the economy. On June 26, there was more startling news—India had closed its mints to silver—and Cleveland met far into the night with Secretary of the Treasury John G. Carlisle. India's action, which left Mexico the only country in the world with free silver coinage, was the event the two men had been waiting for. It threw silverites on the defensive, illustrated once again the primacy of gold in international money markets, and swung public opinion toward the repeal camp. Even moderate silver journals began to waver, wondering if repeal might help after all.[29]

Cleveland let the momentum gather, then, on June 30, he summoned Congress into special session for August 7. The current economic crisis, he declared, "is largely the result of a financial policy . . . embodied in unwise laws." Its solution was equally simple: the unconditional repeal of the Sherman Act. Always sure of himself, Cleveland had staked everything on a single measure—a winning strategy if it succeeded, a devastating one if it did not. Characteristically, too, he would brook no opposition and instructed subordinates to withhold patronage from Democrats who "oppose our patriotic attempt to help the country and save our party."[30]

That afternoon, he slipped away from Washington, ostensibly to rest at his Buzzard's Bay cottage on Cape Cod until Congress met. He boarded a friend's yacht on the East River in New York, and the following day, July 1, as the yacht steamed slowly up the river, surgeons removed much of his upper left jaw and palate. It had been, as Mrs. Cleveland said, a "narrow escape."[31] Fitted with an artificial jawpiece, Cleveland recuperated in secret on Cape Cod, seeing only the closest aides—fishing and relaxing, the country thought. Tanned and rested, though still weak, he returned to Washington on August 5, two days before Congress met. The secrecy worked but at the cost of some criticism of his absence from the capital. Cleveland "is now nursing his fat at Buzzard's Bay," a hostile newspaper complained in mid-July. "He fishes while the country broils."[32]

Fervid silverites were fighting back, stung by the demand for unconditional repeal. They had, to be sure, no special affection for the Sherman Act, which had failed to add as much silver to the currency as they had hoped. But repeal without an effective silver substitute was another matter. "I never did think that the Sherman Bill was a wise piece of legislation," a California senator wrote, "but I believe that if it is unconditionally repealed, . . . silver will be permanently demonetized."[33]

That was exactly the point, silverites felt. Eastern and European financiers had joined in a selfish plot to demonetize silver, "a gigantic conspiracy . . . to establish finally and forever the single gold standard, and to extend it over the world." They had subverted the Sherman Act, dictated the closing of the Indian mints, and caused the collapse of the American economy. Now they had even enlisted the president, who tamely did their bidding.[34]

In such a battle, the stakes were high, silverites were sure, higher than at any time since the Revolution. The working masses were pitted against the parasitic rich, the producers against the speculators, the money of the people against the golden Baal. "The war has begun," Davis H. Waite, the Populist governor of Colorado, shouted to a large rally in Denver on July 11, 1893. "Our weapons are argument and the ballot," but should those not succeed, "it is better, infinitely better, that blood should flow to the horses' bridles than our national liberties should be destroyed."[35] The angry rhetoric, repeated again and again as the repeal struggle approached, alarmed supporters of the gold standard, who, in turn, ridiculed the "Populist cuckoos" abroad in the land. By the time Congress convened, feelings had hardened on both sides of the currency question. Each side laid sole claim to "sound principles" and respectively blamed the "gold trust" or the "silver inflation-ists" for the nation's economic ills.[36]

The special session opened on August 7, 1893, with the chaplain's prayer for divine help "in this time of doubt and perplexity, of unrest and agitation among the nations, and in our own land." That day, the gold reserve stood at $102,291,395, barely above the critical mark. The Southern Pacific Railroad had just laid off 1,000 workers; textile mills in Fall River, Massachusetts, had laid off 7,000. In a few days, the Northern Pacific Railroad would go bankrupt. On August 8, congressmen and senators heard Cleveland's spe-cial message, a calm, reasoned statement that reviewed economic troubles, cited the "evil effects" of the Sherman Act, and urged speedy repeal. The message never mentioned the touchy word *gold* and hinted that quick repeal might lead to an international agreement to boost silver. Cleveland had set out to soothe tempers.[37]

The repeal bill moved quickly through the House of Representatives. Out-numbered, the silverites fought a delaying action, but they could not with-stand the growing public demand for repeal. Democrats—even some silver Democrats—wanted to follow the president, who seemed so sure that repeal would benefit the country and party. Cleveland's floor managers played skill-fully on the feeling, wooing moderate silver men with appeals to support the president, promises of patronage to ease discontent at home, and assur-ances that the administration would sponsor some kind of prosilver mea-sure once repeal had passed. The silver lines bent under the pressure. On August 16, William Jennings Bryan, the attractive young Nebraskan, tried to stiffen resolves. The Democrats, he told a crowded, hushed House, "have come to the parting of the ways," and it was time to choose between arrogant wealth and the "work-worn," "dustbegrimed" people. The country waited for their answer. "[Will they turn] to the rising sun or the setting sun? Will [they] choose blessings or cursings—life or death—which? Which?"[38]

The speech, eloquent and affecting, established Bryan as one of silver's chief spokesmen but changed few votes. Headlines that morning had re-ported the collapse of another railroad, and the pressures for repeal mounted inexorably. House Republicans sat back, tabulating party profits from the Democrats' difficulties. "Let the democrats do the talking and voting," one Republican declared. "It is their funeral."[39] On August 28, after some final maneuvering, the repeal bill easily passed the House by a vote of 239 to 108, a far larger margin than expected. Whereas the Republicans had supported it by 101 to 30, the Democrats had divided 138 to 78. That was ominous for the Democrats, but Cleveland celebrated, certain that the large vote would ease passage through the Senate.[40]

There, he had chosen Daniel W. Voorhees of Indiana to manage the repeal bill. Just a few months before, Voorhees had called unconditional repeal "an outrage," but patronage, dolloped out in lavish quantities, lessened his sense of injustice. As the debate opened, he counted forty-nine senators for repeal, enough to pass the bill if it reached a vote. But Senate rules provided for unrestricted debate, and the silver senators, who disliked Cleveland intensely, were unlikely to help. Matters stalled through August, September, and early October, angering Cleveland, who waved the party lash. If the silver men in the Senate wanted a fight, "he would give them one," he burst out to an aide. Actually, the delay strained the public's patience and strengthened Cleveland's hand. "Times are so hard that people sigh for a change, whatever it might be," a discouraged silverite noted.[41]

The continuing discord worried Maryland's Arthur P. Gorman and a handful of other Democratic leaders in the Senate. A senator since 1881, Gorman was a party man, with impeccable credentials. For a time in the 1880s, he had been closely identified with Cleveland. He managed Cleveland's first presidential campaign in 1884, led his try for an equivocal tariff plank in the 1888 Democratic platform, and helped organize his reelection campaign that same year. Since then, the two men had drifted apart. Subtle and sophisticated, Gorman disliked Cleveland's stubborn self-conceit. He resented the way Cleveland claimed to place principle above party. To him, the two were inseparable: the party *was* a principle and the necessary vehicle to action. Gorman savored organization, preferred quiet work behind the scenes, and labored constantly for Democratic success. Now he saw his party being torn apart, fractured between contending factions, each intolerant of the other. The discord, he was sure, endangered Democratic majorities in at least a dozen states.

Shrewdly, he bided his time, waiting for the proper moment to suggest a compromise that would satisfy both sides. By late October, conditions seemed right, and on October 20, Gorman took his compromise plan to Secretary Carlisle and the Senate Democratic steering committee. He proposed to extend the Sherman Act until October 1, 1894, coin the silver seigniorage in the Treasury, and retire all greenbacks and Treasury notes under $10 in denomination.[42] The administration would get repeal, though not for another year; the silverites would get that year's delay, plus a small additional amount of silver currency. Gorman went over the proposal line by line with

Carlisle and left thinking he had the secretary's tacit approval. The following day, 37 of the 44 Democratic senators signed a letter endorsing the plan.[43]

Cleveland was furious. At a cabinet meeting on Monday afternoon, October 23, he pounded the table "so hard that papers flew to the floor," one cabinet member reported, "and I was afraid he would bruise his hand."[44] Within the cabinet, three of the eight members, perhaps four, favored compromise, but afraid of Cleveland, they dared not say so. Hammering the table, Cleveland vowed to fight until the end, and with that, Gorman's long, patient labors collapsed. Democrats were tired and discouraged. The wily Voorhees seized the moment to cajole the wavering. On October 24, he visited the southern Democratic caucus and, renewing assurances that liberal silver legislation would follow repeal, persuaded a number of southern Democrats to give up the fight. Others decided that they preferred unconditional repeal to compromise, hoping for an early backlash in favor of silver.[45]

The end in sight, senators turned back a silverite proposal to restore the 1878 Bland-Allison Act, 37 to 33, then defeated a free silver amendment, 41 to 31. Ominously for the Democratic party, 22 Democrats voted for the free silver amendment, 20 voted against. Ominously, too, the delegations from sixteen states, all in the South and West, voted unanimously for free silver, whereas the delegations from twenty-one states, almost all in the Northeast and Midwest, voted unanimously against. The lines in the free silver drama were tightening and not in the Democrats' favor. Early in the evening of October 30, the Senate turned at last to the repeal bill itself, which it passed, 48 to 37. The Republicans voted more than two to one for repeal; the Democrats again divided evenly. The gold reserve that day stood at $84,000,000. Cleveland was pleased, and he was the focus of the victory. "He has brought the entire Senate to his feet," one newspaper remarked. On November 1, 1893, he signed the bill into law and ordered the mints to stop purchasing silver. The great repeal battle of 1893, an event that would reshape the politics of the decade, was ended.[46]

At first hopefully, then with mounting impatience, people awaited the promised economic revival. It did not come. The stock market remained listless and even fell a bit the day after repeal. Businesses continued to close, unemployment spread, farm prices dropped. "We are hourly expecting the arrival of the benevolent man who is to pay ten cents a pound for cotton," said the *Raleigh News and Observer* sardonically. Repeal of the Sherman Act was probably a necessary measure. It responded to the realities of international finance, reduced the flight of gold out of the country, and over the long run boosted business confidence. Unfortunately, it also contracted the currency at a time when an expanding money supply might have helped economic recovery. Repeal suffered from the extravagant claims of its sponsors. In the end, it did not even solve the Treasury's gold problem. By January 1894, the reserve had fallen to $65,000,000. A year later, it was down to $44,500,000.[47]

Other troubles emerged with time. A tactical error of vast consequence, Cleveland's unrelenting demand for repeal focused national attention on the silver issue, implicitly reinforcing the silverites' belief in the issue's overriding importance. It intensified the silver sentiment Cleveland had intended to dampen. It also ended the Democrats' hopes of submerging their differences on silver in a campaign to lower the tariff. Years later, as the decade drew to a close, Democrats would speculate on what might have happened to the party if Cleveland, as William McKinley would do in 1897, had sidestepped the volatile silver issue and called a special session of Congress devoted to the tariff. Many of them angrily recalled their own willingness to subordinate silver to the tariff in the 1892 campaign. Cleveland had chosen instead to stress silver, thereby splitting the party and dimming the prospects for tariff reform. "The very memory is enough to make the heart sick," Henry Watterson of Kentucky, an avid tariff reformer, said in 1904.[48]

Spurred by repeal, silver sentiment grew swiftly during 1893 and 1894, sweeping through the South and West and appearing even in the rural regions of New York and New England. Prosilver literature flooded from presses and filled newspaper columns. Pamphlets, some of them distributed by the millions, touted silver's virtues. People read, discussed, and believed. It was a time for solutions, with the economy slumping once more. During 1896, unemployment again shot up; farm income and prices fell to the lowest point in the decade. "I can remember back as far as 1858," said an Iowa hardware dealer that February, "and I have never seen such hard times as these are." Silverites offered a solution, simplistic but compelling: the free and independent coinage of silver at the ratio of sixteen to one.[49]

Free coinage meant that the mints would coin all the silver offered to them. Independent coinage meant that the United States would coin silver regardless of the policies of other nations, nearly all of which were on the gold standard. The ratio of sixteen to one pegged silver's value at sixteen ounces of silver to one ounce of gold, a formulation based on the market prices of the two metals back in the 1830s. Silver had slipped badly in price since then, and the actual ratio was now closer to thirty-two to one, but silverites argued that free coinage would boost the price and restore the old relationship.

The silverites believed in a quantity theory of money: the amount of money in circulation determined the level of activity in the economy. A money shortage—there was not enough gold to support economies around the world—meant declining activity and depression. Silver meant prosperity. Added to the currency, it would swell the money stock and quicken the pace of economic activity. Farm prices would rise. "The blood of commerce will again flow through the arteries of business; industry will again revive; millions of men will find employment; [and] the hand of greed will be stricken from the throat of prosperity."[50]

By 1896, silver had become a symbol. For many, it had moral and patriotic dimensions and stood for a wide range of popular grievances. Cleveland and his fellow gold adherents never understood that. With skillful work, they could have drawn some of the movement's sting, but they instead adopted policies that sharpened its symbolism. Cleveland anointed silver in trying to kill it. For many in the society, silver reflected rural values rather than urban; suggested a welcome shift of power away from the Northeast; gave the nation, acting independently of other countries, a chance to display its growing authority in the world; and spoke for the downtrodden instead of the well-to-do. It represented the common people, as the vast literature of the movement showed. In article after article, pamphlet after pamphlet, farmers and financiers, thrown together in accidental circumstances, debated the merits of silver and gold, with results obvious to all who knew the virtues of common folk and common sense.[51]

William H. Harvey's *Coin's Financial School* (1894), the most popular of all the silverite pamphlets, had the eloquent Coin, a wise but unknown youth, tutoring famous people on the currency. Bankers, lawyers, and scholars came to argue for gold but left shaken, leaning toward silver. Coin used logic and plain sense. He "was like a little monitor in the midst of a fleet of wooden ships. His shots went through and silenced all opposition."[52] *Coin's Financial School* sold 5,000 copies a day at its peak in 1895, with tens of thousands more distributed free by silver organizations. Some political scientists have called it the most widely read campaign document in the history of American politics.[53]

Like Coin, silver profited from illusion. It fed on fears and grew with apprehensions. Its supporters, like the "goldolators" they despised, tended to oversimplify issues, appeal to emotions, imagine conspiracies, and cast

This cartoon of a cow, standing astride much of the country, suggested brilliantly the anger of southern and western farmers who fed the cow the crops they had raised in the South and West but then saw it being milked in the East, with the profits carried off to New York and New England. The gentleman in the foreground sits on a bale of cotton selling for only 7 cents a pound, a price that would not support his crop. (W. H. Harvey, Coin's Financial School [Chicago: Coin Publishing, 1894])

events in terms of good and evil. They also tried to respond constructively to public need and economic hardship. Silver was a social movement, one of the largest in American history, but its life span turned out to be remarkably brief. As a mass phenomenon, it flourished between 1894 and 1896, then succumbed to defeat, prosperity, and the onset of fresh concerns. But in its time, it spoke a mood and won millions of followers. It altered the course of politics. Silver reshaped sectional alignments, changed party outlooks, and helped topple a president. It presided at the birth of a "new" Democratic party.

Little by little, the Democratic party came apart. A word here, a gesture there, an attempt to explain and conciliate might have helped reknit the ranks, but Cleveland had no skill at such things. "He did not know what conciliation meant," said a veteran Washington reporter, "and rubbed out sore spots with a brick."

Discontent surfaced quickly. The 1893 state and local elections turned Democrats out of office across the country. The Republicans prospered, as large numbers of Democratic voters either remained at home or voted Republican. Significantly, the Populists again failed to attract the discontented, except in some areas of the South.[54]

The Republicans swept New York and Pennsylvania. In Massachusetts, they ousted Governor Russell, Cleveland's close friend and once the symbol of Democratic hopes in New England. In Iowa, they defeated Governor Horace Boies, a similar symbol in the Midwest and on the plains. In Ohio, William McKinley crushed his Democratic opponent and won a second term as governor by 81,000 votes, the largest margin in an Ohio gubernatorial race since the 1860s. Ohio and Massachusetts displayed patterns that delighted Republicans. In both states, Republican candidates simply did well everywhere: in rural areas, small towns, and cities and among both old-stock and immigrant voters. They made substantial inroads in Boston, Fall River, Cincinnati, Columbus, Cleveland, Dayton, and other urban-industrial areas.[55]

Disgruntled Democrats spoke of their "Waterloo." "I hope it will be the means of putting a little sense into some heads at Washington," wrote a California Democrat. In January 1894, Cleveland issued $50,000,000 in gold bonds—bonds for which the purchaser had to pay in gold—to replenish the gold reserve in the Treasury. That month, a Republican won a special congressional election in a "safe" Democratic district in New York City. A few months later, Republicans again swept local elections in Ohio, Rhode Island, Michigan, and Connecticut.[56]

The Democrats' spirits dwindled, then reeled under a decisive blow in late March 1894. Looking for a way to soothe silver sentiment and reunite the party, the Democrats in Congress passed a bill authorizing the coinage of the silver seigniorage in the Treasury. The bill was little more than a gesture. It added relatively small amounts of silver to the currency and found its strongest support among Democrats from prosilver districts who had rallied to Cleveland's call for repeal the summer before. A seigniorage law, though largely ceremonial, might placate constituents and answer criticism that the Democrats had no positive approach to the depression.[57]

Would Cleveland sign it? Many Democrats called on him to urge him to do so—it would reinvigorate the party, improve the prospects for tariff reform, and help Democrats in the November elections, they argued—but on March 29, Cleveland vetoed it as unwise and inopportune. It would sap business confidence and weaken the benefits of repeal. On Capitol Hill, reporters had never seen congressmen so angry. Silver Democrats clustered in the cloakrooms and lobbies, cursing Cleveland and complaining of a presidential tyranny that violated Democratic precepts of limited executive power.[58]

Outside the Northeast, the seigniorage veto was a stunning blow to Democrats, a landmark event in the process of party alienation from Cleveland that led to Bryan's nomination for the presidency in 1896. It further isolated Cleveland, confirmed his apparent rigidity, and renewed charges that he pursued a "purely obstructive" policy toward the depression. Moderate Democrats despaired of ever reuniting the party. Retreating into self-righteousness, Cleveland began to complain of the "misconception and prejudice and ignorance and injustice" around him. "There never was a man in this high office so surrounded with difficulties and so perplexed, and so treacherously treated, and so abandoned by those whose aid he *deserves,* as the present incumbent," he wrote a friend bitterly a few weeks after the veto.[59]

For Cleveland and his party, there was more yet to come. In late June 1894, a massive railroad strike broke out at the Pullman Palace Car Company near Chicago, when workers walked out over wage cuts, living conditions, and layoffs. Soon joined by Eugene V. Debs's American Railway Union, the Pullman Strike suddenly paralyzed the western half of the nation. Grain and livestock could not reach markets. Factories began to shut down for lack of coal. In California, fruit rotted in boxcars, stranded on the tracks. Trying to keep peace, Debs instructed strikers to avoid violence and move the mails, lest the federal government intervene.[60]

That made no difference to Cleveland and Attorney General Richard

Olney, who determined to break the strike. Cooperating closely with the railroads, one of the parties to it, they obtained, on July 2, 1894, a wide-ranging court injunction enjoining Debs and the union from interfering with trains carrying the mails or interstate commerce. Cleveland then sent federal troops to affected areas, including Chicago, Los Angeles, and Sacramento, California, in all of which the strike had been peaceful. The Democratic governor of Illinois, John P. Altgeld, protested vigorously, assuring Cleveland that the state could deal with the situation but to no avail.[61]

Hit with soldiers and injunctions, the union never had a chance. By late July, the Pullman Strike was over, with Debs headed for jail, charged with violating the court order. In some quarters, Cleveland for a moment enjoyed public acclaim, but praise came mainly from the comfortable and well-to-do, who lauded Cleveland and voted Republican. Many workingpeople turned against Cleveland and the Democrats, particularly as later investigations documented the administration's collusion with the railroad companies in the strike. Altgeld was bitter. Democrats did not send troops into states capable of handling their own affairs. That smacked of centralized power, Republicanism, and Reconstruction. Relentlessly, Altgeld set out to discredit the hated Cleveland, organizing dissident Democrats in a movement to repudiate the president in 1896.[62]

As if Pullman were not enough, the party reeled again in the debate over its long-promised tariff reform bill. Known as the Wilson-Gorman bill, it had awaited Cleveland's action on repeal of the Sherman Act, then stalled through July 1894 in a House-Senate conference committee. Tempers flared amid the turmoil of the Pullman Strike, and the public's patience began to run out. On July 19, Cleveland intervened, apparently thinking he could bludgeon the Senate as he had in the repeal battle the year before. The bill fell "far short" of desired reform, he wrote in a public letter to William L. Wilson, the bill's sponsor in the House, and amounted to "party perfidy and party dishonor."

Writing the letter was a major blunder, reflecting Cleveland's growing isolation from the party's center. Senate Democrats, including many of his staunchest supporters, erupted in anger and dismay. Cleveland immediately tried to back down, but it was too late. In rapid succession, prominent Democrats took the Senate floor to detail the conditions that had shaped the bill. Senator Gorman was particularly bitter, having worked once again to devise a compromise bill that would hold Democrats together. Cleveland had been consulted at every step and had himself wavered too often on the tariff issue to speak now of such things as party perfidy and dishonor. "The limit of endurance has been reached," Gorman said defiantly. "I hurl back the accusation."[63]

The Senate's mood stiffened, and in mid-August, Wilson and his fellow House Democrats voted to accept the Senate bill. They looked that day "like a grainfield devastated by a hailstorm," Reed later said. Many of them had spent their lives fighting for tariff reduction, and it had come to this. Democrats would not get another chance at the tariff for nearly two decades, until the administration of Woodrow Wilson in 1913.

Cleveland was "depressed and disappointed," he said, uncertain whether to sign the Wilson-Gorman bill. Finally, on August 28, 1894, he let it become law without his signature, ignoring warnings that such a course would further isolate him from his party. William L. Wilson called the new law "a substantial beginning," but people knew better. It was instead a disheartening end, a dismal conclusion to the Democratic party's tariff reform crusade.[64] "The Democrats have given an exhibition of fairly colossal incompetence," Theodore Roosevelt (TR) remarked happily.[65]

With adjournment, congressmen scattered to their homes, to mend fences for the November elections. Sadness and a sense of impending disaster settled over the Democrats. Voters linked them to the depression and to the failure of silver repeal, Cleveland's panacea, to cure it. Republicans were confident, certain the tariff fiasco had sealed their opponents' fate. Cleveland was an easy target, the victim of his own sanctimony. "Isn't he funny?" a Republican wrote as the fall campaigns began. "For solemn stupidity, for the wisdom of un-wisdom, he takes the cake."[66]

Republican and Populist strategists forecast massive defections among normally Democratic voters. Silverites were unhappy with repeal and the seigniorage veto; businessmen and merchants resented the uncertainties of a year's tinkering with the tariff; sheep growers feared hard times from the removal of duties on wool in the Wilson-Gorman Tariff. A story went the rounds about a stranger who came upon a man shearing his sheep backwards, working from the tail toward the head instead of head to tail, as usual. "Well, stranger, I'll tell you," the man drawled, seeing the surprise. "I voted for Cleveland in 1892, and since then I just ain't had the nerve to look a sheep in the face!"[67]

Reed, McKinley, Harrison, and other Republicans hammered at the tariff, the depression, and the inability of the Democrats to govern. McKinley spoke to 371 audiences in sixteen states that fall, helping Republican candidates and building alliances for a possible presidential bid in 1896. Harrison attacked Democratic incompetence: "Can the country afford to educate that party into a capacity for government?" Democrats had trouble finding candidates for major offices; ambitious leaders preferred private life that year to the certainty of defeat. A half-dozen Democrats declined the gubernatorial nomination in New York, and the party turned as a last resort to Senator David B. Hill, who also did not want it. Elsewhere, Altgeld and other dissidents urged voters to distinguish between Cleveland and the party, to repudiate the one and vote for the other. "Judas betrayed his master," Altgeld said a week before the election, "but the world did not therefore condemn all twelve of the apostles."[68]

On election night, Cleveland followed the returns over a private telegraph wire at Woodley, the home in Washington he used as a retreat from the White House. Aides said that he would have no comment on the outcome. It was no wonder. The election buried the Democratic party in state after state. In the largest transfer of congressional strength in American history, the Democrats lost 113 House seats, and the Republicans gained 117. In the Fifty-fourth Congress, the House would contain 244 Republicans, 105 Democrats, and 7 Populists. The Republicans would likely control the Senate as well. The totals were devastating, as was the list of Democratic casualties. Wilson lost by 2,300 votes in West Virginia, in a bid for his seventh term. Richard P. Bland lost in Missouri, William M. Springer in Illinois, William D. Bynum in Indiana. All had been leaders in the House. Prominent senators lost seats as well. "The truth is," as one of the victims said, "there was hardly an oasis left in the Democratic desert."[69]

Twenty-four states elected no Democrats to Congress; six others chose only one Democrat each. A single Democrat (Boston's John F. Fitzgerald, the grandfather of President John F. Kennedy) represented the party's once-bright hopes in New England. As expected, Hill lost badly in New York. The Democrats were decimated in New Jersey and Connecticut, states that were usually closely contested. To their surprise, they even lost some of the "solid" South. West Virginia elected 4 Republican congressmen; Maryland, 3; Kentucky, 4; Virginia, 2; North Carolina, 3; Tennessee, 4; and Missouri, 7. Even Texas elected a Republican congressman. In the Midwest, a vital battleground of the 1890s, the Democratic party was virtually destroyed. Of the 89 congressmen from the region, only 3 now bore the Democratic standard. Eighty-six were Republicans.[70]

The returns discouraged the Populists. Their hopes had again been high as the campaign opened. Hard times might at last break old-party allegiances, moving the large numbers of discontented into the Populist fold.

"The People's Party will come into power with a resistless rush," wrote Eugene V. Debs from jail. Working with Debs and others, the Populists wooed labor and the unemployed, particularly in areas where the Pullman Strike and other labor disturbances had left workers restless and dissatisfied. In the South, they often fused with the Republican party and nominated joint tickets to oppose the dominant Democrats.

None of the plans worked quite as the Populists had hoped. Nationwide, they increased their vote by about 42 percent over 1892 totals, an attractive figure but far short of expectations. They made striking inroads in parts of the South, especially in North Carolina, Georgia, and Alabama, and also gained in Nebraska, Minnesota, and California. Encouragingly, they improved in some urban areas, including Chicago and San Francisco, and did well among miners and railroad workers.[71]

Still, it was far from enough. In a year in which thousands of voters were switching allegiances, the Populists elected only four senators and four representatives. They lost Kansas, Colorado, North Dakota, and Idaho, all Populist states in 1892. Governor Waite failed in his bid for reelection in Colorado. Ignatius Donnelly lost his Minnesota state senate seat. Thomas E. Watson lost another race for Congress in Georgia. The Republicans swept Kansas, once a focus of the Populist movement. Everywhere, the results were disheartening. In Georgia, Alabama, and other southern states, the Democrats continued to use fraud and violence to keep Populist totals down. In the Midwest, the Populists doubled their vote in 1894 yet still attracted less than 7 percent of the vote. From Indiana to California, the discontented had tended to vote for the Republicans, not the Populists. With that, the Populist challenge, once so large with promise and possibility, was nearly over.[72]

The Democrats drifted, torn and discouraged. Administration and antiadministration forces each blamed the other for defeat. Early in 1895, Altgeld declined an invitation to a dinner honoring Jefferson's birthday, certain the celebrants would also praise Cleveland. "Jefferson," he said, "belonged to the American people; Cleveland to the men who devour widows' houses." Administration supporters searched for benefits in their repudiation, enjoying, as one put it, "the spectacle of Hill driven into the ground up to his eyebrows, the picturesque and silver lined hole which Dick Bland pulled in after him, the heap of dust that was once Weaver of Iowa and the shattered prayer wheel which looms on the prairie of Nebraska that was the pious Bryan." William L. Wilson and scores of loyal administration Democrats had also lost, but that drew few reflections. Defeat apparently taught no lessons.[73]

Cleveland retreated into isolation. His mail dwindled, and his name evoked jeers at Democratic gatherings outside the Northeast. Former friends in Congress no longer stopped in to chat. Talented young Democrats who had joined the administration in 1893 went home, disenchanted. Cleveland seldom left the White House, which faithful aides surrounded with guards. There was nowhere to go, except Buzzard's Bay. "I have been dreadfully forlorn these many months," he wrote in February 1895, "and sorely perplexed and tried." During 1895 and 1896, he twice more resorted to unpopular bond sales to rescue the Treasury's gold reserve. A few of his subsequent actions, particularly his blunt opposition to Great Britain in the 1895 Venezuela boundary dispute, brought praise, but they came too late to reverse the tide. Anti-Cleveland feeling spread through society and infected the Democratic party. For millions of people, Cleveland had become a scapegoat, the purveyor of economic ills, the betrayer of his party's great 1890 and 1892 victories.[74]

Attention turned now to the long-awaited presidential election of 1896, an election made even more important by the events of the past few years. Candidates and platforms were yet to be determined, but the issues were already clear, and the stakes were high. Populist prospects looked dim, but elections could always surprise. The silver issue, thanks to Cleveland and the depression, had acquired large and unanticipated importance. The Democratic party had suffered badly but had strong ties to voters in the South and elsewhere. The depression's enormity had changed many voters' views, to which Republicans had responded so far with gratifying success. Confident, they understood they had prospered on the newer issues in 1894 and counted on doing so again in 1896, little knowing that the Democrats still had some important surprises in store.

3

"THE PEOPLE AGAINST THE BOSSES"
THE REPUBLICAN NOMINATION OF WILLIAM MCKINLEY

Until such agreement can be obtained the existing gold standard must be maintained.
—Republican party platform, 1896 [1]

As the year 1896 opened, a large number of Republicans coveted the party's presidential nomination. It was hard not to, in this, a clearly Republican year. Cleveland and the Democrats were enormously unpopular, their ideas and policies discredited in the midst of a harsh depression. Voters seemed eager for change, ready for new directions. They had registered that mood indelibly in elections in both 1894 and 1895, in which they had drubbed the Democrats and for the most part shunned candidates of the People's party. In overwhelming numbers, they had voted for Republican candidates nearly everywhere, an alluring portent of the party's success in 1896, the crucial presidential year.

Inevitably, the early presidential talk turned to former president Benjamin Harrison, now in quiet retirement practicing law in Indianapolis. Harrison never encouraged the talk. He had detested his last year in the White House and thought it undignified for an ex-president to scramble for a nomination. "I do not like to appear to be in the attitude of the little boy that followed the apple-cart up the hill, hoping the tail-board might fall out!" he wrote a party ally. [2]

In a last appeal, an old colleague urged Harrison to run again. No, Harrison replied, he had no desire for the office, and he added, "with twinkling eye, 'Your friend Cleveland is making my administration luminous.'" [3] In February 1896, to the relief of other candidates, Harrison formally withdrew from consideration, leaving the important Indiana delegation up for grabs. Privately, he threw his support to a longtime ally, Senator William B. Allison of Iowa, a venerable Republican who planned to campaign in Harrison's old role as the candidate from the West.[4]

Allison joined a lengthening list of senatorial hopefuls, including Cushman K. Davis of Minnesota, Shelby M. Cullom of Illinois, and Matthew S. Quay of Pennsylvania. All had little chance and wished simply to be in the right spot should lightning strike. In early January 1896, Quay, Thomas C. Platt of New York, James S. Clarkson, a talented and respected party leader from Iowa, and Joseph B. Manley of Maine, secretary of the Republican National Committee, met in New York City to figure out what to do about the nomination. With few other options, they settled on an old and time-tested strategy: establish favorite-son candidacies wherever they could, tie up delegates, and try to block a nomination until they could decide on a candidate they liked. As favorite sons, they would run Thomas B. Reed in New England, the septuagenarian governor Levi P. Morton in New York, Allison in Iowa, Cullom in Illinois, Davis in Minnesota, and Quay himself in Pennsylvania. Combined with the usual "purchasable" delegates from the South, delegations from these states might be enough to slow down other bandwagons and give the group a chance to bargain.[5]

The keys to the strategy were Quay and Platt, two of the era's most powerful and interesting politicians. Sixty-three years old in 1896, Quay had spent a lifetime mastering Pennsylvania politics, not an easy task in a state of that size and complexity. Trained as a lawyer, he had joined the Union army early in the Civil War, left it briefly to become private secretary to the governor of Pennsylvania, and then rejoined to fight in the bloody battle of Fredericksburg in 1862, an act of bravery for which he later received the Medal of Honor. Mustered out, he went full-time into Pennsylvania politics; won a seat in the state legislature; became state treasurer; and in 1887, in the victory he coveted most, was elected to the U.S. Senate.

From 1869 until his death in 1904, Quay was a dominant force in the politics of the Keystone State. Suave, dignified, and well educated, he often departed from the stereotypes of the nineteenth-century party boss. He knew both Greek and Latin, read widely in military and religious history, enjoyed fine wines and foods, and cherished comfortable surroundings. Drawing on his experience with fellow politicians, he once defined American politics as "the art of taking money from the few and votes from the many under the pretext of protecting the one from the other." Renowned for both his learning and his reticence, he knew, critics said, how "to keep silent in sixteen different languages." He often fell asleep with a book across his lap.[6]

Like most political bosses, Quay was also ruthless, prepared to do what was necessary to win. When Quay was six, his father, a minister and missionary, brought home a small sword and pocket Bible for Matthew and his sister. He gave Matthew the first choice and, surprised, heard the boy ask for the Bible. Within hours, the sister had lost interest in the sword—and the young Quay had both possessions, an experience repeated throughout his lifetime.[7] When Benjamin Harrison remarked that "Providence has given us the victory" in the 1888 election, Quay told a journalist: "Think of the man! He ought to know that Providence hadn't a damned thing to do with it." Harrison, he added, "would never learn how close a number of men were compelled to approach the gates of the penitentiary to make him President."[8]

Adept with both feather and knife, Quay had loyal friends around the country, qualities that would prove helpful in the favorite-son strategy this year, in which he planned to keep Pennsylvania's large delegation locked up until the time for bargaining arrived.[9]

In that strategy, he worked closely with his New York counterpart, Thomas Collier Platt, the "Easy Boss," known for the deft touch and the stealthy, polished maneuver. Platt needed both stealth and polish. The Republicans of New York were a fractious group, easy to stampede, difficult to govern, and often divided between the interests of its upstate and downstate wings—that is, the rural northern counties and New York City, respectively. Short in stature, slender, and bald, Platt had gotten his start in the 1870s and 1880s serving the imperious Republican senator Roscoe Conkling, which prompted opponents to call him "Me, Too," a nickname they soon regretted.

Like Quay, Platt entered politics without the usual speaking gifts or public skills. "He could not conduct a conversation, much less make a speech," someone who knew him well said. "He was so little magnetic that even the act of shaking hands he performed listlessly and as though it bored him." Yet he had good judgment at critical moments, patience, and loyalty; he knew how to bring people to his side.[10]

Ruthless and cunning, Platt demanded discipline and organization from his followers, and he asked those qualities of himself as well. Unlike many bosses, he ruled mainly through consultation and consent. "Because Platt played the game for love and not for money, he was not prone to cherish long animosity or to pursue bitter revenges," an acquaintance once observed.[11] In 1896, he wanted a presidential candidate he could control, preferably

Governor Morton, with whom he had long worked. Failing that, he might take Allison or Reed, anyone but the independent William McKinley, whom he feared. During 1895 and 1896, he sent emissaries to other Republican leaders, gathering their support. The emissaries wheedled, bargained, commanded, and in a few cases bribed. Some party leaders listened. "T. C. Platt can not turn time backward, make spotted pigs or produce a three-year-old steer in a minute; but there is little else he can not do if he has the nerve," a loyal lieutenant said on a delegate-hunting trip.[12]

For a time, both Platt and Quay considered supporting Maine's Thomas B. Reed, but they worried about his temper and independence. Throughout the mid-1890s, Reed seemed a formidable front-runner for the nomination, the focus of endless speculation. He wanted it badly, believed his long and valued service in the House of Representatives had earned it, and thought he spoke for the party's most intelligent elements. Campaigning hard for Republican candidates in 1894 and 1895, he had picked up numerous debts to cash in during 1896. He planned to combine solid delegations from New England and the Pacific Coast plus enough scattered support elsewhere to become the nominee. In October and November 1895, Joseph B. Manley, his chief spokesman, paid visits to the Pacific Coast and the South. The trip had no political purpose, Manley insisted, but that of course was doubtful.[13]

In December 1895, Reed won reelection as Speaker of the House, a useful base from which to influence policy and attract publicity. Immediately, he softened his biting wit, as if to establish his presidential timber.[14] In newspaper interviews, he advised Republicans to avoid a return to high tariff duties, a telling jab at his main rival, McKinley. The advice lured western Republicans into the fold and brought important early endorsements from the *Chicago Tribune* and other Republican papers that favored lower tariffs. Some McKinley advisers were sure the bosses lurked behind Reed's candidacy, using New York's Morton as a dispensable diversion. "I think this combination of Quay-Platt-Clarkson and others is for Reed and this Morton candidacy is to throw us off our ground," McKinley's cousin, Will Osborne, warned him.[15]

Still, Reed's momentum flagged unexpectedly as convention time approached. As always, he saw his own handicaps, remarking sardonically that in choosing a candidate, the Republicans "might do worse, and they probably will." A well-intentioned gesture in 1894 to help silver Republicans had backfired and cost him vital support in gold-oriented New England and the Midwest. Enemies combined against him. Geography undermined him, since Maine, his home state, was safely Republican no matter what the ticket. Worst of all, Reed suffered from his own reputation. He seemed brittle and temperamental, too self-centered, somehow unsuited for the demands of presidential leadership.[16]

Geography, temperament, and experience all helped his chief rival, William McKinley, the former congressman and governor of Ohio, who took an early and commanding lead in the race for delegates. McKinley had seemingly spent a lifetime preparing for the presidency. Born in 1843, at Niles, Ohio, the seventh of nine children, he grew up in Poland, Ohio, where he graduated from the Poland Academy at the age of seventeen. After a year in college, angered by the South's attack on Fort Sumter, he enlisted in the Union army, serving in the Twenty-third Ohio under Lieutenant Colonel Rutherford B. Hayes, who took a great liking to him. In letters home, Hayes described McKinley as "a handsome bright, gallant boy" and "one of the bravest and finest officers in the army."[17]

Like so many others in the North, McKinley's war experience attached him firmly to the Republican party. In 1864, he cast his first vote for Abraham Lincoln, using an army ambulance as the election booth and an empty candle container for a ballot box. Admired by officers and men alike, he rose steadily through the ranks, acquiring, even as a commissary sergeant, a reputation for bravery on the battlefield. Breveted a major, a title he carried for the rest of his life, he left the army in 1865, studied law, and moved to Canton, Ohio, a small industrial town in the northeastern part of the state.[18]

Law turned naturally to politics, and in 1876, McKinley won a seat in Congress. There, he devoted himself to the tariff, gradually becoming its chief spokesman. Like James G. Blaine, the Maine Republican whom he idolized, he saw the tariff as the path to prosperity and national greatness, a system of beneficent protection for manufacturers, farmers, and laborers. "It is the tax of patriotism, of home and country, of self-preservation and self-development," he said in 1892. "It has made the youngest country on the earth first in agriculture, the first in mining and the first in manufactures."[19]

Acting upon that belief, he sponsored in the Fifty-first Congress the McKinley Tariff Act, which brought him fame but also narrow defeat in the Democratic year of 1890, when Democrats gerrymandered his district. He toyed again with running for the House in 1892 but decided instead to run for the governorship of Ohio, which he won in 1891 by some 20,000 votes. His record as governor, including efforts to protect the safety of workers, arbitrate labor disputes, and pass a corporate franchise tax, won him another term in 1893, this time by the handsome total of over 80,000 votes.[20]

Through it all, McKinley retained warm friendships. Others envied the way he acquired antagonists but few enemies. "My opponents in Congress go at me tooth and nail," Reed, his main House rival, lamented, "but they always apologize to William when they are going to call him names." McKinley, in turn, thought Reed too mean-spirited for his own good. "Everybody enjoys Reed's sarcastic comments and keen wit," he once said, "except the fellow who is the subject of his satire."[21]

Congressional service honed the Major's legendary ability to manage people. Unlike Reed, he valued diversity and welcomed constructive dissent. He was charming, moderate, cautious, and thoughtful. "The man's genius was for friendship, for judgment of men, for their management," said the wife of a longtime antagonist.[22] Those qualities served him well in February 1893, when Robert Walker, an old Ohio friend, failed in business. McKinley had cosigned some of Walker's loans but safely, he was sure: the notes were for just a few thousand dollars, and Walker was a wealthy man; there was no way he could fail. But the panic of 1893 had caught up with him, as it did with so many others, and it turned out that Walker's debts, in fact, amounted to over $100,000. It was far more than McKinley could repay.

Public sympathy went out to the well-liked Ohio governor, as did personal offers to help. His wife, Ida, rushed home from a visit to Boston to place her property at his disposal. When some urged against it, she replied: "My husband has done everything for me all my life. Do you mean to deny me the privilege of doing as I please with my own property to help him now?" Friends established a trust to repay the debt, and a public subscription brought in additional funds. Refusing at first to accept any gifts, McKinley finally agreed to take only those from people who expected nothing but repayment in return. By June 1893, the sudden crisis was over, and the result, instead of discrediting McKinley, had shown the remarkable public and personal affection for him.[23]

Able, calm, and affable, McKinley had long looked inward for strength. He took pride in old-fashioned values. "Look after your diet and living," he once advised a favorite nephew, "take no intoxicants, engage in no immoral practices. Keep your life and your speech both clean, and be brave." His two children died young, and his wife, Ida, suffered from epilepsy, becoming a semi-invalid requiring his constant attention, a quality the nation admired. For years, he clung to a belief that she would recover. He lowered his voice when around her, took comfort in her nearness, spent hours sitting in closed rooms because she disliked breezes and fresh air. Close beside her, he passed evenings in the dark. He learned how to support her

William McKinley as president. (Ohio Historical Society, Columbus)

weight on his arm and soon knew how to assess her seizures and handle them.[24]

To her, he was always "my dearest," "my precious," and "my precious love." He called her "My darling wife" and closed his letters with "Your faithful Husband and always your lover."[25]

By 1896, he was fifty-three, and he had already been campaigning for the presidential nomination for almost a decade. Ohio, an important state in a critical region, positioned him nicely for a presidential bid and had trained him well for the task. Survival in politics there required "the virtues of the serpent, the shark, and the cooing dove," as a contemporary had once remarked. McKinley had acquired the traits of all three.[26]

In 1894, he had joined Reed and other Republican hopefuls on the stump, himself visiting sixteen states, traveling some 12,000 miles, and addressing nearly 2 million people. He visited New Orleans, spoke in the major cities of the border states, and toured the Northeast and Midwest. Everywhere, he stressed the tariff, the depression, and the disastrous Cleveland administration—"this tariff-tinkering, bond-issuing, debt-increasing, treasury-depleting, business-paralyzing, wage-reducing" administration. In January 1896, with his second term as governor ended, McKinley retired to Canton to spend time with his wife and work on his growing boom.[27]

In Canton, a special telephone line connected him directly with the Cleveland, Ohio, office of his trusted friend and ally Marcus A. Hanna. Contemporaries often misunderstood Hanna. During the 1896 campaign, the Democrats lampooned him savagely, using the ally to get at the candidate. In the *New York Journal,* cartoonist Homer Davenport, who had never even met Hanna, drew harsh caricatures of "Dollar Mark," depicting him as greedy, gloating, and cruel. Dollar Mark bribed delegates, bought nominations, and, as Davenport vividly asserted, controlled his helpless puppet, William McKinley.

Friends and acquaintances knew better. Hanna was genial, well meaning, and affectionate. He was "a man with a good deal of the boy in him," said someone who knew him well, "who would take endless pains to please a child, was sorry when other people were in trouble, [and] liked dispensing happiness under his own roof and widely elsewhere with his left hand." Building on the family businesses, Hanna had made a fortune in Great Lakes shipping, iron ore, and coal mines. Sharing something of Quay's passion for the arts, he owned the Cleveland Opera House, to which he often invited the McKinleys and other guests. Hanna was boyish and shrewd, exuberant and

"HOW CAN HE LOSE ME?" *One of many anti-McKinley cartoons drawn by Homer Davenport of the* New York Journal, *depicting William McKinley as a puppet and Mark Hanna as the money-driven master. (*New York Journal, *October 18, 1896)*

hardheaded, energetic, a millionaire businessman who sympathized with labor, a bluff and open man who enjoyed the secrets of politics.[28]

Politics absorbed and challenged him, especially after he met McKinley, for whom he formed a deep respect. "You are not mistaken in your opinion and standard of McKinley," he wrote a friend in 1892. "He is all you believe him to be and as true as steel." In 1895, Hanna retired from business to devote full-time energies to the McKinley campaign, certain, as he said, that "nothing short of a miracle or death will prevent his being the nominee of the party in '96."[29]

McKinley and Hanna made an effective team. The Major commanded, decided general strategies, selected issues and programs. He stressed ideals. "Mark," he would say, "this seems to be right and fair and just. I think so, don't you?" Hanna organized, built coalitions, performed the rougher work for which McKinley had neither taste nor energy. Importantly, they shared a Hamiltonian faith in the virtues of industrialism, central authority, and expansive capitalism. That faith, triumphant in the 1896 presidential election, became one of the reasons for the vital importance of that election.[30]

A year before the convention, they had settled on an effective strategy: exploit the opposition of Platt and Quay in a campaign of "McKinley against the Bosses" and "the People against the Bosses." McKinley would be featured as "the Advance Agent of Prosperity," the candidate best qualified to lead the nation out of depression. In the race for convention delegates, they would hold McKinley's own Midwest, woo the South, erode Reed's strength in New England, pick up support in the Far West, and wait for others to join the bandwagon. It all worked. As early as March 1896, the bandwagon had become a steamroller.[31]

For Reed, disaster came where he least expected it, in his crucial home base in New England. During the spring of 1896, Republican state conventions in Maine and Massachusetts, as he had hoped, held firm for him, but in late March, New Hampshire, to his surprise, endorsed both McKinley and himself. Far worse, on April 28, the convention in Vermont, in a state almost next door to his native Maine, adopted a resolution expressing a preference for McKinley.[32]

The news dealt a crushing blow to Reed's chances, as did the clear depth of feeling in favor of McKinley throughout New England. "Now we can make no mistake about this," George H. Lyman, chair of the Massachusetts state Republican committee, told a Reed loyalist. "McKinley has out-generaled us all to pieces. I have nothing to say against those who lead our forces, but our sub-Lieutenants are not 'in it' with McKinley's." The McKinley camp "[has] spread through the country a McKinley atmosphere," Lyman added, whereas Reed's campaign "lacks enthusiasm—an element which their campaign possesses to a startling degree."[33]

That was all bad enough, but there was another blow yet to come, this one, unexpected, on the eve of the party's national convention in St. Louis. Manley, Reed's chief adviser, a shrewd and experienced politician who had learned his politics at the knee of the legendary James G. Blaine, suddenly blurted out to a reporter that McKinley had the nomination sewn up on the first ballot. Manley immediately apologized to Reed: "It was a great mistake and I shall regret it all my life," he said, but the damage was done. Reed was appalled. "Manley's conduct is too disgusting to characterize. What bad luck I have had," he concluded, always ready to blame others instead of himself.[34]

Watching these events, McKinley's confidence grew. "Things are looking well all along the line," he had written Whitelaw Reid, editor of the influential *New York Tribune,* as early as February. "Indeed, they could not well look better. Every new entry in the field, it seems to me, has a tendency to weaken the Eastern friends." Reid, in common with other Republicans, agreed but cautioned against complacency. No one should ever take Platt and Quay— those "Eastern friends"—lightly. "Don't let Mr. Hanna underrate the desperation of the combined opposition, or forget that they have all the money they want," Reid warned McKinley.[35]

Encouraging reports were also coming in from the South, long a valued source of Republican convention delegates, though, since the region almost always voted Democratic, not of electoral votes. Knowing their value lay almost solely in their convention votes, many southern Republicans had traded those votes for years, hoping, too, that a lucrative patronage appointment might come their way if their candidate somehow won.

In adopting this approach, black Republicans were simply being realistic. These were the years of Jim Crow, when southern whites used poll taxes, complex voting procedures, court decisions, violence, and a host of other measures to keep African Americans from voting. The numbers of black voters plummeted across the South. In the mid-1890s, to take one example, there were more than 130,000 registered black voters in the state of Louisiana, though relatively few of them actually got to vote. By 1904, there were 1,342.[36]

Although most of them could not vote, blacks could still serve as delegates to conventions, where their votes were greatly valued. That value could confer some social and political status and—in trades with eager national candidates—some much-needed cash. Aware of that fact, Platt had prowled the region in the past, building up alliances and debts. Hanna had, too, working the South tirelessly for his candidates. He did it again in 1895 and 1896, knowing that southern delegates held one of the keys to a McKinley victory.

To make sure of it, Hanna in 1895 acquired a vacation home in Thomasville, Georgia, near the Florida border, to use as a base for gathering McKinley support. In March of that year, he invited the McKinleys themselves to visit—Ida to bask in the South's healing sun, William to hunt for delegates without seeming to do so. They were in Thomasville only for "a little rest and outing," McKinley told reporters, none of whom believed him. There, on Hanna's sun porch, McKinley graciously entertained visiting politicians from across the South, while members of his staff traveled around the region, talking up the Major to those who could not make the trip. In light of later events, it is likely that in some conversations, McKinley hinted at a softer federal policy toward white southerners if he were elected. Buoyed by their reception, McKinley and Hanna made a speaking tour through Florida on the way home, gathering up more delegates before returning to Washington.[37]

The strategy, it was soon clear, paid off handsomely. At the Republican party's national convention, McKinley needed 453½ votes to win the nomination; he received nearly half that number from the South and the border states.[38] To Hanna's special delight, Platt never saw it coming, the New Yorker remaining forever amazed at Hanna's quiet success at collecting delegates in the region. "He had the South practically solid before some of us awakened," Platt lamented in his autobiography.[39]

During March and April 1896, Republican conventions in Ohio, California, Indiana, Nebraska, Michigan, Minnesota, and Wisconsin all instructed for McKinley, signaling the approaching end to the contest. "These McKinley fellows have almost taken our breath away by the enthusiasm they manifest for their candidate," an Indiana Republican noted. Trying to dig up backing in Indiana, supporters of Levi P. Morton found a "volcanic McKinley eruption." In Minnesota, Cushman K. Davis, the state's favorite son, dropped out of the race. "Nothing can stop us now," Hanna said on hearing the news. "All say there is no sense in trying to stem the McKinley tide," a Platt aide wrote. "At present it is one wide yawp and everybody is joining the yell in order to be on the loaded wagon."[40]

A final chance to slow the wagon remained—the delegate-rich state of Illinois, whose convention would meet on April 30. Many had long thought Illinois offered the best opportunity to stop McKinley's rush for the nomination.

*Mark Hanna, the head of McKinley's campaign, who adopted new
methods of organization, fund-raising, and efficiency that shaped later
presidential elections. (Frederick Meserve Collection, by permission of the
Houghton Library, Harvard University, Cambridge, Massachusetts)*

"We must gather up our loins there," Allison's manager had written in December 1895, "for that is the heart of it all."[41]

The strategy depended on one thing: the ability of veteran Illinois senator Shelby M. Cullom to hold on to his own state, but embarrassingly, he, like Davis in Minnesota, could not do it. "The McKinley forces are organized all over my State," Cullom noted as early as March. "They have their agents tramping around, organizing McKinley clubs and doing anything in their power to make the State solid for McKinley." The results showed at the April convention, where the delegates drubbed a resolution backing Cullom— beating him even in his own county—and endorsed McKinley. "The very air is full of McKinley," an Illinois Republican wrote the Major.[42]

The decisive win in Illinois gave McKinley enough delegates to ensure his victory at St. Louis. Quay signaled Platt to tone down his statements against McKinley, and he himself visited Canton to make peace. "The walls of the anti-McKinley Jericho are knocked too flat by the blast of the Illinois trumpet to be rebuilt," the *New York Evening Post* commented. "Quay and Platt and Manley make a dismal pretense of continued cheerfulness, but they see the fatal drift away from them, and know it cannot be checked."[43]

The *Evening Post* was right. On June 16, when the Republican convention opened in St. Louis, McKinley and Hanna were in full control. McKinley's face and name were everywhere: on buttons, badges, banners, and canes made of the famous "McKinley tin." South Carolina delegates peddled a drink they called "the McKinley," made of bourbon whiskey, lemon juice, and sugar. On a wall inside the convention hall, a large banner proclaimed "Republicanism Is Prosperity," a keynote for McKinley's upcoming campaign, which would feature him as "the Advance Agent of Prosperity" and sponsor of "the Full Dinner Pail," two effective slogans that would soon adorn the new pin-back buttons.[44]

Hanna had arrived early, to see to last-minute details. With McKinley's nomination in hand, the platform took up most of his attention, especially the plank on the currency. Initially, he and McKinley had wanted to emphasize the tariff, play down the gold-silver controversy, promise to work for international bimetallism, and pledge to maintain "our present standard" of currency, which everyone knew, without mentioning the actual word, meant gold. They had hoped to let McKinley's mild bimetallic record speak for itself, but silence invited ridicule:

My words have been for silver,
My silence stood for gold,

And thus I show the teaching
Of some great sage of old.
And if there is a question
As to just what I meant,
I'll answer that quite fully—
When I am president![45]

Where there was ridicule, there was sure to be Reed, who happily remarked that in most circuses, "there was always at least one first class acrobat who could ride two horses at once."[46]

Like many Republican congressmen, McKinley had a mixed record on the currency. Though always opposed to free silver, he had long favored some use of the white metal, a view that found support among many of his constituents. As a result, he had voted in his first term in the House for the Bland-Allison bill favoring silver and then voted to override President Hayes's veto of it. A few years later, he had also voted for the Sherman Silver Purchase Act of 1890.[47]

But the situation was different now. Lines had hardened on the currency issue; depression had swept the land; and McKinley was a likely nominee for the presidency, not just a candidate for Congress from an Ohio district. In that light, both he and Hanna soon came to believe a firm statement for gold might prove useful. It could drive the Democrats toward a divisive stand for free silver and win praise in the East and Midwest, both crucial regions for a Republican victory.

Through the spring of 1896, McKinley hesitated, but he began to lean more and more toward including in the platform the key word *gold*. Once he had made his own decision, he shrewdly played a waiting game, letting sentiment gather among Republicans for an unequivocal plank, a strategy designed to build consensus and avoid bitter divisiveness within a party that contained members favoring gold, silver, or both.[48]

The plan was "to harmonize all sections," as Mark Hanna remembered in 1900, "and prevent any discussion of the subject outside the [Platform] Committee which would line up any factions against it (except the ultra silver men). In that I succeeded, and felt willing to give all the credit claimed by those who assisted."[49]

Dozens claimed the credit, including Platt, Theodore Roosevelt, and Senator Henry Cabot Lodge of Massachusetts, who canvassed hotel hallways and meeting rooms arguing urgently for a firm statement for gold. They did have some helpful effects: Lodge, for example, devised the attractive pledge in the platform to work for an "international agreement" for silver. Platt, who had hoped to use the issue to sidetrack McKinley's nomination, long claimed that the adoption of the gold plank at St. Louis was "the greatest achievement of my political career." But McKinley had made that decision well before the convention opened. "Tell our friends at St. Louis they can't make the platform too strong for me," he had told a key lieutenant on convention eve.[50]

On Thursday morning, June 18, the platform committee was ready to report, beginning with an attack on the Cleveland administration, a reaffirmation of the party's commitment to tariff protection, and then the crucial fifth plank:

> The Republican party [it said] is unreservedly for sound money. (Great applause). It caused the enactment of a law providing for the payment of specie payments in 1879. Since then every dollar has been as good as gold. (Applause). We are unalterably opposed to every measure calculated to debase our currency or impair the credit of our country. (Applause). We are therefore opposed to the free coinage of silver, except by international agreement with the leading commercial nations of the earth— (The speaker," the official convention Proceedings noted, "was here interrupted by a demonstration of approval on the part of a large majority of the delegates which lasted several minutes).
> (Continuing . . .)
> which agreement we pledge ourselves to promote, and until such agreement can be obtained, the existing gold standard must be maintained.[51]

The cheering continued. The plank was everything gold-standard Republicans could have wished.

That same afternoon, the delegates listened with respect as Senator Henry M. Teller of Colorado, a white-haired veteran of Republican politics and one of the founders of the party back in the 1850s, proposed a free silver substitute for the gold plank. His eyes filled with tears, Teller warned the convention that the statement in favor of gold meant continued depression and Republican disaster. He told the delegates:

> I contend for [the substitute] because in this year of 1896 the American people are in greater distress than they ever were in their history. I contend for it because this is in my judgment the great weight, the great incubus, that has weighed down enterprise and destroyed progress in this

favored land of ours. I contend for it because I believe the progress of my country is dependent on it. I contend for it because I believe the civilization of the world is to be determined by the rightful or wrongful solution of this financial question.[52]

That last statement was quite a mouthful, a vivid measure of the importance some silver men were giving the issue this year. If the convention voted for the gold plank, Teller went on, "I must, as an honest man, sever my connection with the political organization that makes that one of the main articles of its faith. (Applause)."[53] Teller stood on the stage, sobbing. The delegates cheered and sympathized, respecting his many years of service to the party, but defeated the substitute by a large margin, 818½ votes to 105½.[54]

At that, Senator Frank Cannon of Utah, another silver Republican, went to stand beside Teller on the platform. Cannon, at Teller's request, planned to speak for the silverites who were about to walk out of the hall, but he was young, relatively new to the party, and lacked the many relationships Teller had built up over the years. He never had a chance.

"Who's that?" Hanna asked a congressman sitting next to him. "Cannon," was the reply. "Who's Cannon?" Hanna asked. "How did he break in?" "Senator—Utah," replied the congressman. "Perty, ain't he?" Hanna said. "Looks like a cigar drummer!"[55]

Someone in the galleries soon interrupted Cannon with a shout, "Goodbye, my lover, goodbye!," and as he tried to go on, delegates and spectators began to yell: "Put him out," "Let him print it," and "Go to Chicago," the site of the upcoming Democratic National Convention.[56]

Twenty-three silver Republicans, far fewer than Teller had hoped, marched up the aisles. Teller was still in tears. ("Silver is, we think, the first raw metal that has ever been wept over," The Nation, an eastern gold journal, jeered.) A Vermont senator grabbed Senator Fred T. Dubois of Idaho, saying, "Oh, Fred, don't leave; go back, go back and stay where you belong." Himself in tears, Dubois replied, "I hated to do it, but as an honest man, true to my people and my convictions, I must go."[57] In the Ohio delegation, Hanna stood on a chair screaming, "Go! Go! Go!" William Jennings Bryan, there as a special correspondent for a Nebraska newspaper, climbed on a desk to get a better view.[58]

Outside the hall, the Republican silverites caucused briefly and met with a delegation of Populist leaders who had come to St. Louis in anticipation of a walkout. The two groups reached "a perfect agreement as to the future," Herman E. Taubeneck, the People's party chairman, announced, "and henceforth we will work along the same lines." They would try to unite Populists, silver Republicans, and silver Democrats against McKinley and the "money power," with Teller, they hoped, as the group's presidential nominee.[59]

The platform settled, the delegates turned eagerly to the nomination for president, though the outcome, as they all knew, was already determined. As expected, Iowa nominated Allison; Maine (through Massachusetts) named Reed; New York named Morton; Pennsylvania, Quay.

Back in Canton, McKinley sat in his library, near the telephone and telegraph lines that connected him to his lieutenants in St. Louis. His wife and mother and a few friends chatted in the parlor across the hall. From time to time, McKinley walked over to have a word with Ida or, smiling, ask her friends, "Are you young ladies getting anxious about this affair?"[60]

In St. Louis, it was soon Ohio's turn. Governor Joseph B. Foraker, a long-time McKinley rival in the state, had agreed to place the Major in nomination, McKinley in turn agreeing to support Foraker for a coveted seat in the U.S. Senate. Foraker was a powerful and eloquent orator, and he easily carried the delegates with him. Like the speakers before him, he began with an attack on the Cleveland administration, establishing a dominant Republican theme for the election campaign that year:

> [It has been] one stupendous disaster, . . . a disaster, however, not without at least one redeeming feature. It has been fair—nobody has escaped. It has fallen equally and alike upon all sections of the country and all classes of our population. The just and unjust, the Republican and the Democrat, the rich and the poor, the high and the low, have suffered in common. . . . Over against this fearful penalty we can set down one great blessed compensatory result. It has destroyed the Democratic party. The proud columns that swept the country in triumph in 1892 are broken and hopeless in 1896.[61]

People clearly wanted something different in their president this year, "a man," he said, "who . . . typifies in name, character, record, ambition and purpose the exact opposite of all that is signified by the present free trade, deficit making, bond issuing, labor starving, Democratic administration." The delegates, cheering loudly, savored the words and the rolling rhythms. "I stand here," Foraker continued, "to present to this Convention such a man. His name is William McKinley."[62]

At this, the first mention of McKinley's name, delegates rushed into the aisles, shouting and cheering, throwing hats and canes in the air. Others stood on chairs and yelled, waved fans and flags, and blew on horns. McKinley, at home, sat back in his chair and then leaned forward again to listen over the telephone line to a curious hum, something no presidential candidate had ever heard before, the sound of the demonstration in his behalf in far-off St. Louis. The telephone operator, distracted by the cheering, had left the receiver off the hook, and McKinley heard himself being cheered, "like a storm at sea, with wild, fitful shrieks of wind," said a veteran reporter who was there.[63]

Being interrupted in the middle of a speech was difficult, "like stopping a race horse in full career," McKinley remarked to those around him. The operator in St. Louis returned to the telephone, and McKinley could hear Foraker continue: "You seem to have heard the name of my candidate before," the Ohioan was saying. "Ah," McKinley said, "that is like him. He knows what he is doing and is all right."[64]

"And so you have," Foraker went on. "He is known to all the world." "No other name so completely meets the requirements of the American people; no other man so absolutely commands their hearts and their affections." Elect him, Foraker concluded, "and he in turn will give us an administration under which the country will enter upon a new era of prosperity at home and of glory and honor abroad."[65]

As the balloting unfolded, McKinley followed it carefully, making notes as he went. It took only one ballot, his ranks holding firm. When Ohio was reached on the roll call, he needed only twenty votes for the nomination; Ohio itself had forty-six, all of course pledged to its native son. Rising from his chair, McKinley again crossed the hall to the room where his wife and mother waited. "Ida," he said, "Ohio's vote has given me the nomination." He kissed her, then turned and kissed his mother. The two women cried.[66]

Outside, a large crowd stood in Canton's town square, watching the bulletins as they came in from St. Louis. When McKinley's nomination was announced, the big fire gong sounded in City Hall tower. Steam whistles, cannons, guns, calliopes, bells, and firecrackers went off; bands played; and Canton's streets crowded with people shouting in triumph. The noisemakers, a reporter said, "all united to create a commotion that might have startled the man in the moon and the dwellers in Mars."[67]

Horsemen and bicyclists raced up North Market Street to McKinley's home. People crowded on the front lawn, while some of his companions fled out the back door. "You have my sympathy," one of them remarked as he left.[68] Early souvenir hunters began to pluck flowers from his flowerbeds and steal pieces of his fence. Pickpockets were already working the crowd out front, evidenced in a score of empty purses found at the end of the day.[69]

Back in St. Louis, the final totals gave McKinley 661½ votes to 84½ for Reed, 61½ for Quay, 58 for Morton, and 35½ for Allison. The Major's triumph was overwhelming, positioning him nicely for the campaign. The convention then named Garrett A. Hobart of New Jersey for vice-president, after Reed turned it down. A well-to-do corporate attorney, Hobart was popular in New Jersey and surrounding states, states that were important for McKinley's election, and he added strength to the ticket. Had he not died of heart disease in November 1899, he, not Theodore Roosevelt, would likely have become president after McKinley's assassination in 1901.[70]

In Canton, delegations from nearby towns were already pouring in, met at the railroad station by mounted escorts and led to the McKinley home. Some 2,000 people arrived from Alliance, Ohio. Massillon sent nineteen carloads, the cars so jammed that people clung to the sides and tops of the coaches. More arrived from other neighboring towns, including Niles, McKinley's hometown. The Niles delegation carried tin buckets and tin banners, tin canes, tin whistles, and tin horses, all reminders, of course, of the provision in the McKinley Tariff that had helped start a tin factory in Niles. In the group was Henry Mason, the only one there who had known McKinley as a boy: "He was a good steady young fellow, as I remember," Mason told a reporter.[71]

Standing on a chair on his porch, welcoming the crowd, McKinley immediately established the themes that would dominate his campaign: a sound currency, a tariff to protect American business and labor and put money in the Treasury, and a return of prosperity. "What we want in this country is a policy that will give to every American workingman full work at American wages," he told the crowd. "A policy that will put enough money into the Treasury of the United States to run the Government. A policy that will bring back to us such a period of prosperity and of plenty as that we enjoyed for more than thirty years prior to 1893."[72]

McKinley spoke to 50,000 people that day, all between 5 p.m. and midnight, a signal of the strategy he would follow until November.[73] He retired after midnight, exhausted. Planning for the campaign would start the next morning. Republicans were pleased and confident. They had a popular, experienced candidate, a respected vice-presidential nominee, and an attractive platform. The defection of the silver Republicans might cause trouble, but a strong stand for the tariff and sound currency should overcome that. For the moment, the gold plank brought relief, a thankfulness to have the matter settled. Hanna would head the campaign, ensuring an energetic and effective organization. The Democrats carried the twin burdens of depression and Grover Cleveland. Surely, McKinley would win.[74]

4 DEMOCRATS DIVIDED
THE DEMOCRATIC CONVENTION AT CHICAGO

You shall not press down upon the brow of labor this crown of thorns,
you shall not crucify mankind upon a cross of gold.
—William Jennings Bryan[1]

Nearing their national convention, the Democrats staggered under their burdens. They were tired and discouraged, torn by anger and dissension. Administration Democrats fought antiadministration Democrats. Gold men fought silverites; section battled section; leaders such as Gorman and Bryan and Wilson argued over the party's future. Cleveland sulked, alternating between periods of withdrawal and feverish bursts of activity. He fished, protected the gold reserve, and paid careful attention to personal investments. "I find I am developing quite a strong desire to make money," he wrote his financial adviser in 1895, "and I think this is a good time to indulge in that propensity."[2]

That was an interesting thought, this making of money: in 1895, the nation Cleveland led continued to suffer under grave economic hardship. It was the third year of depression. Millions remained unemployed; many had lost hope. Farmers went bankrupt, their farms auctioned off to pay their debts.

In June 1894, Susan Orcutt, a young farm woman from western Kansas, wrote her governor a letter. She was desperate. Like thousands of others, she had no money and nothing to eat. "I take my Pen In hand to let you know that we are Starving to death," she wrote. Hail had destroyed their crops. "My Husband went away to find work and came home last night and told me that we would have to Starve. He has bin in ten countys and did not Get no work. . . . I havent had nothing to Eat today and It is three oclock."[3]

Conditions were no better in the cities, as the records of the Massachusetts state medical examiner illustrated: "K.R., 29," suicide by drowning: "Out of work and despondent for a long while. Body found floating in the Charles [River]." "F.S., 29," suicide by arsenic: "Much depressed for several weeks. Loss of employment. At 7:50 a.m., Jan. 1, she called her father and told him she had taken poison and wished to die." "R.N., 23," suicide by bullet wound of the brain: "Out of work. Mentally depressed." Shot himself in the right temple. "Left a letter explaining that he killed himself to save others the trouble of caring for him."[4]

The files of medical examiners across the country told a similar tale. Hardship lay everywhere, as did anger and bitter disillusionment. Fed up, many Democrats in the Midwest, Far West, and South had had enough; they wanted to disavow Cleveland and set a new course but recognized the strength of party loyalty and the powers of incumbency. Rarely in American history has a political party repudiated its sitting president. It happened to Grover Cleveland in 1896.

It started early. In 1894, more than twenty Democratic state platforms came out for free silver. That fall, the elections accelerated the trend, decimating the Democrats in the Northeast and Midwest. Power within the party suddenly shifted to the South, where it remained for decades. The party's base narrowed; its outlook increasingly reflected southern views on silver, race, and other issues. Elsewhere, the elections persuaded worried Democrats of the need to move in fresh directions. John P. Altgeld, the head of the Illinois party, led the way. A shrewd and sensitive politician, Altgeld recognized silver's potential. It enabled Democrats to dissociate themselves from the hated Cleveland, disavow past mistakes, and revive their flagging fortunes. It turned dejected Democrats into spirited ones. The fight for silver "has stirred up our people" and "put new life into the Democratic party here," Altgeld told party leaders in other states.[5]

Altgeld moved early, conscious of the need for quick action to head off opposition from the Cleveland Democrats. In June 1895, over a year before the Democratic National Convention, he called a special state convention to place the Illinois party on record for free silver. Party organizations in several other states immediately followed. In August, silver Democrats formed a Bimetallic Democratic National Committee, a "shadow" group to parallel the Cleveland-run regular committee. It monitored administration activities and lobbied for free silver platforms. In Iowa, Horace W. Boies, the former governor, eased his party toward silver, hoping to use the issue for a presidential bid in 1896. Richard P. Bland, at fifty-eight the elder statesman of the silver cause, had similar ideas in Missouri. A Jacksonian Democrat, Bland wanted to reunite the West and South in a crusade for silver and the common man.[6]

Out in Nebraska, William Jennings Bryan sensed an opportunity. Dissident Democrats had their issue, but they lacked a leader. Boies and Bland, Bryan thought, would surely stumble, and Altgeld, the most influential among them, could not run for president because of his German birth. Some strategists touted the Republican Henry M. Teller, but Democratic partisanship made his nomination unlikely. Aside from scattered dark horses, that left Bryan—the "logic of the situation," as he liked to tell friends during 1895 and early 1896.

Few Democratic leaders agreed. Bryan was young, barely thirty-six, and came from a Republican state west of the Mississippi River. He had served two terms in the House of Representatives, hardly enough experience for presidential responsibilities. If anything, he seemed a man for the future rather than the present. The influential Altgeld thought so, reminding Bryan: "You are young yet. Let Bland have the nomination this time. Your time will come."[7]

Bryan did not relinquish prizes so easily. He dreamed, and he had worked tirelessly to turn dream into reality. Growing up in rural Salem, Illinois, he had graduated from Illinois College as valedictorian in 1881. In college, he had studied diligently, become an award-winning orator, and courted Mary Baird, one of the many remarkable women of the late nineteenth century. Mary Baird Bryan was winsome and intelligent, most ambitious, a lawyer in her own right, and totally wed to her husband's interests. A few years after marrying, the young couple moved west to practice law in Lincoln, Nebraska. Only moderately successful as an attorney, Bryan discovered himself in politics. He loved people and won them over by showing it. As in everything he did, he worked hard at politics, polishing his skills, especially his extraordinary speaking ability. Bryan was a captivating public speaker, tall, slender, and handsome, with a beautiful voice that, in an era before microphones, projected easily into every corner of an auditorium. Practicing at home before mirrors, he rehearsed his speeches again and again, as Mary Bryan listened to pick out errors in tone or substance.[8]

In 1890, he won election to the House. A low tariff Democrat who switched to free silver, he symbolized his party's transition during the 1890s. He supported Cleveland in 1892, then broke with him over the depression

William Jennings Bryan, the famed "Boy Orator of the Platte," who captured control of the national Democratic party in 1896 and embarked on an unprecedented whistle-stop campaign that brought him close to victory. (Library of Congress, Washington, D.C.)

and the currency. Seeing the mounting public interest in silver, Bryan studied the issue and made it his own. Opponents thought him shallow and unsophisticated, a creation of his own voice, but he attracted a growing following. In 1893, he helped lead the fight against unconditional repeal of the Sherman Silver Purchase Act, and a year later, the object of Cleveland's bitter hostility, he retired from Congress to work full-time for silver. Between 1894 and 1896, Bryan canvassed the nation, courting editors, wooing potential delegates, and fanning interest in the silver cause. He turned down few invitations and spoke in almost every state. As always, his speeches built on each other, progressively bringing together favorite ideas and sentences from previous efforts. In December 1894, Bryan found a phrase he liked—"I will not help to crucify mankind upon a cross of gold"—and saved it for future use.[9]

Unlike McKinley, Bryan drew on the Jeffersonian tradition of rural virtue, suspicion of urban and industrial growth, distrust of central authority, and abiding faith in the powers of human reason. Jefferson, he once said, "placed man above matter, humanity above property, and spurning the bribes of wealth and power, pleaded the cause of the common people." Bryan pleaded the same cause. He believed in human progress, but unreflective, he never thought deeply about its processes or ends. He ably led and only dimly understood. Professionals scoffed at his presidential ambitions, and Bryan himself recognized the distant odds. His prospects depended on silverite control of the party and luck at the national convention. As 1896 approached, he seemed no more than an attractive dark horse, with strong ties to the discontented in the South and West, helpful friends among the Populists, and a broad network of party allies built up during years of relentless campaigning. In retrospect, he was the logical candidate, the embodiment of the forces reshaping the Democratic party.[10]

Tensions mounted through early 1896, as Democrats of different persuasions battled for control of the party. Everything rested now on the state conventions, some forty of them, that would meet between April and June to adopt platforms and choose delegates to the national convention. In February, Democrats in Congress voted almost two to one for a free coinage bill, an initial victory for the silverites. Bland, Boies, and Bryan—the "busy bees," Cleveland's secretary of agriculture, J. Sterling Morton, sourly called them— redoubled efforts for silver delegations.[11]

Cleveland lashed back, determined to hold the party for gold. He was sure the Democrats would lose that year, but he wanted a sound money candidate and platform to keep the record clean. Carlisle, Wilson, Morton, Hoke Smith, and other spokesmen went west and south to undermine silver and defend administration policy. The experience was sobering. Old friends shunned them; audiences jeered. Morton got a hostile reception on the Pacific Coast that included threats on his life. "The silver sentiment is universal all over the West, and it is growing," he growled to reporters on his return to Washington.[12]

In selecting a presidential candidate, some loyal Democrats argued that Cleveland should again be the choice—"having wrecked his party, he is the man who should be compelled to sit up and watch the ruins," the Republican *New York Tribune* jested—but even Cleveland's staunchest allies realized that his nomination was out of the question. Cleveland himself did not make his intentions known, hoping the continued use of his name might keep the sound money forces in his party together.[13]

Secretary of the Treasury Carlisle had some supporters, but he withdrew in April, saying he was much more concerned about the party platform than about its candidate. That may have been true, but Carlisle also knew that, linked to the unpopular Cleveland, he stood little chance of winning. Other possible gold candidates included William C. Whitney and David B. Hill of New York, Robert E. Pattison of Pennsylvania, and William E. Russell of Massachusetts. In Illinois, William R. Morrison said that he would accept the nomination if it came without a fight, an unlikely possibility.[14]

For months, some of those close to Cleveland still held out hope for a gold candidate. His Michigan friend Don M. Dickinson wrote him in mid-June 1896 that, after all, the gold men controlled the national committee, had "the right" on their side, and could count on the help of honest and principled delegates who "will be worth more than all the free-silver shouters in the Southern delegations to the Convention." Surely, "radicals" such as Altgeld and "Pitchfork Ben" Tillman of South Carolina would horrify undecided delegates, pushing them into administration ranks.[15] New York's Tammany Hall, Dickinson added, would send experienced men to help in the cause, an irony in light of the fact that Cleveland had first made his reputation by fighting that organization.[16]

Dickinson was wrong, very wrong. Overcoming party traditions and loyalties, the silver men won several early victories. In April, Oregon Democrats, the first to meet, went for silver. Washington, Colorado, Missouri, Alabama, and Mississippi followed, and the Nebraska party split in two, with separate conventions, platforms, and delegations. As expected, Pennsylvania, Massachusetts, and Rhode Island soon countered for gold. The gold men eagerly awaited news from Michigan, where Dickinson, with hard work, managed in late April to hold the state for gold. "Light out of darkness," Wilson re-joiced in his diary, adding the next day, "The silver men seem dazed by the victory of the Administration forces."[17]

If so, they were not dazed for long. In May, Tennessee, Iowa, South Caro-lina, Wyoming, and Oklahoma all declared for silver. "Now we find perverts where we least expected them, and a madness that cannot be dealt with or, indeed, scarcely approached," Wilson said sadly on May 26.[18] By the end of that month, twelve state conventions had met and favored silver, and only eight had gone for gold. "I have never seen the masses of the people so wild over a question they know little or nothing about," Wilson wrote on May 27, close to giving up on efforts to beat back silver sentiment in his own West Virginia district. "To reason with them is as impossible as to talk down an angry cyclone, and they turn away from all those whom they have been wont to follow in public matters with contempt." They were rallying instead, Wil-son lamented, behind "the loudest and emptiest demagogue who can rail at 'Goldbugs,' denounce Wall Street, and shout free silver."[19]

On June 3, Kentucky, Carlisle's own state, declared for silver, with effects that were felt throughout the South. The next day, Virginia Democrats voted 1,276 to 371 for a free silver platform. It was not even close. Silver Democrats nationwide sensed victory. All doubt soon vanished: during the rest of June, Kansas, Texas, Arkansas, North Carolina, Georgia, Louisiana, Ohio, Indiana, Nevada, New Mexico, Idaho, Montana, North Dakota, Utah, and California all went for silver.[20]

Cleveland made a final try, issuing a message to Democratic voters in mid-June. Although he had not counted heads, he said, "I refuse to believe that when the time arrives for deliberate action there will be engrafted upon our Democratic creed a demand for the free, unlimited, and independent coinage of silver." To adopt a free silver plank would be "unpatriotic" and "foolish," would harm the country, and would result in "lasting disaster to our party organization."[21]

By then, attention had turned to Illinois, whose delegates were scheduled to meet in late June. "What ups and downs we are having in this fight," the anxious Wilson wrote. "Before the Michigan Convention, we were very blue. After that, the fight seemed won. With Illinois under Altgeld's control, we may yet lose the Convention."[22] They would, indeed, and by an overwhelm-ing margin. On June 23, the Illinois state convention, with 1,065 delegates, voted unanimously for free coinage. For the gold men, it was a devastating blow. Of the twenty-three states that held conventions in June, eighteen went for silver.[23]

Equally noticeable, delegates in a large number of the conventions had hissed the name of Cleveland. The South Carolina platform denounced him outright. In Ohio, a delegate called him an "arch traitor," the "Benedict Arnold of the Democratic party."[24] At the Illinois convention, the keynote speaker prayed for forgiveness for Cleveland's nomination in 1892: "May God forgive us for it. There must be a limit even to divine wrath, for we have since then been beaten as with a scourge of scorpions." The statement evoked a "hurricane of cheers," a newspaper said, and yells of "Say it over again," "Hit him again," and "Tell the reporters to put that down," followed by another round of loud applause.[25]

As silver strength grew, so did the presidential hopes of a growing number of silver candidates. In the weeks before the convention, the press tended to focus on three: Henry M. Teller, the stalwart silver Republican from Colorado; Boies, the former governor of Iowa; and Missouri's Richard Parks Bland, a man so identified with the silver cause that he carried the nickname "Silver Dick."[26]

Teller, the fervent silverite who had walked tearfully out of the Republican convention, had a number of supporters, but many of them were Populist leaders who hoped the Democrats would name him and save them from having to endorse a Democrat. There was little chance of that. Silver Democrats were hungry for victory—and for the patronage jobs that went with it. "Young man, when we win a Democratic victory we want a Democrat," a veteran senator told a reporter. "I have served long in the Senate with Mr. Teller and I respect him, but the next Democratic President will be a Democrat and fill the offices with Democrats."[27]

Though he still had a following among silverites in the Midwest, Boies found that his prospects had also begun to flag well before the convention met. His rise had been fast, starting with his move to Iowa at the age of forty to practice law. A lifelong Republican, he grew impatient with the party's defense of high tariff rates, and in 1884, he cast his first Democratic vote for Grover Cleveland. Taking advantage of his switch, Iowa Democrats in 1889 named him for the governorship, which he won against great odds in this Republican state. Reelected in 1891, he immediately became a potential presidential candidate, reflected in his showing at the 1892 Democratic National Convention, where he placed a strong third in the balloting, behind Cleveland and Hill.[28]

But Boies had important disadvantages as well. His reputation was largely regional, confined to a handful of states in the Midwest. He had little backing within his own state organization, which was controlled by sound money men, and worse, he had voiced warm approval for Cleveland's use of troops in the Pullman Strike, a position that angered many silverites. Still, as late as July 1896, on the eve of the Democratic convention, the respected journal *Review of Reviews,* surveying presidential candidates, chose Boies as "more likely perhaps than any other man to receive the nomination."[29]

That left Richard P. Bland of Missouri, for many months the acknowledged front-runner for the nomination. A consistent spokesman for free coinage, he had the support of more silver Democrats around the country than any other person. In 1877, he had steered through the House of Representatives a free coinage bill, later watered down in the Senate. His name was part of the Bland-Allison Silver Purchase Act of 1878, an important victory for the silver cause. He had backed the Sherman Silver Purchase Act in 1890 and helped lead the fight to prevent its repeal in 1893. Those favoring him also argued that for this year at least, Missouri was well positioned between the West and South, making a Missouri candidate appealing to both sections. "Surely if the servant were worthy of his hire—and Bland was— Bland should have been chosen," a reporter later said.[30]

Bland himself thought his chances were good. The Republican convention, he believed, had helped him greatly. "The coming fight . . . ," he said when it was over, "is to be between the productive masses of the United States, and what might be called the fund-owning classes." Everyone knew where Bland stood in that fight.[31] He planned to stay away from the convention, working on his farm near Lebanon, Missouri, but ready to have his picture taken. He pretended disinterest: "I hope," he said, "they will not nominate me . . . if they can find a stronger man." In fact, Bland hovered near the telegraph in hopes of good news. He asked his doctor for something to calm his nerves. "Do you think you will be nominated, Mr. Bland?" the doctor asked. "Yes, I am sure of it. I do not want it but it seems to be coming my way."[32]

Yet Bland, like everyone else, had important issues working against him. Many colleagues, even some of his close friends, thought him old and uninteresting, a respected remnant of the past. A nice man, "he pulled no wires, and was artless as a child," a fellow Missouri politician said. A fervent and lifelong Democrat, he had little appeal for the Populists except for his devotion to silver. A Presbyterian, he had married a Catholic and raised his children as Catholics, leaving him open unfortunately to the anti-Catholic sentiment that was widespread in the period. In all this, Bland retained his popularity, but he had weaknesses that might harm him within an unusually fluid convention.[33]

Unlike Bland, there was one candidate eager to exploit that fluidity, the energetic and popular young Nebraskan William Jennings Bryan. Bryan himself liked his prospects. He was, as he often told friends, "the logic of the situation," and indeed there was some logic to it. In the spring of 1896, he explained it all to the wily political veteran Champ Clark of Missouri, who, stunned, had not even counted Bryan among the candidates. It lay in a simple process of elimination, Bryan said to Clark. "Bland will not be nominated, because it is too early to nominate a candidate from one of the old slave states. I have no prejudice on that subject, but others have." Boies was not well enough known. Senator Joseph C. Blackburn of Kentucky and Vice-President Adlai E. Stevenson, two other candidates, had little support. That left only himself, Bryan told Clark—"[and] I will get it."[34]

He had certainly worked hard for it. With relentless energy, he had spent a half-dozen years attending prosilver conferences, drawing up silver platforms, and lobbying state Democratic conventions. Along with his talented wife, Mary, he had written countless letters to party leaders and accepted almost every invitation to speak. "I perhaps was personally acquainted with more delegates than any other man who was mentioned as a candidate," he said once the convention was over. No doubt he was.[35]

He had also won the admiration of men like Pitchfork Ben Tillman of South Carolina, not a normal ally, by urging silver Democrats to take over the Democratic party, not form a new one. Once a hopeless strategy, it was, remarkably, about to come to fruition. "Bryan is the biggest man among us; he is the wisest man in our party," Tillman was now saying in the spring of 1896. He "advised that we keep the machinery, stay in the boat and let other fellows jump overboard if they wanted to. I know now that he was right, because it is certain that our crowd will control the next National Convention."[36]

Despite his confidence, Bryan knew that he remained something of a long shot for the nomination. For one thing, his chances depended upon a series of unforeseen events at the convention, nearly all of which would have to break his way for him to win. For another, he needed for now to remain a dark horse, to stay out of the limelight in order to head off attacks from the leading contenders, a strategy that turned out well—so well, in fact, that as the convention neared, several newspaper polls placed him last in the field. Some polls did not mention him at all.[37]

Watching events from Republican party headquarters, Charles G. Dawes, who knew Bryan and his talents well, thought differently, remarking to McKinley and Hanna that for the first time in American history, the two parties would nominate candidates with the same first name. The two men looked at him and laughed. Bland, they were sure, was a shoo-in for the Democratic nomination.[38]

It revealed a great deal about Bryan that he could even focus on the convention. On June 27, shortly before it opened, he attended the funeral of his old friend and law teacher Lyman Trumbull in Chicago. That same day, his beloved mother died unexpectedly in Salem, Illinois, at the age of sixty-two. He rushed home for the funeral. He wept, spoke eloquently of her influence on his life, and recited with others the verse from 2 Timothy that had been read at his father's funeral sixteen years before: "I have fought the good fight, I have finished the race, I have kept the faith." The words summed up Bryan's life as well.[39]

His mother buried, he once more displayed his deep devotion to politics, leaving Mary and the children in Salem to return to Chicago. He was eager to join the many silver men who were meeting there to plot strategy for the Democratic convention, intent on taking command of the proceedings from the start. They had also just learned that William C. Whitney, one of Cleveland's most formidable advisers, had decided at the last moment to go to Chicago to lead the fight for gold.[40]

Fifty-five years old in 1896, Whitney was already a legend in American life. One of his ancestors, a brigadier general in the Revolutionary army, had helped George Washington cross the Delaware. Whitney himself had married the daughter of a millionaire partner in the Standard Oil Company, who left him a large fortune on her death. A New York lawyer, he had served as secretary of war in Cleveland's first cabinet, managed Cleveland's triumphant reelection campaign in 1892, and had his fingers on every pulse—"the most influential man in the [Democratic] party," the New York Times said. In business or politics, no one took him lightly.[41]

He had planned on taking a European vacation but, heeding pleas from Cleveland and others, decided to go to Chicago instead. "Now is the time," he had written William E. Russell two weeks earlier. "Come with me to Chicago and we will do one of two things—either beat down this craze or save the *esprit de corps* of the Eastern Democracy by most emphatic action. This last is probably all we can do, but there is more duty in that at the present time than in anything else."[42]

With his usual flair, he hired a special train of three luxury railroad cars to take himself and his allies to Chicago. On Thursday, July 1, the cars left New York, carrying Whitney, David B. Hill, Russell, and other state Democratic leaders: the press promptly dubbed it the Gold Train. "The fight is being keyed up in the sound money states," Whitney said as they pulled out of the station, "and there is a great increase in the spirit and determination of Democrats who are going to Chicago to fight free silver."[43]

Whitney, for all his acumen, was in for a surprise. Arriving in Chicago, he found a city alive with silver badges, silver hats, and silver banners. Hurrying to his suite in the Auditorium Hotel, he dispatched allies to size up the situation. They returned, startled, with news that there were silverites everywhere. "For the first time I can understand the scenes of the French Revolution!" one of them said. It was a theme that gold Democrats would repeat throughout the campaign.[44]

In a lifetime accustomed to winning, Whitney still had hopes he could pull out a victory. His strategy was twofold. First, unlike Cleveland, he planned to offer a softer position on the currency, focusing on working for international bimetallism, an offer that might sway some moderate silverites. Second, he would make every effort to stop the silverites from gaining control of two-thirds of the delegates. If he could do that, Whitney and his allies might use the party's two-thirds rule to force the convention into accepting a compromise candidate and compromise platform.[45]

Undeterred, silver Democrats had long since done their own counting. "The two-thirds rule will not stand in our way long," Senator James K. Jones of Arkansas, head of the Democratic National Bimetallic Committee, said bluntly. "A majority can make its own rules. We will not abrogate the two-thirds rule unless it is necessary, but a majority is going to control the next Democratic convention."[46]

The Chicago Coliseum, home of the convention, was at the time the largest permanent exhibition hall in the world; it took up an entire city block, covering five and a half acres, and could seat 20,000 people, which it often did. Buffalo Bill's Wild West Show had just played there. Years later, Theodore Roosevelt and his cousin Franklin D. Roosevelt won presidential nominations there. In 1969, it hosted the final convention of the radical student group Students for a Democratic Society.[47]

In an era before artificial amplification, its size challenged the vocal chords of even the most expansive speakers. The room was huge, as large as a Gothic cathedral; the ceiling was low, and the echoes unpredictable. For the first time in the history of national conventions, managers hired a medical staff of sixteen doctors to take care of delegate ailments. Knowing the size of the delegates, they had also ordered special chairs, the kind, they specified, "that a three hundred pound man can jump on all day without weakening it." It was a wise decision in an emotional convention whose delegates often climbed on their chairs.[48]

Silverites filled the city's streets. "At this hour," a Populist leader wrote home to California, "all that is known is that the silver forces are in full control, and all Chicago rages with universal discussion of the money question." Pleased, Altgeld put the finishing touches on the Bland campaign. Bland supporters moved through the crowd distributing "Bland cornfield handshakes"—a shake of the right hand with a free glass of whiskey in the left. Supporters of Boies and Teller also worked the crowds. David B. Hill looked glum, telling one questioner, "I never smile and look pleasant at a funeral."[49]

As Whitney planned, the Democratic National Committee, meeting the day before the convention, recommended Hill of New York for temporary chair. To oppose Hill, silverites put up Senator John Daniel of Virginia. The vote was 27 to 23 for Hill, a far narrower margin than gold Democrats had hoped for. Clearly, there were already some defections in their ranks. By the same vote, the committee seated the gold delegates from Nebraska, which left Bryan out of the convention.[50]

But with those votes, gold had won its final victory. The next day, the convention's third day, the silver delegates happily displayed their strength. In a stunning party reversal, they defeated Hill for temporary chairman, seated contesting silver delegations, including Bryan's, and put together a platform that shocked administration Democrats. The financial plank said:

We demand the free and unlimited coinage of both silver and gold at the present legal ratio of 16 to 1, without waiting for the aid or consent of any other nation.

("The speaker," the official convention Proceedings noted, "was here interrupted by demands all over the hall that he read this paragraph again.")

Senator JONES: If the Convention will be quiet, I will read it as many times as they want to hear it. But I am hoarse, and I must appeal for order, because my voice is in bad condition, and I cannot hope to be heard unless the gentlemen of the Convention will be quiet. I will read it again.[51]

The Cleveland Democrats were prepared for that. They were not prepared for planks that denounced nearly every policy Cleveland had pursued since 1893. The platform called for lower tariffs and governmental economy; attacked the "arbitrary interference by Federal authorities in local affairs," a slap at Cleveland and the Pullman Strike; censured Cleveland's bond issues and his "trafficking with banking syndicates"; and chided the Supreme Court, which in 1895 had declared the income tax unconstitutional. Horrified, some Cleveland men immediately packed their bags and left for home. Others, resolving to fight on, drew up a substitute platform that defended the gold standard and praised the administration.[52]

Bryan had already had several strokes of good fortune. There had been talk, for example, of making him temporary chair, which would have placed him in the spotlight too soon. His name came up again for the post of permanent chair, but that idea was also set aside. Bryan thus lost two early opportunities to address the convention, which, he rightly thought, was no loss at all. It saved for him the one opportunity he wanted most: to address the delegates during the debate over the platform.[53]

But the order of that debate mattered, too. Some party managers had wanted Bryan to give the opening argument, which by tradition would review the details of the platform. Bryan, for his part, wanted nothing to do with a review of platform details. He wanted to make an emotional appeal to delegates who, he knew, were hungry for just that sort of appeal.[54]

In that process, Tillman's enormous ego unwittingly helped out, another break for Bryan. After everyone agreed to allot an hour and fifteen minutes to each side in the debate, Bryan asked Tillman if he wished to open or close for the silver side. He preferred to close, Tillman replied, but would need at least fifty minutes to do so, nothing less. Hill would surely oppose a closing speech that long, Bryan responded, and at that, Tillman agreed to let Bryan make the shorter, closing argument, precisely what Bryan had hoped for all along.[55]

Those who knew Bryan's skills on the platform were delighted. "I have heretofore spoken of the talk for Bryan for president," a newspaper friend of his said that night. "Tomorrow night there will either be a great deal more talk of this sort or what there has been will come to an end. I think there will be more."[56]

Bryan thought so, too. The evening before he was to speak, he, Mary, and a few friends ate a late supper at a restaurant near their hotel. Outside, bands marched, and people cheered for their favorite candidates. Many sported the new pin-back badges for Bland and Boies, the two preconvention favorites. Only a few supported Pitchfork Ben Tillman, but they wore the most eye-catching badge of all: a silver, three-pronged pitchfork, with a helpless gold-bug—Cleveland, Carlisle, and Republican senator John Sherman—impaled on each prong.[57]

Bryan watched the scene "in smiling confidence," a friend at the dinner later said. "These people don't know it, but they will be cheering for me just this way tomorrow night. I will make the greatest speech of my life tomorrow in reply to Senator Hill. . . . I will be at my best. Hill is the brains of the opposition, and when I have answered him it will dawn on the convention that I am a pretty good man to lead the fight."

"Don't you think that Mr. Bryan has a good chance to be nominated?" Mary Bryan chimed in, glancing at another friend at the table. Bryan did not wait for the answer: "So that you may both sleep well tonight, I am going to tell you something. I am the only man who can be nominated. I am what they call 'the logic of the situation.'" He alone, he said, had the kind of broad appeal to discontented farmers and laborers, silver Democrats, Populists, and silver Republicans that could win the election.[58]

The next day, a newsman standing near the front of the convention hall overheard another reporter predict Bryan's nomination. Who was this fellow Bryan? the newsman asked, and he was directed to "a youngish man with a smooth face, high forehead, and pronounced jaw. . . . He has on a short black alpaca coat, and is sucking a lemon." Why was he going to win? the newsman asked. He was sucking a lemon to clear his throat, the reporter replied, and that meant he was going to speak. The silverites were desperate for a leader. "If Bryan gets before them while they're in this condition, they're gone."[59]

As agreed, Tillman opened the debate, his hair uncombed, collar wilted, necktie undone. He looked like a "train robber," a respected reporter said. Worse, he quickly lost the audience with an agitated speech that combined an appeal to sectionalism with rabid abuse of Grover Cleveland. "I come to you from the South—from the home of secession—from that State where the leaders of—," he announced, drawing loud hisses from the audience, who wanted to hear nothing about the Civil War and sectional animosity.[60] "Mr. TILLMAN (resuming): 'There are only three things in the world that can hiss—a goose, a serpent, and a man.'" At that, more hisses broke out.

Tillman done, it was Hill's turn, and as he moved toward the platform, Clark Howell of the *Atlanta Constitution*, an old friend of Bryan's, passed the young politician a note. "You have now the opportunity of your life," Howell told him. "Make a big, broad, patriotic speech that will leave no taste of sectionalism in the mouth and which will give a sentiment that will touch a responsive chord in the heart of the whole country. You can make the hit of your life." Bryan, reading the words, quickly wrote back: "You will not be disappointed. . . . I will speak the sentiment of my heart and I think you will be satisfied."[61]

A speaker with long experience, Hill gave a "very strong speech," Bryan thought. "I would say at the outset, I am a Democrat; but I am not a revolutionist," Hill began cleverly, spurning Tillman's sectionalism, and then he urged delegates to vote down "this unnecessary, ridiculous, and foolish platform." "Be not deceived," he pleaded to the convention. "Do not attempt to drive old Democrats out of the party, who have grown gray in its service, to make room for a lot of Republicans and Populists and political nondescripts who will not vote your ticket at the polls."[62]

While Hill was speaking, a friend of Bryan's leaned over to whisper advice on how to answer his arguments. "I shall not spend a minute arguing those points," Bryan quickly replied. "I do not intend to make an argument for silver. The time for argument has passed. The time for action has come."[63]

Following Hill, Senator William F. Vilas of Wisconsin, a loyal administration supporter, provided a mind-numbing defense of Cleveland's financial policy, and delegates could barely hear former governor Russell of Massachusetts, whose voice, sadly, was hoarse from an illness that would kill him in scarcely a week.[64]

Toward the end of Vilas's speech, Russell, fearing that Vilas had eaten up too much time, asked that he be given extra time. Seizing the opportunity, Bryan, agreeing, asked that his own time be extended as well. It gained him ten minutes more, "and I needed it for the speech I was to make," he later said. "This was another unexpected bit of good fortune. I had never had such an opportunity before in my life and never expect to have again."[65]

As his own time approached, Bryan felt nauseous, as he often did before a major speech, and wished he could lie down. A reporter walking around the convention floor found him munching on a sandwich to calm his stomach. "Who will be nominated?" the reporter asked. "Strictly confidential, not to be quoted for publication," Bryan replied, "I will be."[66]

"Wait until you hear Bryan," the silver delegates were whispering as Russell came to a close. A stir of anticipation flashed across the floor. Spectators in the galleries stood up to get a better view. Loud cheers broke out.[67]

"I can see Hill yet, bald and short, with his dipping, pointed nose and his badger-like ferocity, gesturing with short strokes, as if with a broad sword, as he predicted the disgrace and the overthrow of the party," Edgar Lee Masters, the author, said. "Suddenly I saw a man spring up from his seat among the delegates, and with the agility and swiftness of an eager boxer hurry to the speaker's rostrum. He was slim, tall, pale, raven-haired, beaked of nose." Delegates caught at his coat as he made his way to the platform, "as if to bid him God-speed."[68]

He climbed the platform "two steps at a time," a reporter for the *New York World* said, with the look of a "strong-limbed, strong-lunged" athlete: "Ear-splitting noises were heard; waves of scarlet fans danced in the galleries." Another reporter, positioned about fifty feet away, saw "a man in the full energy of ambitious life—flashing, gleaming eye, broad-shouldered, straight as an arrow, the physique of a gladiator, the spirit of a crusader; voice clear and vibrant; 15,000 spectators emotionally following every word, every gesture."[69]

Bryan, as he often did with major speeches, had tested parts of this one before. He had tried out the cross of gold image in remarks in Congress. He had used most of the speech in a debate at Crete, Nebraska, just a week before the convention. As usual with important speeches, he and Mary had also practiced it over and over in front of a mirror at home.[70]

Nervous a few moments before, Bryan suddenly felt, he later said, "as composed as if I had been speaking to a small audience on an unimportant occasion." He extended his right arm toward the delegates in an appeal for silence. It took some time, but at last the crowd fell quiet. "I never addressed an audience which seemed to act in such perfect harmony; it reminded one of an immense chorus trained to sing in concert," Bryan recalled.[71]

Waiting for the delegates to quiet down, it struck Bryan that the earlier speakers had positioned him nicely for what he was about to say: Tillman had been angry and vituperative; Hill, cold; Vilas, dull; and Russell hard to hear.

Stepping forward, he lowered his hand to his side. "I would be presumptuous, indeed," he began in a soft voice,

> to present myself against the distinguished gentlemen to whom you have listened if this were a mere measuring of abilities; but this is not a contest between persons. The humblest citizen in all the land, when clad in the armor of a righteous cause, is stronger than all the hosts of error. I come to speak to you in defense of a cause as holy as the cause of liberty—the cause of humanity.

Bryan had the delegates from the start. Almost like a trained choir, they rose, cheered each point, and sat back to listen for more.

The silver issue, he said, was the most important issue ever discussed in America's politics, a judgment that overlooked much of the country's history but again measured the importance both sides were giving the currency issue this presidential year. For years, silver men had devoted themselves to this moment, to winning a silver platform in a national convention, and they were there, consequently, "not to discuss, nor to debate, but to enter up the judgment already rendered by the plain people of this country."

Easterners praised businessmen but forgot that laborers, miners, and farmers were businessmen, too:

> The man who is employed for wages is as much a business man as his employer; the attorney in a country town is as much a business man as the corporation counsel in a great metropolis; the merchant at the crossroads store is as much a business man as the merchant of New York; the farmer who goes forth in the morning and toils all day—who begins in the spring and toils all summer—and who by the application of brain and muscle to the natural resources of the country creates wealth, is as much a business man as the man who goes upon the board of trade and bets upon the price of grain.

Wild applause echoed through the hall; the galleries were "a mass of white because of the handkerchiefs waving." Bryan then spoke of the men who worked in the mines, in contrast to the few misers who spent their time conspiring for gold:

> The miners who go down a thousand feet into the earth or climb two thousand feet upon the cliffs, and bring forth from their hiding places the precious metals to be poured into the channels of trade are as much business men as the few financial magnates who, in a back room, corner the money of the world.

Cheering wildly, delegates stood on those load-bearing chairs and waved hats, canes, and banners. "Go after them, Willie," a man shouted, and another yelled, even louder, "Give it to them, Bill."[72]

Bryan had coined the words about the businessman the night before, and he always regarded them as the most powerful part of the speech.[73] Many in the audience agreed. High up in the gallery, a farmer had said to a friend that he was ready to leave, not caring to listen to "that crazy Populist, Bill Bryan of Nebrasky." The friend urged him to stay. For the farmer, it was worth it.

When Bryan spoke of the businessman, he threw his hat high in the air, slapped his coat on the seat in front of him, and shouted: "My God! My God! My God!"[74]

Bryan continued:

Our war is not a war of conquest; we are fighting in the defense of our homes, our families, and posterity. We have petitioned, and our petitions have been scorned; we have entreated, and our entreaties have been disregarded; we have begged, and they have mocked when our calamity came. We beg no longer; we entreat no more; we petition no more. We defy them!

Shouts echoed through the hall, and delegates again pounded on their chairs.

Savoring each cheer, Bryan defended the platform and the primacy of the money issue. Silver would make the masses prosperous and lead to other reforms.

If they ask us why we do not embody in our platform all the things that we believe in, we reply that when we have restored the money of the Constitution all other necessary reforms will be possible; but that until this is done there is no other reform that can be accomplished.

"You come to tell us," Bryan then said, turning to the gold men who were listening nearby,

that the great cities are in favor of the gold standard; we reply that the great cities rest upon our broad and fertile prairies. Burn down your cities and leave our farms, and your cities will spring up again as if by magic; but destroy our farms and the grass will grow in the streets of every city in the country.

A few more words and then the famous peroration came:

Having behind us the producing masses of this nation and the world . . . we will answer their demand for a gold standard by saying to them: "You shall not press down upon the brow of labor this crown of thorns, you shall not crucify mankind upon a cross of gold."

Bryan first moved his fingers down his temples, suggesting blood trickling from his wounds. He ended with his arms outstretched, in a crucifixion stance. Letting the silence hang, he dropped his arms, stepped back, then started to his seat.[75]

The delegates, transfixed, sat in a silence that Bryan found "really painful." For a moment, he thought he had failed, but suddenly, there was pandemonium.[76] Delegates shouted, cursed, and threw hats, coats, handkerchiefs,
and other objects into the air. They cheered, laughed, and cried. The famed
Illinois lawyer Clarence Darrow, who knew something about swaying an
audience, had never seen people so moved. "That is the greatest speech I
ever listened to," Darrow's friend Altgeld said in the midst of the shouting,
though, as a fervent supporter of Bland, he soon tried to divert attention elsewhere. From the platform, a reporter watched two old men embrace, tears
streaming down their cheeks. Delegates seized state banners and paraded
around the hall. Men who had traveled to Chicago to nominate other candidates were drawn into the excitement, including even some gold delegates
who "caught the infection," a newspaper said, and cheered. Outside, crowds
danced through the streets.[77]

As Bryan walked back to his seat, delegates fell over each other trying to
touch him. The aisles filled with yelling men. Bryan found himself in the
midst of a shouting, pushing mob, every man anxious to grasp his hand.
"Under the spell of the gifted blatherskite from Nebraska, the convention
went into spasms of enthusiasm," the hostile *New York Times* reported. Roar
after roar of cheers rose and fell "like the noise of a tremendous storm."
Thousands in the Coliseum were shouting at once, creating, a reporter said,
"a perfect Niagara of sound."[78]

It sounded like "one great burst of artillery," another reporter wrote.
The delegates stood on chairs and waved hats, canes, flags, and umbrellas.
"Some, like demented things, divested themselves of their coats and flung
them high in the air," an onlooker remarked. Surrounded by cheering men,
Bryan looked "bewildered, half-frightened, panting, yet proud and satisfied,"
a reporter thought.[79]

Jones passed Bryan a note: "You could be nominated on the first ballot.
Shall the voting begin?" No, Bryan answered: "If my boom won't last overnight, it won't last until November." To ensure there would be no nomination that night, he instructed his own Nebraska delegation to join in a call
for adjournment.[80]

The question came up again that evening as Bryan rode back to his hotel
with two friends from Nebraska. "Aren't you afraid that the adjournment
of the convention will spoil your chances for the Presidency?" they asked.
Bryan shook his head. "Don't rush things," he said. "If my candidacy won't
keep overnight it will wilt pretty soon on a canvass."[81]

The silver Democrats had found their leader. To Bryan, it was a moment touched with magic, a rare and perfect union of audience and speaker. He also knew that years of careful groundwork had prepared the way. When the tumult subsided, the delegates defeated the substitute platform and adopted the majority silver report, 628 to 301. With a sense of happy release, they also voted 564 to 357 against a resolution commending the Cleveland administration.

On the morning of July 10, balloting got under way.[82] From his hotel, Bryan had sent the Nebraska delegation his final instructions: "There must be no pledging, no promising, no trading on any subject with anybody. No delegation must be permitted to violate instructions given by a state convention. Our delegation should not be too prominent in applause. Treat all candidates fairly."[83]

On the first ballot, Bland led as expected, with 235 votes to 137 for Bryan and 67 for Boies. Though Bland did take the lead, he had already lost important ground. His managers had claimed to control the delegates from the South, but Bryan had won the votes of Georgia, Louisiana, Mississippi, and North Carolina. Most gold men, refusing to support the silver platform or a silver candidate, abstained from voting throughout the balloting.[84]

Both Bland (281 votes) and Bryan (197) gained on the second ballot. Boies, with only 37 votes, had already dropped well behind. The next ballot showed 291 for Bland, 219 for Bryan; Bryan was clearly gaining. As the fourth ballot got under way, Alabama, which had voted for Bland during the last two ballots, switched to Bryan, followed by Idaho and Kansas. As the crucial roll call ended, Bryan had finally overtaken Bland, 280 votes to 241.[85]

Across the convention floor, delegations caucused, weighing whether to join the Bryan bandwagon. Eyes fixed on Illinois, which throughout the first four ballots had cast its crucial 48 votes for Bland. At the end of the fourth ballot, its delegates demanded a caucus. "For God's sake, stand by Mr. Bland!" an Arkansas delegate said to Altgeld, holding tightly to his arm. Altgeld's face "was white as death," someone remembered, and no wonder: he had lost control of his own delegation. Bryan now led Bland by 4 votes within it, and under the unit rule, the entire Illinois delegation would switch to Bryan on the next ballot. Back in his hotel room, Bryan read the bulletin that Illinois was leaving the hall. "That settles it," he quietly said.[86]

On the fifth ballot, it was all Bryan. He gained votes from California and Florida. The convention cheered when the chair of the Kentucky delegation withdrew Blackburn. As the roll call unfolded, Bryan gained 1 to 5 votes from a variety of states, then Tennessee transferred its 24 votes from Bland to Bryan. Cheers again swept across the floor. Virginia gave Bryan 24 votes more. Shortly thereafter, the Illinois delegation returned to the hall, and Altgeld announced 48 votes for Bryan. At that, Ohio moved its 46 votes into the Bryan column.[87]

Although Bryan was still short of the nomination, the Bland leaders knew they had lost. The chair of the Missouri delegation stood and read a letter from Bland himself, asking the convention to withdraw his name whenever another silver candidate had a majority. With that, Missouri's 34 votes went to Bryan. Iowa finally withdrew Boies. Arkansas changed from Bland; Virginia followed. Texas switched to Bryan, followed by Utah, and a delegate moved to make the nomination unanimous.[88]

Pandemonium broke loose across the floor. Bands played "Hail to the Chief." Flags of other state delegations surrounded the Nebraska banner and were carried jubilantly across the hall.[89] Amid the cheering, abuse of Bryan had already begun. "Lunacy having dictated the platform," the *New York World* said, "it was perhaps natural that hysteria should evolve the candidate." "His speech to the convention was an appeal to one of the worst instincts of the human heart—," *The Nation* added, "that of getting possession of other people's property without the owners' consent. That is what is meant by free coinage at 16 to 1."[90]

Friends quickly congratulated Mary Bryan, who had watched the voting from a seat in the gallery. "I think my husband will try to deserve the great honor these men have conferred upon him," she told a reporter. "I appreciate it, I assure you. If his wife's aid is of value in the endeavor to elect him, he will have all possible assistance from me."[91]

That evening, at Bryan's hotel, police tried to keep the crowds from overwhelming him. The candidate stood in the door of his room, shaking hands as people passed by. Tired, he napped for twenty minutes, but people continued to walk in and out just to catch a glimpse of him. Awakening, he went back to shaking hands. "I seem to have plenty of friends now, but I remember well when they were very few," he said to someone nearby.[92]

When his room became too crowded, he walked down to the hotel lobby and shook hands for almost an hour. At one point, he reached for a piece of paper and wrote a telegram via the newspapers to the American people, promising, if elected, to serve only one term. Later in the evening, retreating to a bathroom to draft it, he sent a lengthy telegram to William Randolph Hearst, the influential owner of the *New York Journal*, inviting his support.

VOL. 31 NO. 773   AUGUST 8 1896   PRICE 10 CENTS

Judge

ENTERED AT THE POST OFFICE AT NEW YORK AS SECOND CLASS MATTER. COPYRIGHT 1896   BY THE JUDGE PUBLISHING CO.   TITLE REGISTERED AS A TRADE MARK.

"THE BOY STANDS ON THE BURNING DECK.
WHENCE ALL BUT HIM HAVE FLED."

"THE BOY STANDS ON THE BURNING DECK WHENCE ALL BUT HIM
HAVE FLED": A popular anti-Bryan cartoon depicting "Boy Bryan"
standing stubbornly on his ship's "Burning Deck," on fire because of his
"Silver Platform," "Populism," "Anarchy," and "Repudiation," all feared
by Republican and many middle-class voters. (Judge, August 8, 1896)

In the end, though Hearst himself opposed silver, the *Journal* became the only major eastern paper to back him.[93]

In newspaper interviews that evening, Bryan remained modest, thinking in particular of the venerable Bland. "My nomination," he told one reporter, "is due to the peculiar circumstances which surround this campaign and not to any superior merit of my own. In fact, had the convention considered who was most deserving the honor would have fallen upon another."[94]

In financial circles, there were many who wished it had. At the news of Bryan's nomination, the stock market faltered, and there was a rush for gold.[95]

That evening, Bryan and other party leaders met to discuss his running mate, to be chosen the following day. The names of Bland and Boies came up, but neither would take the job. A few who were there argued that someone poor should be named, to symbolize once again the Democratic campaign against privilege. Others, more pragmatic, urged the nomination of a candidate with enough money to help finance an already-bankrupt campaign.[96]

In the end, the delegates chose Arthur Sewall of Maine, who was sixty-one years old, a well-to-do shipbuilder, and a board member of a Maine railroad and bank, two entities many Bryan Democrats and most Populists did not like. In his favor now, he was one of a few significant business figures in the country who openly supported silver.

Bryan himself had never met Sewall until the man rushed over on the convention floor to praise Bryan's speech and urge his immediate nomination.[97] A member of the Democratic National Committee, Sewall had voted, the day before the convention opened, against Hill for temporary chair, and his colleagues on the Maine delegation had promptly removed him from the committee. He wired his wife that he had left politics for good. Several days later, he was the Democratic nominee for the vice-presidency.[98]

Sewall's nomination would pose large problems for Bryan and his Democratic allies. He favored silver, to be sure, but his interests in banking and railroading made him an easy target for Populists and others who preferred a candidate with a very different background and outlook. Bryan never quite figured out how to deal with the problem, nor did many of the Populists who would meet soon in their own national convention. The unfortunate Sewall would become a drag on both campaigns.[99]

To his delight, Bryan discovered that he and Mary had spent about $60 during the convention, "a sum," he later wrote, "probably as small as anyone has spent in securing a presidential nomination." The Pullman Palace Car Company offered him a private car for the trip home, but he turned it down, not wanting to seem to accept favors from railroad companies. On the way home, the Bryans were surprised to find people already standing along the railroad tracks, hoping for a glimpse of the candidate or, even better, a speech. When they reached Lincoln, cheering crowds filled the town.[100]

Along the way, Bryan realized that his newfound fame had preceded him, and there was a sense that he had done something remarkable at Chicago. He had somehow interpreted hundreds of delegates to themselves, voicing their sufferings, hopes, and fears. Champ Clark, the wise Missouri politician, recognized it immediately: "The reason of the astounding effect of its delivery was that he was expressing tersely, epigrammatically, and eloquently what two-thirds of that convention thought and wanted to say, but did not know how to say. In him they had found a mouthpiece—an interpreter. He set them on their heads and stole away their hearts."[101]

Edgar Lee Masters called the speech "the beginning of a changed America," and he in turn promptly changed his own life, dropping his study of classical economists and English literature and throwing himself into the cause. To many such as Masters, Bryan seemed a new Thomas Jefferson, perhaps a new Andrew Jackson, a man who could lead a nation once again on a crusade against privilege.[102]

"The fountains in the hearts of men were stirred," said Josephus Daniels, the influential North Carolina newspaper editor, and "like the others, I had been swept away on the tide of hero worship." People believed, he added, that Bryan was "a young David with his sling, who had come to slay the giants that oppressed the people and they felt that a new day had come and, with it, a new leader."[103]

Through the genius of the telegraph, famed Kansas journalist William Allen White later said, "the continent thrilled to that speech, and for a day a nation was in a state of mental and moral catalepsy. . . . If the election had been held that summer day, Bryan would have been chosen President." "It was the first time in my life and in the life of a generation," White added, "in which any man large enough to lead a national party had boldly and unashamedly made his cause that of the poor and the oppressed." White's reflections were generous, but they happened to have come years later. In July of 1896, he felt quite differently: "I was moved by fear and rage. . . . To me, he was an incarnation of demagogy, the apotheosis of riot, destruction, and carnage."[104]

There were many in the society who agreed. Bryan had stirred diverse forces in a divided nation, as White, a keen observer, had noted. There is no evidence that he would have won had the election occurred that July day in 1896. He would almost certainly have not—a speech that charmed the delegates might not carry a nation—but in any event, he and William McKinley still faced the trial of a long and important campaign, a campaign that became a legend in the ongoing story of American presidential politics.

5

BRYAN TAKES THE STUMP

A large portion of my voice has been left along the line of travel, where
it is still calling sinners to repentence.
—William Jennings Bryan[1]

After it was over, Bryan remarked that there had been few national conventions in American history as dramatic as the meeting in Chicago. There were contests, he noted, over candidates; deep-seated tensions over issues; and fights surrounding the temporary chairmanship, the seating of delegates, the platform, and the nominations themselves. And through it all ran a bitter struggle for control of one of the country's major political parties, a party that traced its heritage to Jefferson and Jackson and, for the outnumbered gold men in the convention hall, to Grover Cleveland as well.

"It was a great contest," Bryan said of the convention. "I venture the assertion that never before in the history of this country did any party have such a contest within its ranks as that which ended in Chicago."[2]

There was more drama yet to come. Almost from the moment Bryan won at Chicago, he began to receive letters that touched him deeply. Scribbled on torn sheets of paper, they told him of the difference his nomination had already made in people's lives. He was "the new Christ of Humanity," as one of them said, brought forth "to loose the chains of plutocracy from the people." "You are the first big man that i [*sic*] ever wrote to," an Iowa farmer said. "Dear father of our Country . . . ," an Indiana supporter wrote, "God has sent you amongst our people to save the poor from starvation and we no [*sic*] you will save us." During the campaign, Willa

Cather, the novelist known for her keen personal observations, saw "rugged, ragged men of the soil weep like children" as Bryan spoke to them in Red Cloud, Nebraska.[3]

Eugene V. Debs, the outspoken labor leader whom Bryan greatly admired, said much the same thing, calling him "the people's standard bearer in the great uprising of the masses against the classes":

> You are at this hour the hope of the Republic—the central figure of the civilized world. In the arduous campaign before you the millions will rally to your standard and you will lead them to glorious victory. The people love and trust you—they believe in you as you believe in them, and under your administration the rule of the money power will be broken and the gold barons of Europe will no longer run the American government.[4]

"The new Christ of Humanity," the "father of our Country," "the hope of the Republic—the central figure of the civilized world": these were heady words, and many candidates would have taken pains to sidestep them. Not Bryan, who saw himself, in fact, in those very terms. He believed his candidacy was the "first battle," as he later put it, in people's hope to improve their lot, fend off those hated gold barons, and regain their rightful role in a swiftly changing society.

The feeling, importantly, went beyond common folk and the leaders of labor. E. C. Wall, a prominent and well-to-do Cleveland Democrat in Wisconsin, believed in gold but supported Bryan, saying, "The fight today is, in my judgment, whether there shall be a republic or not. Whether a few men of wealth shall govern this land or the people."[5]

For many Americans, this sense that earthshaking issues were at stake lasted throughout Bryan's storied campaign. The day before the election, twenty-three married couples from central Pennsylvania joined in a letter to thank him for a noble campaign in which he had "pilloried plutocracy . . . and revealed to the people the privileged class, in all its revolting nakedness." Mary Bryan they thanked as well, for "risking health and life" to make "the cause of her husband, the people, her cause." Certain that Bryan would win the presidency the next day, they were eager to watch him free "a monopoly cursed people" from "the power of mammon."[6]

Thoughts of that sort gave a special urgency to Bryan's efforts, and on August 7, after a short rest at home, he set off on a political campaign that became an American legend. Weighing his options, he had decided to open it in New York City, to arouse, he said to close friends, "the enthusiasm of

our supporters to attack the enemy first in the stronghold of the gold sentiment." That decision was weighty enough, but he made another one as well:
he chose to read the speech in New York rather than deliver it extemporane-
ously, knowing, he later said, that he might disappoint thousands in the hall
but reach more effectively the hundreds of thousands who would read his
remarks in print.[7]

Phrases about the "enemy" were harmless enough when muttered in private but unfortunate when used in public. As the Bryans left Lincoln for the
trip to New York, he told the crowd at the railroad depot that he had wanted
to accept the nomination at home but had decided instead upon New York,
"in order that our cause might be presented first in the heart of what now
seems to be the enemy's country, but which we hope to be our country before this campaign is over." The phrase *the enemy's country*, so lightly said,
haunted him through election day.[8]

It may also have been a mistake not to rest along the way. By his own
count, Bryan spoke thirty-eight times on the trip to New York, including
speeches to large crowds in several major cities. Frequently, he was awakened during the night and spoke to trackside crowds, sometimes in his
nightgown. Joined on the train by his defeated rival Bland, he even stopped
off in Canton, McKinley's home, and graciously praised McKinley for his
"high character and great personal worth."[9]

"My dear," McKinley said to his wife, "this is Mr. Bland whom Mr. Bryan
defeated for the democratic nomination for president." "Bland," he said, as
Bryan looked on, "you should have been nominated; you were the logical
candidate and the strongest man your party had." "I am satisfied if my party
is," Bland replied, offering a polite close to a scene that was surely bizarre.
It was night when the Bryans reached New York City, "quite fatigued by the
journey," Bryan later wrote.[10]

The evening of the speech, 12,000 people crowded into Madison Square
Garden to hear the fabled "Boy Orator of the Platte." Another 15,000 stood
outside, unable to get in. It was unbearably hot: ninety-seven degrees, the
thermometers said. Significantly, David B. Hill stayed away, as did all but a
handful of New York State's Democratic leaders. Conservatives were openly
apprehensive, fearful that Bryan might rouse the unemployed to a new pitch
of discontent.

Governor William J. Stone of Missouri, introducing Bryan, did him no fa-
vors, delivering a long-winded speech that covered six closely printed newspaper pages.[11] Boos from a crowd eager to hear Bryan finally drove Stone
from the stage. Unfolding his manuscript, Bryan followed his plan, "only

laying the manuscript aside when near the conclusion," he recalled. He read for two hours. Half the audience had left by the time he finished, though it may have been the heat as much as the speech that drove them away. "The delivery was a disappointment to those present, as I knew it would be," Bryan said.[12]

It was, but in some ways, it still served Bryan's purpose. For two hours, he did his best to reassure voters that he and his platform offered no menace to private property, traditional institutions, or the social order. There was no plan to abolish the Supreme Court, as some opponents were already claiming, just a hope it would reverse its decision on the income tax. He explained at length his views on the money question and urged sectional unity and national honor.

Opponents charged that he stood for revolution, Bryan emphasized, but he did not.

> Our campaign has not for its object the reconstruction of society. We cannot insure to the vicious the fruits of a virtuous life; we would not invade the home of the provident in order to supply the wants of the spendthrift; we do not propose to transfer the rewards of industry to the lap of indolence. Property is and will remain the stimulus to endeavor and the compensation for toil.[13]

All in all, it was an acceptable performance, especially in light of the difficult circumstances. Some friends wished he had not read the speech and taken advantage of the compelling speaking skills that, after all, had drawn the thousands to the Garden. Friendly newspapers wished, too, that he had spoken at greater length on the income tax or the use of court injunctions against labor, both popular topics among urban workers. Instead, he had dwelled on silver, "the paramount question of this campaign," as he had told his listeners.[14]

Opponents, of course, had an easy time making fun of him. They pointed happily to his vanishing audience, scoffed at his "radicalism," and even gibed unfairly that Mary Bryan had worn the same dress to two different receptions. "To put it in blunt, sincere language, the great Bryan demonstration in the Madison Square Garden last night was a disappointment," the *New York World* said the next morning. "Mr. Bryan read a speech, temperate in tone and beautifully phrased, but he failed to fire the great multitude which came to see and hear him." With clear relief, conservative New Yorkers began talking derisively of the "Boy Reader of the Platte."[15]

The criticism did not faze Bryan at all. Though a deeply sincere man, he was also fairly unreflective, sure of his mission, wedded to his moral purposes, and certain that he stood for the right.

Back in Lincoln, he plotted his strategy for victory. There was, if he let himself look at it, plenty of room for discouragement. In early September, gold Democrats meeting in Indianapolis named a separate presidential ticket, obviously designed to take votes away from him. Democratic newspapers were deserting him in droves. In New York City alone, the *World, Sun, Herald, Times,* and *Evening Post* had already repudiated him, as did the *Herald, Globe,* and *Post* in Boston; the *Times* and *Record* in Philadelphia; and the *News* and *Sun* in Baltimore. With the defection of the *Chicago Chronicle,* the Democrats had no spokesperson at all in that city. In the South, the *Louisville Courier-Journal, New Orleans Picayune, Charleston News and Courier,* and *Richmond Times* refused to support Bryan and Sewall. All were widely read; all could usually be counted on to back the Democratic ticket. Hearst's *New York Journal* became the only Democratic newspaper in New York City and virtually the only paper in the whole Northeast that supported Bryan.[16]

Campaign cash was also hard to come by, and Bryan knew from the outset that he would have to campaign on a shoestring. Traditional Democratic donors were sending their money to McKinley or watching from the sidelines, eager for Bryan's defeat. By late August, a key checkpoint in the campaign, Bryan's funds were in such disarray that his campaign manager had to plead for contributions in an open letter to the American people. "No matter in how small sums, no matter by what humble contributions," he asked, "let the friends of liberty and national honor contribute all they can to the good cause." The "friends of liberty" doubtless did the best they could, but many of them had been struggling for years simply to keep their own lives afloat.[17]

As expected, Hearst and the *New York Journal* made one of the largest contributions to the campaign, nearly $41,000, Hearst himself chipping in $15,000 of the total. Marcus A. Daley, a Montana silver mine owner, reportedly sent $50,000, but contrary to campaign legends, little support came from the owners of silver mines.[18] Fervent in his backing for Bryan, the influential Henry M. Teller did everything he could to tap that source but with little success, thanks in part to the collapse of the silver market after 1893. "Times are dreadful hard here," he told another silver senator in September 1896. "We could have raised $100,000 four years ago easier than we can raise 10 now."[19]

All told, Bryan collected about $300,000 for his entire campaign, a dramatic contrast to McKinley's fund of $3,500,000. Those two figures alone measured some of the enormous challenges Bryan faced.[20]

Lacking money, Democrats could do little in the way of distributing campaign documents, only a small fraction of the materials the Republicans were sending out. In all, they managed to distribute only 10 million speeches and pamphlets, fewer than the Republicans mailed every few days, and 125,000 copies of *Coin's Financial School*, the prosilver pamphlet, once widely popular, that had just about outlived its usefulness. The National Silver party managed to add some 8 million documents, a woeful amount in this important campaign year.[21]

Like the Republicans, the Democrats established their headquarters in Chicago, with a branch office in Washington, D.C. Two of the party's allies, the People's party and the National Silver party, both chose to work out of Washington, in part to save scarce campaign funds. In one of his first decisions, Bryan chose Senator James K. Jones of Arkansas, head of the Bimetallic Democratic National Committee, to lead his campaign. The choice was tricky because Jones had the benefit of close ties with silverites but very difficult relations with southern Populists, whom he had once advised to join with "the negroes where they belong," a statement he quickly denied. Jones had also never led a national campaign, a disadvantage that became clear at several points during the canvass.[22]

There were other significant hurdles as well. The party of states' rights and limited government, the Democrats had long worked comfortably within a weak national party structure, which was not an advantage during a difficult national campaign. In normal years, they might profit from several electoral advantages over the Republicans—dominance in the so-called solid South, for example, and a lasting appeal to many voters in the North and Midwest—but this, of course, was not a normal year. The party was badly split between the Cleveland and Bryan wings; it suffered from voters' perception of its inability to deal with the hardships of the depression, and it had the task now of figuring out what to do about the challenge of the People's party. This, it was clear from the start, would not be an easy campaign.[23]

Fortunately for his party, Bryan had his own answers to these problems, built largely on his experiences during the early years of the decade. First, bypass traditional party organizations and pull on the help of the thousands of silver men and silver clubs he had met in his years of campaigning. Second, forget all the newspapers that were deserting him; if he made enough news on the stump, they would have to send reporters along on his train, print his speeches, and cover his campaign.[24] Third, finance the campaign by minimizing expenses and inviting small contributions. And finally, place Bryan the candidate on the national stump, where the same alluring voice that had helped him win the nomination might just land him in the White House.

"When I see this assemblage tonight," he told a large and cheering crowd in Chicago early in the campaign, "and when I remember what the newspapers in the city say (loud and continued hissing) I am reminded of what one of our friends said to me: 'Nobody is on our side except the people.'"[25]

Seizing on these ideas, many of them new to American politics, Bryan struck boldly. Skirting party leaders, newspapers, and organizations, he took his campaign directly to the voters. Contrary to legend, he was far from the first to do so. William Henry Harrison had campaigned in 1840, Stephen A. Douglas in 1860, Horatio Seymour in 1868, Horace Greeley in 1872, and James G. Blaine in 1884.

But he *was* the first presidential candidate to make a *systematic* tour of the states he needed for election. In a display of remarkable stamina, he traveled, by his own reckoning, 18,009 miles and delivered 570 speeches in 29 states, speaking to audiences totaling 2 or 3 million people. "It used to be the newspapers educated the people," he said to an August rally in Iowa, "but now the people educate the newspapers."[26]

Reporters who accompanied him never knew whether to scoff or praise. At the beginning, he had no staff and little organization. He looked up his own train schedules, bought his own tickets, carried his own bags, rode in public cars, and changed trains in the middle of the night to make connections. Often, he walked from the station to the hotel.

In early October, the Democratic National Committee finally leased a private railroad car for him, named *The Idler*—"a most inappropriate name, it seemed to me," Bryan said—which added both to his comfort and to his efficiency. The Bryans ate many of their meals in the car and slept better than they did at hotels, an important consideration in a tiring campaign.[27]

Leaving home again on September 9, Bryan spent every day except Sundays campaigning. Speaking so often, his throat naturally worried him: "I tried," he remembered, "a cold compress, and a hot compress, and a cold gargle and a hot gargle, and cough drops and cough cures and cough killers in endless variety and profusion," but he finally abandoned the remedies and relied on his own stamina. He spoke, on average, 80,000 words a day, a remarkable total. Fortunately, he could fall asleep at a moment's notice and in odd places, such as in a chair or stretched out on the floor of the railroad

William Jennings Bryan, on the left, and Mary Baird Bryan, on the right, welcoming crowds from the rear platform of their campaign train, The Idler, *during their remarkable eighteen-thousand-mile campaign. (Library of Congress, Washington, D.C.)*

car. He slept for ten or twenty minutes at a time, waking up for the next talk.[28]

Awakened, he was instantly ready to speak. As he did through most of his life, he ate huge meals, as many as six a day. After reporters mentioned his fondness for radishes, women at his stops would hand him bunches of the plant for the next part of the trip. Aides fanned him in the heat and gave him rubdowns with gin to loosen his muscles. The smell of gin also drove people from the railroad car, another benefit, though from time to time, he mounted the speaker's stand "smelling like a wrecked distillery."[29]

In a typical day, Bryan might speak twenty or thirty times. Some days, he made as many as thirty-six speeches. At stops in major cities, he frequently spoke at least twice in the same evening, once to a large audience outdoors and then again to a different audience in a local meeting hall. Endowed with enormous energy, Bryan wore out most of those who accompanied him. He "likes it all, . . . " a Washington correspondent said, "the early rising, the crowded days, the bands, the turmoil, the shouting and applause. . . . He can sleep anywhere at any time." "Living near him is like living near Niagara," Willa Cather, his fellow Nebraskan, said. "The almighty ever-renewed force of the man drives one to distraction." Reporters could barely keep up. "Mr. Bryan has a damnable habit of going to bed at 12 o'clock and getting up at 1:30 for work," as one of them said.[30]

Bryan was an evangelist by nature, and his campaign had many of the hallmarks of a revival meeting. At scheduled stops, people arrived hours or days early, pouring in from nearby towns and farms. Awaiting his arrival, they held parades, sang hymns, and listened to speeches from lesser orators. Welcoming committees prepared elaborate receptions based on the sixteen-to-one theme, often sixteen young girls in white dresses and one small boy in a gold-colored suit. Finally, almost always late, *The Idler* pulled in from the previous rally thirty or forty miles away. Eagerly, the crowd pressed forward to see Bryan, touch him, and take his hand. Women held up babies they had named after him.

Warmed by the crowd, Bryan summoned strength for yet another speech. Tired, his voice hoarse, he would say in apology that "a large portion of my voice has been left along the line of travel, where it is still calling sinners to repentance," a line that nearly always drew a laugh. For ten or twenty minutes, he would talk briefly of silver and the common people, of justice and righteousness, and of the need for the people to reassert control over the affairs of the nation. The talk finished, the crowd pressed forward again, hoping for a last touch or handshake, and *The Idler* pulled out for another town and, somehow, another speech.[31]

It did not matter that he only spoke for a few minutes, a historian of the campaign has noted. "Everyone knew his arguments anyway; the people had come to marvel at his appearance, to stand near the man who promised to redeem the land they loved from the grasp of the forces of Evil."[32]

Some, lured by his talent at public speaking, came simply to hear him. After a speech in a western state, one of his listeners told him, "I have ridden fifty miles to hear you speak tonight. I have always read every speech of yours that I could get hold of. I would ride a hundred miles to hear you make a speech. And, by gum, if I wasn't a Republican, I'd vote for you."[33]

Bryan's moralistic campaign excited many voters—that was clear from the large and cheering crowds at stop after stop on his famous tour—but it put off many voters as well. The problem, so serious that it ultimately contributed to his defeat, surfaced first in Chicago, where he had adopted the rhetorical technique of "polarization"—an attempt to persuade his listeners to abandon the middle ground and commit to him and his cause—to win over the delegates. The technique had worked well in Chicago, helping him to gain the presidential nomination, but it fared less well in front of a national audience.[34]

During his speech at the convention, he had employed strong rhetorical strokes. He had reminded listeners of the language of the Civil War ("In this contest brother has been arrayed against brother, father against son"); used military metaphors ("We are fighting in the defense of our homes, of our families, and posterity"); compared silver Democrats to Christian crusaders at war with the infidels; spoken approvingly of "the avenging wrath of an indignant people"; and blamed the nation's problems on the well-to-do ("What we need is an Andrew Jackson to stand, as Jackson stood, against the encroachments of aggrandized wealth"). From start to finish, his language was consciously defiant: "We beg no longer; we entreat no more; we petition no more. We defy them."[35]

There was one truth, Bryan had said at Chicago, a theme he repeated over and over during his campaign. "If there is one lesson taught by six thousand years of history it is that truth is omnipotent and will at last prevail," he announced in Salem, on the lawn of the courthouse where he had first practiced law. "You may impede its progress, you may delay its triumph; but after awhile it will show its irresistible power, and those who stand in its way will be crushed beneath it."[36]

"The Democratic party has begun a war of extermination against the gold standard," he said in Albany, New York. "We ask no quarter; we give no quarter. We shall prosecute our warfare until there is not an American citizen who dares to advocate the gold standard."[37]

"We have commenced a warfare against the gold standard," he told a crowd in Indianapolis, "and we expect to continue that warfare until there will not be a man in this country who will dare to raise his voice in favor of the gold standard."[38]

To an audience in Louisville, Kentucky, he said: "I call your attention to the fact that in this campaign the lines are drawn between Plutocracy and Democracy. In such a fight there is no middle ground; those who are not for us are against us."[39]

In Cleveland, Ohio, he stated: "We have the gold standard. It came to us without our desire." In opposing it, "we have begun a war that knows no truce, we ask no quarter, we give no quarter. It is war, war, war."[40]

Bryan spoke that way throughout his campaign, in words and phrases that were often confrontational—*crushed beneath it, extermination, warfare,* and *war, war, war*—reinforced in turn by his frequent comparisons of himself and his cause to stories in the Bible, stories his Bible-reading audiences knew by heart. In Chicago, he had taken on the role of Jesus Christ himself, "crown of thorns," "cross of gold," and all. On other occasions, he summoned images of himself as David against Goliath, as Moses, as Saint Paul, or as Solomon, the wise rule-giver. Opponents he likened to Judas Iscariot, and though warned against it again and again, he continued throughout the campaign to call them "enemies."

Other voices in his entourage built on the same imagery. Josephus Daniels of North Carolina, who sometimes traveled with him, praised Bryan "because he has rolled away the stone from the golden sepulchre in which Democracy was buried." Others found it wonderful that "this country has witnessed a new Pentecost and received a new baptism of fire." A party leader in Illinois happily reported that many Republicans "have come forward like sinners in a religious revival and joined us with public denunciations of their old party affiliations." Others spoke of "evangelists in the cause" and "converts."[41]

As typical in these years, people took up the imagery in song:

No crown of thorns to its brow shall press,
Never again, say we, no cross of gold mankind distress;
Never again say we.
We'll loosen all the cords that bind;

VOL. 31 NO. 779   SEPTEMBER 19 1896   PRICE 10 CENTS

Judge

ENTERED AT THE POST OFFICE AT NEW YORK AS SECOND CLASS MATTER, COPYRIGHT 1896   BY THE JUDGE PUBLISHING CO.   TITLE REGISTERED AS A TRADE MARK

THE SACRILEGIOUS CANDIDATE.

No man who drags into the dust the most sacred symbols of the Christian world is fit to be president of the United States.

"The Sacrilegious Candidate," a harsh attack on Bryan's use of religious imagery, depicting him standing on the Bible, clutching the cross and the crown of thorns, with the subtitle "No man who drags into the dust the most sacred symbols of the Christian world is fit to be president of the United States." (Judge, September 19, 1896)

Give equal chance to all mankind,
And here a new Redeemer find,
Leading to victory.[42]

Through much of his career, Bryan had used the language of religion and confrontation, and in some settings, it had worked well for him. Those settings, however, were almost always narrow and focused—a race for Congress in Nebraska or an address to a prosilver conference—but in this national campaign, it tended to drive people away. Many religious leaders questioned it, especially its use of sacred images for political purposes, and they delivered sermon after sermon against it. Many voters did not like it, a fact that McKinley and the Republicans quickly exploited.[43]

In his own campaign, McKinley purposely established a different tone. "It is their intelligence we seek to reach," he said of those who might vote for Bryan; "it is their sober judgment we invoke; it is their patriotism to which we appeal. . . . It is to persuade, not to abuse, which is the object of rightful public discussion."[44]

The contrast was both vivid and clear, the two candidates' language measuring some of the important differences between them. McKinley, no less than Bryan, believed deeply in personal salvation, but he described the experience in terms that were tolerant and inclusive. Bryan thought otherwise. "If this [being born again] is true of one [person], it can be true of any number," he argued again and again. "Thus, a nation can be born in a day if the ideals of the people can be changed." Bryan's campaign aimed for exactly that: a nation that had been "born again," resting on bedrock values, acting on one "truth," conscious always of a sacred cause.[45]

Still, people came to hear Bryan by the thousands, and the Nebraskan spoke to crowds, as he himself said, that could be "measured by the acre rather than the head." He attracted encouraging audiences in the upper South, including 70,000 in Louisville, Kentucky; in North Carolina, they were the largest in memory. In West Virginia, newspapers estimated that he spoke at one time or another to fully half the voters in the state. Asked once if he ever became tired of having so many people come to see him, Bryan quoted an esteemed southern senator: "Yes, it does nearly kill me, but if they did not do it, it would entirely kill me."[46]

Students at Yale University heckled him so much that he refused to continue his speech there, but elsewhere in the Northeast, he spoke to large and enthusiastic audiences. Crowds in Connecticut and Massachusetts averaged

15,000 people. In a speech on Boston Common in late September, there were at least 50,000—some guessed 70,000 or more—in the audience, which heartened Bryan, though aides recalled seeing factories with large placards threatening layoffs and closings should he win. "Probably the only passage in the Bible read by some financiers is that about the wise men of the East," he burst out. "They seem to think that wise men have been coming from that direction ever since."[47]

He conferred briefly with Arthur Sewall in Maine and then, leaving New England, paid a second visit to New York City, where he drew crowds so large that Josephus Daniels complimented him on the enthusiasm. Yes, Bryan replied, these crowds were excited, but come watch his rallies in the Midwest and on the plains. "These people," he told Daniels, "have given us a great welcome in the East, but the West is on fire."[48]

One of those places on fire, the small town of O'Neill, Nebraska, "buzzed [that summer and fall] with political disputation from dawn till next dawn," a longtime resident recalled. Instead of tearing down the arbor they had built for their annual Fourth of July picnic and dance, townspeople decided that year to keep it and make it a place for campaign discussions. "By day and by night men and women . . . met there to talk about the Crime of '73, the fallacies of the gold standard, bimetallism and international consent, the evils of the tariff, the moneybags of Mark Hanna, the front-porch campaign of McKinley," the resident wrote. "They read W. H. Harvey's *Coin's Financial School* to themselves, their friends, and opponents.. . . They read Bryan when they couldn't go off to listen to him."[49]

Whenever they could, people went off to listen to him. Recognizing the region's crucial importance, Bryan spent much of the last month of his campaign in the Midwest, especially in the Ohio and Upper Mississippi river valleys, Illinois, Indiana, Ohio, and Michigan.[50] There, he continued to stress the quantity theory of money, the silverites' conviction that economic well-being depended on the amount of currency in circulation. Some nations might prefer gold, Bryan argued, but there was simply not enough gold in the world to sustain economic activity. McKinley, if he wished, could go on and on urging the opening of the mills instead of the mints, but if people did not have the money to buy what the mills produced, the mills would shut down again. Without an adequate money supply, farmers were poor and restive, and "the farmers of the country are the Samsons, and when they fall they will pull down the pillars of the temple with them."[51]

"My friends," he said at a campaign stop in Ohio, "we believe that free coinage of silver, the opening of the mints to the free coinage of silver at 16 to i, without waiting for the aid or consent of any other nation on earth, means the advancement of the interest of the people and of general prosperity."[52]

"He's talking silver all the time and that's where we've got him," Mark Hanna famously exclaimed at one point in the campaign.[53] Hanna in a large sense was right—a careful reading of Bryan's campaign speeches amply confirms it—but Bryan did "talk" from time to time about issues other than silver. At various campaign stops, he praised labor unions, called for the arbitration of labor disputes, backed the income tax, spoke in favor of civil service reform, and urged measures to curb the trusts. On his second trip to Madison Square Garden, he focused on issues of the income tax and the use of injunctions against labor, as his supporters there had earlier hoped he would.[54]

He spent Labor Day 1896 in Chicago, where he reminisced about a recent trip through Iowa and the hogs he had seen there. That took him back to his own boyhood on his father's farm, and he recalled that they had put rings in the noses of their hogs to let them get fat but not eat more than they should. "And then it occurred to me that one of the most important duties of government is to put rings in the noses of hogs," to restrain the growing size of large businesses, he suggested, which was not profound thinking but a significant departure from the outlook of the old Cleveland Democrats.[55]

Remarkably eloquent, he could carry audiences to new levels of thought, as he did in a speech in St. Louis in October:

I was born after the war. I belong to that generation which has never had an opportunity to prove its love of country upon the battlefield; but, oh, my countrymen, never in the history of this country has there been such an opportunity as there is today for the citizen to prove his love, not only of his country but of all mankind and of his God. The battle that we fight is fought upon the hilltop, and our contending armies are visible to all the world. All over this globe, in every civilized nation, the eyes of mankind are turned toward this battlefield. Show me, anywhere, a man oppressed, show me a man who has suffered from injustice, show me a man who has been made the victim of vicious legislation, and I will show you a man from whose heart goes up a silent prayer that we may win.[56]

The large crowds that had turned out in state after state gave Bryan hope, in fact, that he might win. During a stopover in Chicago, he visited with his old friend Charles G. Dawes, Hanna's top aide, whom he had known well when they both lived in Lincoln. They had a good chat, but Dawes, who knew that

McKinley by that time was well ahead in the campaign, came away struck by Bryan's remarkable confidence that he would win. "Bryan, somehow, imagines he has a chance to be elected President," Dawes wrote that night in his diary. "He . . . gave me a conditional invitation to visit at the White House."[57]

The size of the crowds had also worried Republican leaders, including John Hay, who wrote a friend: "The last week of the campaign is getting on everybody's nerves. There is a vague uneasiness among Republicans. . . . I do not believe defeat to be possible, though it is evident that this last month of Bryan, roaring out his desperate appeals to hate and envy, is having its effect on the dangerous classes."[58]

Those "dangerous classes," in fact, had heard Bryan speak less to hate and envy than to hope and possibility, to the liberating potential of silver, to priorities that offered hope to the downtrodden, to the intervention of government in national problems. He spoke to those people, as he often put it, who were sure that "there are two ideas of government. There are those who believe that, if you will only legislate to make the well-to-do prosperous, their prosperity will leak through on those below. The Democratic idea, however, has been that if you legislate to make the masses prosperous, their prosperity will find its way up through every class which rests upon them"—an argument that would resonate through Franklin D. Roosevelt and the New Deal.[59]

And now he was ready for the end of the grueling campaign. "My hand has been used until it is sore, but it can handle a pen to sign a free-coinage bill, if I am elected," he told a crowd in Ottumwa, Iowa, as he headed home. "I have been wearied with work, but I still have the physical strength to stand between the people, if they elect me, and the Wall street syndicates which have been bleeding this country."[60]

Back in Lincoln, he wired Jones at party headquarters in Chicago that gold men, fearful of defeat, might try to keep silverites from the polls. "The gold syndicates and the trusts are fighting for existence and we must be prepared to meet them at every point," he told Jones, urging him to post loyal men at key voting places.[61]

On the day before the election, the Bryans and their daughter Grace embarked on one more trip of their campaign, touring Nebraska in a last-minute attempt to help Democratic congressional candidates. Bryan's final day lasted nearly eighteen hours, and he gave twenty-seven speeches, one of the largest number of any day during the canvass. The following morning, they took an early train home to Lincoln, and Bryan went to his polling place. There, a prominent Republican suggested that everyone remove their hats as a mark of respect for their townsman, a gesture that pleased Bryan greatly.[62]

With no train to catch the next day, Bryan felt unusually tired that night, a sign of the end of the daily campaign demands, and he went to bed at 6:30 in the evening. "After two days' rest I will be as sound and as strong as when I began, and able to begin again," he told Mary. "If they elect McKinley," he added, "I will feel a great burden lifted off my shoulders." Just after midnight, betting in New York City closed at almost three to one in McKinley's favor.[63]

"The campaign was over, and its conclusion brought to me a sense of relief," Bryan later wrote. "No matter what the result might be, I felt I had done all within my power to bring success to the principles for which I stood." Bryan had every right to think he had done all he could. In a spirited and principled campaign, during which he had introduced new methods to American politics, he had taken his message to voters across the nation, and for the moment, he could rest content. Now it was time to wait for the morrow.[64]

6

*[The Democrats] say we must fuse, but their idea of fusion is that we
play minnow while they play trout; we play June bug while they play
duck; we play Jonah while they play the whale.*
—Thomas E. Watson[1]

Once he had won the Democratic presidential nomination
at Chicago, Bryan had immediately returned home to Lincoln where he answered telegrams and letters of congratu-
lation and talked to delegates who were on their way to the
Populist and National Silver party conventions at St. Louis.
Anxious to assemble a winning coalition, he eagerly awaited
news from those conventions, hoping for their support in
the upcoming campaign. "The action of the National Silver
Convention was known in advance," he later said, "but there
was considerable uncertainty as to the result of the Populist
Convention."[2]

There was, indeed. On the eve of their own convention,
the Populists were in trouble, and they knew it. At the beginning of 1896, they had staked everything on the assumption
that neither major party would endorse silver. The Republicans seemed safe for gold or, at least, a cautious plank for bimetallism, and surely Grover Cleveland, with all the powers
of the national administration, could keep a silver plank out
of the Democratic platform. As it turned out, the Populists
guessed right about the Republicans, wrong about the Democrats. The nomination of Bryan on a bold silver platform
abruptly presented them with a set of difficult choices.[3]

Those choices also fed on angry disagreements within
their own ranks. Since the mid-1890s, the Populists had

fractured into factions, at war with each other over leadership, tactics, platforms, and ideas. One large faction, with Thomas E. Watson, William A. Peffer, and a few others at its head, bitterly opposed the efforts of some Populists to focus solely on silver that year. Disliking the thought of cooperating with these new Bryan Democrats, they wanted to mount the party's usual broad reform campaign that included, along with free silver, tough measures to regulate the railroads and telegraphs, laws to open up the political process, an income tax to raise revenue and even out incomes, protections for labor, and other long-standing measures. To stake out their position, they adopted the name "middle-of-the-roaders," or "mid-roaders," signaling their desire to avoid narrowing the platform. The mid-roaders had some appeal in the West but were strongest in the South, where tensions between Populists and Democrats had always run high.

As so often in the Populist movement, the mid-roaders defined themselves in song:

> Side tracks are rough, and they're hard to walk,
>   Keep in the middle of the road;
> Though we haven't got time to stop and talk
>   We keep in the middle of the road.
> Turn your backs on the goldbug men,
> And yell for silver now and then;
> If you want to beat Grover, also Ben,
>   Just stick to the middle of the road.
>
> Don't answer the call of goldbug tools,
>   But keep in the middle of the road;
> Prove that the West wasn't settled by fools,
>   And keep in the middle of the road.
> They've woven their plots, and woven them ill,
> We want a Weaver who's got more skill,
> And mostly we want a Silver Bill,
>   So we'll stay in the middle of the road.[4]

Herman E. Taubeneck and James B. Weaver, leading an opposing "fusionist" faction, thought such arguments foolish. The Populists had done poorly in elections in 1894 and 1895, and they needed now the kind of additional support Bryan and the silver Democrats could bring. Silver did narrow the Populist platform, that was true, but the mid-roaders themselves had often seen the wisdom of that. Why not exploit silver's wide popularity to win the election this year and then enact other important Populist reforms once in office? In the Midwest and on the plains, Populist leaders were reporting rank-and-file enthusiasm for Bryan "bordering on hysteria," a sentiment that might be fatal to ignore.[5]

"The supreme hour for action has arrived," Weaver, a respected old reform campaigner, argued emphatically. "If we would be victorious we must make common cause with the heroic men who dominated the Chicago convention." "I care not for party names," well-liked Kansas congressman Jerry Simpson agreed; "it is the substance we are after, and we have it with William J. Bryan."[6]

Simmering for years, the fight between the two factions came to a head in January 1896 during a dispute over the timing of the party's national convention. Mid-roaders in general wanted to hold the convention early in the year, even as soon as February or March, in order to beat the other parties to a broad platform that would capture national attention and rally the forces of reform. "An early convention will head off and give a quietus to the movements of the 'new silver party,'" a leading Populist newspaper noted, "and will force into line or out of the party those ambitious populists who advocate leaving the middle of the road."[7] Peffer agreed: "I think the Populists should adopt their own platform, name their own candidate for President, and maintain [their own] organization."[8]

Those favoring a focus on silver, by contrast, argued for a late convention, timed to take advantage of the voter discontent they foresaw once both the Republicans and Democrats had blundered on the financial issue. Taubeneck in particular was sure that, after the other two parties had declared for gold, the Populists could easily gather up the nation's disaffected in a "grand union of the reform forces," as he put it. "I am a middle-of-the-road man," Weaver said, "but I don't propose to lie down across it so no one can get over me. Nothing grows in the middle of the road."[9]

At the crucial meeting of the party's national committee that January, the fusionists won the debate. Defeating the arguments of the mid-roaders, they scheduled the Populist convention for July 22, well after the dates already chosen by the Republicans and Democrats. Making sure that no one missed the point, they also appointed a committee to confer with silverites in the other parties, to work to bring together everyone "friendly to financial reform" in support of the same candidates for president and vice-president.[10] It was a fateful blunder, exposed barely six months later with Bryan's victory at Chicago in early July.

Ignatius Donnelly, a leading mid-roader, was furious, charging that

Taubeneck and the others had been "flimflammed" by the silverites, but in fact, they had simply gambled and lost. Shrewd observers such as Peffer had seen the possibility coming, with Peffer giving this headline to an earlier article in his newspaper: "IF THE DEMOCRATIC NATIONAL CONVENTION DE- CLARES FOR FREE SILVER COINAGE, THEN WHAT OF THE PEOPLE'S PARTY?"[11]

It was a good question, but unfortunately, there were few good answers. After Chicago, the Populists faced a painful choice: nominate an independent ticket and risk splitting the silver and reform forces or nominate Bryan and give up a good deal of their identity as a party. Either way, they were certain to lose. "If we fuse," as one of them said plaintively, "we are sunk; if we don't fuse, all the silver men we have will leave us for the more powerful Democrats."[12]

Further limiting their options, the Populists in neither faction had a candidate of their own strong enough to defeat Bryan for their party's nomination. Old hands such as the fusionist Weaver were well known, but they had run the race too often and were unsuited now for the needs of a new national campaign. Minnesota's mid-roader Donnelly, imaginative and articulate, often acted in ways that seemed odd and eccentric, difficult to keep on task. Marion Butler of North Carolina, though growing in popularity, was a recent convert to the ranks. Among mid-roaders, there was some talk of the stalwart Peffer, but his support centered on his own area on the plains. Eugene V. Debs, widely popular among those hoping for a broad campaign, refused to run. More and more, Populists lamented the unexpected death of Alliance president Leonidas L. Polk back in June 1892.[13]

Thinking ahead, Taubeneck and other fusionists had once had a plan to solve the problem: nominate for president the Republican Henry M. Teller, who could bridge the gap between Populists and silver Democrats. Teller was respected both in the South and in the West; he had courageously walked out of his own party's national convention; and although he was calling for a campaign focused on silver this year, he saw the issue as only a beginning of the effort toward broader reforms. But the outcome at Chicago again changed the situation, Teller immediately declaring his unyielding support for Bryan. "I will not be a party to any movement to divide the friends of silver in this campaign," he made it clear to fellow silverites, "and if we fail to concentrate on Mr. Bryan . . . the fault will not be with the friends of silver who heretofore acted with the republican party."[14]

For southern Populists, these decisions were particularly painful. They had struggled for years against desperate Democratic threats and violence to establish their party's separate identity. To endorse Bryan and Sewall now meant retreat from that struggle, humiliation, and almost certainly the end of their party. It might, in the Democratic South, even mean injury or death at the hands of vengeful Democrats. In the aftermath of Chicago, southern party leaders did not know what to do: they generally liked Bryan and cheered for silver; they also hated the Democrats. Even under Bryan, as Tom Watson put it, the Democrats "say we must fuse, but their idea of fusion is that we play minnow while they play trout; we play June bug while they play duck; we play Jonah while they play the whale."[15]

"For God's sake don't indorse Bryan," a Texas Populist pleaded with delegates to the Populist convention at St. Louis. "Our people are firm, confident and enthusiastic; don't betray their trust. Don't try to force us back into the Democratic party; we won't go." "Five hundred Populists say never surrender," Dallas County's Populists wired their representative at the convention. "Bryan means death."[16] Bitter, another southern Populist put it even more strongly: "If the Savior of mankind himself was nominated by the Democratic party on a platform of the 10 commandments, I would vote against him," he said. "That is how I feel about the Democratic party."[17]

Angry mid-roaders from twenty-three states caucused in St. Louis on July 21, the day before the party's convention opened, determined to come up with a candidate and a strategy. They came up with neither but did agree on one thing: they would not accept the nomination of both Bryan and Sewall. In the light of party principle, that decision made considerable sense, but it still left them with few winning alternatives of their own. Canvassing the choices they had, they settled on a ticket headed by Colonel Seymour F. Norton of Illinois, a Chicago newspaper publisher, longtime reformer, and author of the greenback tract *Ten Men of Money Island,* for president and Frank Burkitt of Mississippi, a state senator and real estate attorney, for vice-president—men so little known in most of the country that the slate alone revealed a great deal about the dilemma of the mid-roaders.[18]

When the convention's opening gavel finally fell, the delegates were understandably bewildered, many with a sense that events had already spun out of their control. This was a party—and a cause—for which they cared passionately. They had lived and fought for it for years. Many of them were poor; most were hopeful and dedicated. Some delegates had no shoes; others took off their shoes when they were not in the convention hall in order to save the leather. They slept in parks and other public places, ate sparingly, and walked miles to the convention hall to save cab and trolley fare.[19]

Reflecting the party's principles, women played a much larger role than they did in the conventions of the other parties. Mary E. Lease sat on the platform, a member of the Populist executive committee. She wanted the delegates to endorse the nomination of Bryan and Sewall and would soon campaign throughout the Midwest for Bryan. Silver orator Helen M. Gougar of Indiana addressed the convention, denouncing the "thieves of Wall Street" who were supporting McKinley.[20]

It was an unruly gathering, onlookers noted, filled with the voices of people who cared and wanted to be heard. Delegates often broke out in their favorite song, "We'll Shoot the Gold Bugs, Every One." "It was a convention made up of men and women," a visitor said, "of hundreds of people dissatisfied with existing conditions, groping for something, they hardly knew what, which would restore power to the people. Everybody was allowed to talk; it was a convention of free speech." "This dramatic and historical scene," another onlooker wrote, "must have told every quiet, thoughtful witness that there was something at the back of all this turmoil more than failure of crops or the scarcity of ready cash."[21]

In his opening address, Senator Marion Butler of North Carolina, chosen as temporary chair, went on the attack, accusing the Democrats of stealing the People's party platform in order to avoid "uniting the silver forces to win a great victory."[22] By a wide margin, the delegates then made a crucial decision, electing William V. Allen, a Nebraska senator, Populist, and close friend of Bryan's, as permanent chair. The vote, another blow to the mid-roaders, was not even close, obviously reflecting pro-Bryan sentiment within the convention. Mounting the platform, Allen could see banners in the hall bearing the words "Keep in the Middle of the Road." Pointing to them, he urged Populists to demand more and "occupy the whole road."[23]

He did not stand before them to urge Bryan's nomination, Allen said several times, and then he proceeded to do just that. "It is for you to choose and not for me," he said, but he told the delegates that if they put a third ticket in the field, they would defeat free coinage; defeat government ownership of railroads, telephones, and telegraphs; defeat an income tax; and "foist gold monometallism and high taxation upon the people for a generation to come."

When he returned home to report to his constituents, he said, "I do not want them to say to me that the Populists have been advocates of reforms when they could not be accomplished, but when the first ray of light appeared and the people were looking with expectancy and with anxiety for relief, the party was not equal to the occasion; . . . it was stupid; it was blind;

it kept 'in the middle of the road' and missed the golden opportunity." The message, despite Allen's denials, was clear: endorse Bryan or give up on the reforms for which the People's party had long campaigned.[24]

The Committee on Resolutions, with Weaver as chair, recommended a platform that endorsed the broad reforms of the party but, in a final blow to the mid-roaders, focused on free silver. The financial question, the platform said bluntly, was "the great and pressing issue of the pending campaign."[25]

Recognizing the strength of the Bryan forces on the convention floor, some mid-roaders had begun to toy with a different idea. When it came time to nominate a president, why not let the fusionists have Bryan but name someone other than Sewall, preferably a Southerner, for vice-president? In that way, they could maintain a semblance of party independence and give Populists a candidate to rally around during the coming campaign. Jones, Bryan's campaign chair, who was in a St. Louis hotel room urging the Populists to back the Bryan-Sewall ticket, unwittingly pushed delegates in that direction. Refusing to bargain with the Populists in any way, he enabled mid-roaders to argue that the Bryan Democrats wanted only to take over and destroy the People's party.[26]

To many delegates, at a loss for what to do, the strategy was persuasive. "Populists were willing to swallow Democracy gilded with the genius of a Bryan," as Donnelly put it, but they did not wish to "stomach plutocracy in the body of Sewall." "If we elect Bryan," another delegate warned, "and he should be killed by some assassin by order of the money power, we would want a different man from Sewall."[27]

Swayed by the idea, a minority of the convention's rules committee recommended that the delegates choose their vice-presidential nominee first, and by a small margin—738 to 637—the convention, to the surprise of many, agreed. Learning of the vote, the Bryan Democrats knew at once that the convention would choose a Populist for the post. "Populists nominate Vice-President first," Jones wired Bryan, who was at home in Nebraska. "If not Sewall, what shall we do? Answer quick. I favor your declination in that case." "I entirely agree with you," Bryan immediately replied. "Withdraw my name if Sewall is not nominated." Jones quickly informed key Populist leaders of Bryan's decision, hoping it would sway the convention to endorse the Bryan-Sewall ticket, adopt an appropriate platform, and adjourn.[28]

It did not. Confused delegates, starved for news, had no idea what to think. Rumors ran back and forth across the convention floor. Some said that Bryan and Jones had agreed to drop Sewall from the Democratic ticket if the Populists named a different vice-presidential candidate. Other reports said that Bryan had declared he would hold firm for Sewall. Strangely, there were even denials of any exchange of telegrams at all between Bryan and Jones, though the telegrams had been published that morning in the St. Louis newspapers.[29]

Those favoring a separate nomination had already sounded out the popular Thomas E. Watson of Georgia, who met their main criteria: he was from the South, articulate, independent, committed to the cause, and widely respected in Populist ranks. Watson, who was not at the convention, at first turned down the idea, but when leading mid-roaders promised him that Democratic leaders had agreed to withdraw Sewall, he gave in. "Yes, if it will harmonize all factions," he wired supporters in St. Louis. It was a decision he would greatly regret.[30]

On the first ballot, Watson received 539¾ votes to only 257 for Sewall, a measure of the delegates' distaste for the Maine Democrat. It was late evening, and as Watson's supporters moved to make his nomination unanimous, the lights suddenly went out in the convention hall. Reporters lit candles. A voice shouted that Watson had been nominated at exactly sixteen minutes before one o'clock, and cheers erupted from the floor: "Sixteen to one! Sixteen to one!" The delegates then nominated Bryan for president, 1,042 to 321 for Norton.[31]

As Sewall did for the Bryan Democrats, Watson soon brought trouble to the joint Democratic-Populist campaign. Spirited, eloquent, and forceful, he was an effective campaigner, but he was also notoriously outspoken, quick to anger, and eager to find an affront. The Populist convention had barely adjourned when he was writing in his *People's Party Paper* that the delegates had done it all wrong: "We thought before the convention met, and we think now," he wrote, "that the welfare of our party, and of the principles it represents, demanded that we nominate our own ticket, and put upon that ticket two Populists, tried and true."[32]

Their convention over, the Populists debated about what to do. Some urged negotiations with Bryan for the withdrawal of Sewall in favor of Watson. Feelers along those lines were extended to the Bryan camp but met with quick rebuff. Bryan Democrats had little reason to negotiate. They wanted Populist votes, to be sure, but they had no need for the party organization, which was close to disintegration in any event. Populist voters, they knew, had nowhere else to go. The Democratic party chairman, James K. Jones, put it bluntly: "Mr. Sewall will, of course, remain on the ticket, and Mr. Watson can do what he likes."[33]

The Populist endorsement probably hurt Bryan as much as it helped. It

Thomas E. Watson, the fiery Georgia politician who was a leader of the southern wing of the People's party and the party's controversial vice-presidential candidate in the election of 1896. (Watson Papers, University of North Carolina–Chapel Hill)

won him relatively few votes, since many Populists—perhaps most—would have voted for him no matter what. It identified him as a Populist, which he was not, and enabled opponents to place him at the head of a ragtag army of malcontents, anarchists, and misguided fanatics. The Sewall-Watson squabble underlined the point, suggesting the fragility of an unnatural alliance. How could such a coalition govern? Would Sewall or Watson be vice-president? Might Donnelly and Taubeneck join Altgeld and Tillman in a jumbled "Demopop" cabinet? The prospect worried moderate voters and highlighted McKinley's program of progress with stability. It also helped unite Bryan's opponents, who set out, as the Republican Henry Cabot Lodge declared, to crush "the revolutionary resolutions put forth by the Democratic party, which has passed completely into the hands of the Populists."[34]

William C. Whitney and his colleagues on the so-called Gold Train returned to New York City on Saturday evening, nine days after they had left so hopefully for Chicago. A "weary-looking party of men stepped slowly from the cars and walked up the passageway," a reporter who was there to interview them said. "Whitney led the way. His face was haggard. The fight at Chicago had told on him." "Where is the band?" he said jokingly to one of the reporters. "They're out here going over their music getting ready to play 'Silver Threads among the Gold,'" someone replied. Asked about the convention, Whitney declined to comment on it. "I have nothing to say," he remarked. "Indeed, there is nothing to say. Later in the week we may have something to tell the newspapers and the public. But there is nothing now. We must see and confer with others."[35]

That was true for most gold Democrats, who wanted a moment to reflect on the outcome at Chicago and think about their options. There were a few, of course, who decided to act more quickly. The *New York Sun,* an influential Democratic newspaper, came out against Bryan the day before he was even nominated. Cleveland's secretary of the navy, Hillary Herbert of Alabama, also repudiated Bryan immediately. Well before the Chicago convention adjourned, McKinley sat on his Canton porch reading letters and telegrams from important Democrats and Democratic newspapers pledging their support in his campaign.[36]

Cleveland himself urged silence until conditions cleared. "I have an idea, quite fixed and definite," he wrote his longtime friend and cabinet member Daniel S. Lamont, "that for the present at least we should none of us say anything. I have heard from Herbert today. He says he has declared he will not support the ticket. I am sorry he has done so. We have a right to be

KILLING THE GOOSE THAT LAID THE GOLDEN EGG.
An Eastern opinion of the Chicago Convention.
From the *Herald* (New York).

"*KILLING THE GOOSE THAT LAID THE GOLDEN EGG*": *Populism, armed with the "Free Silver" axe, joined by "Altgeldism" and "Tillmanism," killing the Democratic party goose at the Democrats' Chicago convention of 1896.* (New York Herald, n.d., in Review of Reviews, August 15, 1896) quiet—indeed I feel that I have been invited to that course. I am not fretting except about the future of the country and party." "I'm a good deal dazed politically," he told another cabinet member, Hoke Smith, "but my judgment is that it is best for the present to think much and *talk none*."[37]

Unwilling to wait, some leading gold Democrats began to adopt strategies that reflected their own temperaments, policies, and needs. Hoping for rewards, Pennsylvania's ex-governor Robert E. Pattison, the only gold Democrat who had been willing to accept a nomination at Chicago, endorsed both Bryan and the silver plank. Unable to stomach either Bryan or silver, David B. Hill of New York found no comfort in that strategy, but neither could he bolt his party, which he had served—and which had served him—his entire life. Hill chose, therefore, simply to step away from the national race, saying in a famous phrase, "I am a Democrat still—very still."[38] Arthur Pue Gorman, the consummate party man, worked for Bryan. William L. Wilson spoke privately against free silver but tried to avoid a public stand. Smith of Georgia, secretary of the interior, owned an important Atlanta newspaper and felt he had no choice but to endorse Bryan in the interests of his paper and, even more, the racial feelings in his state. Unsympathetic, Cleveland thought he had made the wrong decision and accepted his resignation from the cabinet.[39]

Significantly, the representatives of New York City's old and powerful Democratic organization, Tammany Hall, returned from Chicago the same way they had gone there: on different trains than William C. Whitney. Professional politicians, they had different interests and ambitions than Whitney and the men around him. They, too, had no love for Bryan and silver, but valuing power, they would quietly ignore the ticket and focus their efforts on electing their congressional, state, and local candidates.[40]

For Tammany, the strategy worked. Bryan lost, McKinley won, Tammany maintained its place in its home city and, with occasional exceptions, managed for years to remain in power.

The tactics worked elsewhere as well, including, importantly, among the urban Irish in the Midwest, who generally remained loyal to the Democratic party. Like Tammany, they did not expect Bryan to win the White House but following quietly along, focused on their own local candidates and their own local ambitions. Again, the strategy paid off. Taking their licks in 1896, McKinley's year, the midwestern Irish in elections in 1897 and 1898 regained power that would endure for decades to come. Within a month of McKinley's inauguration, Democrats defeated Republican mayors in Chicago, Akron,

Dayton, Springfield, Zanesville, Cincinnati, Columbus, Detroit, and even Canton, McKinley's hometown. In the next twelve months, the Democrats regained control of New York City, Cleveland, and Milwaukee.[41]

Soon, more and more gold Democrats decided they needed to take some kind of emphatic action, unwilling to accept Bryan's "foul pit of repudiation, socialism, [and] anarchy," as William L. Wilson put it.[42] Bryan's nomination reminded them of the crisis of 1861, an attempt to divide the country into sections—then into North and South, now into South and West against the East. Bryan and his followers, they thought, also planned to divide it into classes, the haves and the have-nots: "to take property from the hands of those who created it and place it in the hands of those who covet it."[43]

What should they do? they had asked themselves over and over again in the days after Chicago. They were lifelong Democrats, committed to their party. Should they stay with that party and somehow swallow Bryan, hope for his defeat, and wait for a chance to recapture the organization in 1900? Should they back McKinley, a distasteful option to people who had spent their lives opposing the policies he stood for? McKinley, it was true, was backing gold this year, but he also supported tariffs, with his very name attached to the 1890 tariff act they had fought so hard to defeat. Reflecting these feelings, Secretary of State Richard Olney wrote Cleveland that "so far as personal qualifications for the Presidency are concerned, I should as soon take my chance with Bryan as with McKinley."[44]

Before long, their answer became clear: they would form a third party to defend traditional Democratic doctrines and divert votes from Bryan, even if most of those votes actually helped McKinley. They also hoped that a separate ticket might preserve something of their own party organization, lay the groundwork for a return to power in 1900, and influence the election of members of Congress, making it possible, even if Bryan won, to prevent him from passing a free silver law.

A leading gold Democrat from Illinois put the reasoning well:

> Our crowd will name a third ticket. We are still democrats. We are not leaving the party. We want to hold the party together, preserve it, in other words, until it should come together again. We who are in this fight for the gold standard—we who are democrats—stand between two fallacies, the republican fallacy of protection and the democratic fallacy of free silver. We can in conscience support neither. So the third ticket will come in.[45]

And so it did, coming in at a Gold Democratic convention in Indianapolis in early September 1896, where delegates from forty-one states and three territories chose the name of the National Democratic party and adopted a vigorous platform that praised the Cleveland administration; attacked the tariff and the free coinage of silver, both "schemes for the personal profit of a few at the expense of the masses"; declared for the gold standard; and defended the Supreme Court.[46]

In choosing a presidential candidate, a number of delegates wanted to name Cleveland himself, but he declined, "unalterably opposed," he said, to the thought. It was a wise decision. An unpopular president, he would only attract bitter personal attacks and distract from the purpose. There was also talk of J. Sterling Morton of Nebraska, Cleveland's crusty secretary of agriculture, and William L. Wilson of West Virginia, the loyal postmaster general, neither of whom wanted the nomination. "I shall do all I can to direct attention to Senator Palmer," Wilson wrote in his diary, "and in any event away from myself."[47]

To Wilson's relief, the venerable Senator John M. Palmer of Illinois actually wanted the honor, and Simon Bolivar Buckner of Kentucky was willing to accept the nod for vice-president. The ticket united former Union and Confederate generals, and it was also old, the oldest in the country's history. Palmer in 1896 was seventy-nine, Buckner seventy-three. Bryan, as newspapers soon noted, was the youngest presidential candidate ever nominated, Palmer the oldest. Palmer was already forty-three years old when Bryan was born.[48]

Cleveland was delighted, calling the new ticket "a delicious infusion of fresh air. Every democrat after reading the platform ought to thank God that the glorious principles of the party have found defenders who will not permit them to be polluted by impious hands." He preferred McKinley to Bryan and hoped Palmer and Buckner would divert enough votes from Bryan in the border states and Midwest to defeat him. Henry Watterson, the famous editor of the Democratic *Louisville Courier-Journal,* called it "building a bridge to McKinley" to ensure the Republican's election.[49]

Hanna also had a strong hand in building that bridge, secretly subsidizing the Palmer campaign in a number of close states, including Delaware, Virginia, West Virginia, and Kentucky, where it might help to tip the balance to McKinley.[50] After the election, McKinley gave Palmer and the Gold Democrats credit for having aided "materially" in his election. "I have a rather soft feeling for them," Hanna added. "I know that they consulted our wishes at every step."[51]

Drawing on its network of traditional Democrats, the newly formed National Democratic party was able to put up electoral slates in all but seven states, a remarkable achievement in such a short time. Remarkably, too, it also fielded portions of state and congressional tickets in at least twenty states, including campaigns for governor in several states, another sign of its deep-seated hold on the loyalties of many Democrats.[52]

Bryan was furious, angry that the National Democrats would dare even to adopt the name Democrats, which belonged now, he argued, to the majority of the party that had won a fair contest at the Chicago convention. Worse, these so-called Democrats had nominated a separate ticket not as real Democrats, hoping to win, but to help elect a rival party, an act, he later wrote, that "introduces into national affairs a new kind of warfare which, in my judgment, history must condemn."[53]

When word reached Bryan that the Gold Democrats were thinking of adopting Andrew Jackson's old hickory tree as their new party's symbol, it was the final straw. "Take a hickory stick for their emblem?" he asked witheringly. "Why do they not take something more appropriate? Why do they not put upon their ballot the picture of an owl? Nothing could be more appropriate. It looks wise and does its work in the dark. Or, if they do not like the owl, let them take the mole. It is a smooth animal and works underground all the time."[54]

Palmer, despite his age, campaigned vigorously—speaking at sizable rallies in New York's Madison Square Garden, a number of states in the Midwest, and most of the cities east of the Mississippi River—though he had no expectation of winning. But no matter: his task was to take Democratic votes from Bryan and help McKinley. "I promise you, my fellow Democrats," Palmer said in a speech in Missouri in the final days of the campaign, "I will not consider it any great fault if you decide next Tuesday to cast your ballots for William McKinley." "The way to make [your] votes count," a West Virginia senator told Gold Democrats at the close of the campaign, "is to throw them to McKinley."[55]

Still, friends were amused that thoughts of the White House itself had gone to Palmer's head. "You would laugh yourself sick could you see old Palmer," a Gold Democrat said in late September. "He has actually gotten it into his head he is running for office."[56]

On a very different mission, the Populists clung as best they could to their hopes in the election. To organize their campaign, Marion Butler established the party's national headquarters in the old Wormley Hotel in Washington,

D.C., adjacent to the headquarters of the National Silver party. He also set up a small office in Chicago, an effort to coordinate campaign activities with the Democrats who were located there. In a sign of the organization's challenges, the party's national treasurer stayed away from both headquarters, arguing that he needed to remain at home in Indiana to look after his personal business.[57]

But then, there was little money for him to count. Early on, Butler decided not to take on debt during the canvass, which meant, of course, that Populist headquarters could afford to distribute few pamphlets, which was a significant disadvantage in an educational campaign. For the first few months, they required advance payment for orders from local organizations, a requirement that led inevitably to harmful delays in filling requests. Often, they had to refer orders for pamphlets and other literature to the headquarters of the Democrats, a major embarrassment for a party struggling to seem independent.

The Washington office ran on as little as $150 a week, not even enough to defray the costs of rent and postage—quite a contrast to the funds at Hanna's disposal. Most workers, necessarily, were volunteers, devoted to the party and willing to contribute their time and energy to advance the cause. At one point, Butler appealed urgently to Populist voters to contribute a dollar each to the campaign, but few could afford to do even that. Out on the stump, there were not a lot of straight-out Populist speakers, but those who were there often had to pay their own expenses.[58]

In Washington, Butler and his colleagues devoted their efforts to the crucial process of "fusion," forging agreements with the Democrats in specific states and congressional districts to trade candidates—or electoral votes or both—to establish a place on the ballot. Negotiations proceeded slowly but ultimately produced unified Democratic-Populist presidential tickets in twenty-eight states, mostly in the West. Usually, the two parties divided presidential electors on a joint Bryan-Sewall-Watson ticket, which would offer Bryan-Sewall and Bryan-Watson ballots at an agreed-upon ratio. In California, Nebraska, Minnesota, the Dakotas, and other states, they also fused on congressional and state races. In Kansas and Colorado, the Populists capitulated to the Democrats and campaigned for the Bryan-Sewall ticket.

Not surprisingly, fusion fared less well through the South, and in all but four states, the Populists simply withdrew the Bryan-Watson ticket. In Louisiana, the Populists fused with the Democrats on national offices and with the Republicans on local offices. In North Carolina, they fused with the Democrats on the presidential ticket, fused with the Republicans on the congressional and legislative tickets, and ran a separate ticket for governor, lieutenant governor, and auditor. Populist leaders understandably reeled under the confusion, trying to sort out tickets and mediate between factions. "The uncertainty on Watson & Sewall is tearing our party to pieces," a Tennessee leader said that summer.[59]

A major victim of that uncertainty, Watson kept urging party leaders to get Sewall off the ticket, a position he made clear in his first campaign speech in Atlanta in early August. "You cannot fight the national banks with any sincerity with a national banker as your leader," he told the crowd angrily. "You can't fight corporations with a corporation king as your leader."[60] "This is a movement of the masses," he said a short time later to a cheering audience in Dallas. "Let Bryan speak for the masses and let Watson speak for the masses and Sewall talk for the banks and railroads." Sewall, he added bluntly, was "a wart on the party. He's a knot on a log. He is a dead weight on the ticket."[61]

Frustrated, Watson embarked in September on a tour of the South and West, hoping by dint of cause and personality to forestall fusion and perhaps even force Sewall to withdraw from the race. "You must burn the bridges if you follow me," he told an enthusiastic crowd of 5,000 in Dallas, one of his first stops. "I am for straight Populism (cheers) and I do not propose to be carried to one side of the road or the other (wild cheering)."[62]

The large crowds in Texas, long a center of agrarian protest, encouraged Watson, but as he moved further west, the cheers grew a good deal fainter. Audiences in Colorado and Nebraska, once bastions of populism, were small and unenthusiastic. In Kansas, which used to be populism's banner state, the party's headquarters flew flags for Bryan and Sewall, not Bryan and Watson. Angry, Watson again demanded the withdrawal of Sewall. "I took my political life in my hands when I extended the hand of fellowship to your Simpsons, your Peffers, and your Davises in Georgia," he told the Kansans. "The Georgia Democrats murdered me politically for that act. I stood by your men in Congress when others failed. I have some rights at the hands of Kansas. I have counted on your support. Can I get it?"[63]

The answer, clearly, was no, but Watson decided to try once more, this time in Bryan's own Nebraska. "I am not here to make a little two-by-four silver speech," he said to a small audience in Lincoln, Bryan's hometown. "I am a Populist from my head to my heels. I am not ashamed of my cause, nor afraid to unfold my banner anywhere and fight under it." Fight Watson had plenty of, but it was getting lonelier and lonelier under that banner. Bryan, his running mate on the Populist ticket, did not bother to acknowledge his visit to Lincoln. Discouraged, Watson soon gave up and retreated home to Georgia, where he remained for the rest of the campaign.[64]

Things were no better there. In Georgia, incredibly, Tom Watson did not even appear on the ballot, state party leaders having decided to list only Bryan and Sewall. "I am out of the race in Georgia," he said to his old constituents in one of his last speeches. "There are two tickets you can vote—for Bryan and Sewall, or for McKinley and Hobart; or if you can't stand either you can stay away from the election next Tuesday and not vote at all."[65]

Many chose to vote for Bryan-Sewall or stay away, there and elsewhere, which was a sad ending to the great agrarian crusade of the late 1880s and early 1890s. "Alas and Alack!" the eloquent Donnelly wrote in his diary shortly after the election. "It seems useless to contend against the money power. Every election marks another step downward into the abyss, from which there will be no return save by fire and sword." Bryan had offered such hope of success this year, Donnelly thought. "We had a splendid candidate and he . . . made a gigantic campaign; the elements of reform were fairly united; and the depression of business universal, and yet in spite of it all the bankrupt millions voted to keep the yoke on their own necks. . . . I tremble for the future."[66]

So did many others, including Luna Kellie, a prominent Great Plains Populist and newspaper editor, who soon sold her paper, unable to continue. "Hardly a reform paper remained alive," she said, "and the abuse was hard to bear. I was supposed to send in editorials but to save my life I could not say anything that I felt I had not said before and had not done any good." "And I dared not even think of what hopes we had had," she added. "It meant sleepless nights and nerves completely unstrung." Kellie lost all interest in politics.[67]

William A. Peffer, one of the most thoughtful and devoted Populists of them all, lost a bid for governor of Kansas on the Prohibition ticket in 1898 and campaigned for McKinley and the Republicans in 1900. Weaver continued to work with the Democrats but with little power. Taubeneck, once the energetic head of the proud new People's party, retired to private life. William Allen, who had exercised such large influence as the chair of the 1896 Populist convention, practiced law.

Marion Butler, the attractive North Carolina senator, gradually became a member of the Republican party. Ignatius Donnelly continued to work with the People's party until he died of a heart attack in 1901. Jerry Simpson, one of the People's party's most talented leaders, lost his Kansas House seat in 1898 and moved to New Mexico Territory to sell lands for the Santa Fe Railroad, an organization he had once bitterly fought. Not long ago, he had hoped for reforms as big as a diamond.[68]

7

THE FRONT PORCH CAMPAIGN
MCKINLEY AND THE REPUBLICANS IN THE 1896 ELECTION

This is a year for press and pen.
—*William McKinley, September 1896* [1]

Initially, McKinley and Hanna planned the kind of campaign traditional in American politics. McKinley the candidate would say little, except for the usual formal letter to the country accepting the nomination. After Labor Day, Republican speakers, like the Democrats, would take the stump, in their case attacking Bryan and extolling their candidate's virtues. The campaign would then peak in the days just before the election, with massive parades and mass meetings aimed at rallying voters.

In line with that plan, Hanna had scheduled a vacation cruise along the New England coast sometime in August; McKinley looked forward to a quiet summer and early fall at home in Canton. But Bryan's nomination suddenly changed all that. "The Chicago convention has changed everything," Hanna wrote McKinley on July 16. "It has knocked out my holiday and cruise . . . ," and now, the campaign will be "work and hard work from the start. I consider the situation in the West quite alarming and business is all going to pieces and idle men will multiply rapidly. With this communistic spirit abroad the cry of 'free silver' will be catching." [2]

Hanna's fears about free silver and idle men reflected worries quickly spreading among Republican leaders. "I am not so sure as you are about the 'great victory,'" one party veteran wrote another in mid-July. "The political situation was entirely changed by the Chicago performance." The usual Democratic ticket they could have beaten "without half trying," he concluded, "but the new movement has stolen our thunder."[3]

Deepening the worries, early polls suggested that in a number of states in the Midwest and West, Republicans who favored free silver were thinking of voting for Bryan. In Iowa, the head of the Republican state committee reported in mid-August that the situation looked "threatening." "A large percent of our republican farmers," he said, were seeing free silver as "a remedy for the present hard times," so much so that in many Iowa counties, "the free silver craze has taken the form of an epidemic." Another Iowan noted "whole counties swept from under us by the Silver craze, places where all the County Chairmen and subcommitteemen have left us." Surveys indicated that as many as a quarter of Iowa Republican farmers favored free silver.[4]

Similar reports flowed in from other important states in the Midwest, which both sides regarded as a crucial battleground in the election. Ohio, Indiana, and Michigan suddenly seemed doubtful, and free silver, it was said, had a worrisome following in Illinois. In August, veteran Republican managers concluded that of all the states between the Appalachians and the Rockies, only Wisconsin appeared safe for McKinley. Theodore Roosevelt came away from a September visit to Republican headquarters in Chicago convinced that political conditions in the Midwest were "very doubtful," reflecting, he thought, "the savage hatred of the unprosperous for the prosperous."[5]

James J. Hill, owner of the Northern Pacific Railroad, had sources of information all along his tracks, and the news, in his opinion, was not good. Letters and telegrams were pouring in from Chicago to the Pacific Coast, reporting "an epidemic craze" among farmers and some laborers. "I take the liberty of . . . hoping," he told the powerful financier J. P. Morgan, "that you will urge those who are to manage the McKinley campaign that they should get to work *at once*."[6]

If Bryan's nomination upset McKinley's and Hanna's careful calculations, his decision to undertake a dramatic whistle-stop speaking tour stunned them both. Without much thought, Hanna quickly urged McKinley to take the stump as well. "You've got to stump or we'll be defeated," he told his friend. "You know I have the greatest respect for your wishes," McKinley replied, "but I cannot take the stump against that man."[7]

"Don't you remember that I announced that I would not under any circumstances go on a speech-making tour?" he asked an aide who also urged him to travel. "If I should go now it would be an acknowledgement of weakness. Moreover, I might just as well put up a trapeze on my front lawn and compete with some professional athlete as go out speaking against Bryan. I have to *think* when I speak." Besides, Bryan would always undercut him, no matter what he did. "If I took a whole train, Bryan would take a sleeper; if I took a chair car, he would ride a freight train. I can't outdo him, and I am not going to try."[8]

There was a better plan, McKinley thought, one that would take advantage of his own strengths rather than playing to Bryan's, a plan that had worked on a smaller scale for Benjamin Harrison in 1888. Instead of going to the people as Bryan planned to do, why not bring the people to him? It was, it turned out, a brilliant strategy. McKinley's "Front Porch Campaign" became a legend in American political history.[9]

There were some stumbles at first, but before long, the Front Porch Campaign unfolded with impressive precision. Anyone who wanted to visit Canton needed only to write McKinley headquarters saying a delegation of farmers or steelworkers or merchants or railroad men hoped to call on McKinley on a given day. Someone at headquarters would then invite the delegation's leader to Canton, where he was asked what he planned to say. "Oh, I don't know; anything that occurs to me," he often replied. "That will hardly do," McKinley would gently say, determined to avoid the kind of impromptu remark that had defeated presidential candidates in the past.[10] "Write out what you are going to say and let me see it a week or ten days ahead. . . . With your permission I shall make some suggestions and return it to you." "Now that was politics," a McKinley aide said admiringly. He was right. It was politics, and it worked like a charm.[11]

When a delegation of visitors arrived in Canton, they marched from the railroad station down Main Street and under the ornate plaster McKinley Arch, where they paused to give earlier groups time to make their speeches and start back to the depot. While they waited, one of the McKinley Home Guards, a boy given a mount just for that purpose, dashed through the streets on horseback to McKinley's home to let aides know who was next in line. The aides then retrieved McKinley's draft remarks for that group and prepared him for the visit.

Released at the arch, members of the new delegation made their way up the hill to McKinley's modest North Market Street home. Spirited troops of mounted horsemen, cheering townspeople lining the streets, and local bands that played music tailored to their state or industry accompanied them all the way. In a large tent near McKinley's house, "wets"—those who drank—were offered two glasses of beer and a sandwich, "drys"—those who did not—a cup of coffee and two sandwiches. Amid flags and bunting and curious neighbors, the visitors then massed on McKinley's front lawn, as the spectators cheered and the bands played on. "What poor McKinley has to endure moves my compassion," Thomas B. Reed remarked sympathetically. "I hope he don't hate a brass band." If he did, he never let on.[12]

Standing on his front porch, McKinley listened to the leader's remarks as if he had never heard them before, "like a child looking at Santa Claus," a friend amusingly remembered. In the spirit of the campaign, the visitors often sported gold badges, gold ties, and gold hats or carried items made of tin, recalling again McKinley's sponsorship of that "infant industry" back in 1890. They sang ditties of their own composition, as did one proud delegation from Vermont:

The mills are a'stoppin' and the markets are a'droppin,'
    We want yer, McKinley, yes we do.
The last four years of Grover, thank the Lord, are almost over,
    An' our hearts are a'turnin,' Mac, to you.
We've been thinkin' till we're sad of the good
        old times we had
    Up to eighteen ninety-two.

Have you heard from the front, way up in old
        Vermont,
    Where the sugar maple tree grows high,
Where the butter is pure gold an' the people can't
        be sold
    By any old silver-plated lies:
        Where they believe in protection—but not repudiation—
            For the people are honest an' true;
They'll stand up for the right with all their
        brawny might.
        An' they send, sir, their best regards to you.[13]

Looking on through it all, McKinley then climbed on a chair or box to reply, first welcoming the visitors to his home and his town. Confirming the welcome, they could often see Ida waving by his side or standing, smiling, in the front window. If the reply he had drafted was short, he memorized it; if it was long, he read it, again making sure there were no dangerous mistakes. Finished, he invited the visitors to walk across the porch, shake his hand, and have a glass of lemonade or two before they marched back, chanting

Standing on a box or chair, William McKinley spoke to hundreds of thousands of visitors at his Canton, Ohio, home in his famous Front Porch Campaign, which became a legend in American political history. (Ohio Historical Society, Columbus)

and cheering, to the station to catch their train home. With them, they often took a piece of McKinley's fence or lawn, as well as stories about meeting the handsome, genial, well-spoken candidate.[14]

Delegations passed through Canton at an eye-opening rate, enabling McKinley at home to rival the impact of Bryan on tour. Between June 19 and November 2, 1896, the key dates of the campaign, 750,000 people came, in over 300 delegations from 30 states. Railroads reported carrying 9,000 cars filled with passengers, most of them traveling on excursion fares, slashed so low that a round-trip ticket from Chicago fell to $3.50, making a trip to see McKinley, Democratic newspapers complained, "cheaper than staying at home."[15]

The Front Porch Campaign was a remarkable success. As the weeks wore on, Bryan inevitably showed the wear and tear of his exhausting tour. McKinley, on the other hand, remained rested, able, as he had said, to "think through" his remarks, and ready every day to post fresh copy for the next day's newspapers.[16]

While McKinley spoke to the crowds, Hanna organized the campaign. He did it brilliantly, assembling a team of talented individuals to staff a highly efficient organization. Looking over the field, he and his advisers saw from the start that they had little chance to win in the Deep South, dominated by Democrats since the end of Reconstruction, or in the silver-producing states of the Far West. The Northeast, they felt, was safe; opposition to Bryan's candidacy was spreading swiftly there. That left the Midwest as the main battleground, and there they decided to focus their efforts. On that basis, McKinley and Hanna chose Chicago as the headquarters for the campaign, the first time that city had served as the actual headquarters of a major party. With fund-raising in mind, they established another, smaller office in New York City, the usual home of presidential campaigns.[17]

To oversee the work in Chicago, they named Charles G. Dawes, a former lawyer in Bryan's hometown of Lincoln, Nebraska, who had moved to Chicago and begun a successful gas business. Dawes was tall and slender, with a dangling red mustache and large ears. Seeing him for the first time, Hanna could not take his eyes off the ears but soon realized that major talent lay between them. "He doesn't *look* much," Hanna said, but he grew to admire Dawes's efficiency and business-like approach to politics. Dawes, in turn, was totally devoted to McKinley, whom he had met as a youth, and the Major returned the affection. "You have won exceptional honor," he wrote Dawes about his work in 1896. "You had long ago won my heart."[18]

A photograph of a flag-filled parade down Market Street in Canton, Ohio, taking visitors from the town's railroad depot to the McKinley home for speeches and songs. (Ohio Historical Society, Columbus)

Keeping close watch on campaign accounts, Dawes required competitive bids in doling out contracts, a new tactic in American presidential politics. He hired most of his close associates from business, not politics, and set up a careful accounting system that relied on business models, including those of his own gas company. Campaign staffers, at his direction, focused on process and on results. Known as "the General" among subordinates, Dawes rivaled Hanna in energy and efficiency. Together, they constructed a campaign that has rarely been matched in American politics. It also set key precedents for future elections.[19]

Charles Dick, age thirty-eight, one of Hanna's close aides, served as secretary of the Chicago office. William M. Hahn, former chair of the Ohio Republican committee and a McKinley friend, took charge of the Speakers' Bureau, and Perry S. Heath of Indiana, an ex-newspaperman who had organized Benjamin Harrison's publicity efforts in 1888, supervised the Literary Bureau, a task of special importance in this "educational campaign." William McKinley Osborne, the candidate's cousin and close friend, headed the office in New York.[20]

Hanna himself chaired the Republican National Committee, vowing to oversee the campaign from both New York and Chicago: "I will be in the saddle, so to speak, and be found at both places at different times." For others on his committee, he drew, as Republican tradition would have it, on defeated champions of rival candidates, including Matt Quay, Joseph Manley, and Tom Platt. He assigned Quay to oversee the campaign in the South, Manley to look after New England, Platt to help out in New York. These were all feared and powerful men, but everyone knew who was in charge. "There is only one man in the National Committee," James S. Clarkson, one of the shrewdest of Republicans, wrote. "That man is Hanna, of course."[21]

Hanna's first task was to raise money for the campaign. Dawes, his key associate, feared for a time that that would be difficult, knowing how hard the panic and depression of the 1890s had hit potential contributors. "I am afraid that we are mistaken in assuming that we are going to have more funds than in 1892," Dawes warned McKinley in early August. "While the interest of business men is greater, in our contest, it is more difficult for them to spare the money for subscriptions."[22]

Dawes, it turned out, had nothing to fear. Suddenly alarmed by the prospect of Bryan's election, well-to-do Republicans and some gold Democrats opened their wallets, putting together a war chest that Dawes himself placed at $3,570,397.13, an extraordinary figure. It was twice what Republicans had spent just four years before, nearly ten times as much as Bryan would have for his own campaign in this crucial year.[23]

To raise the money, Hanna shuttled between Chicago and New York, warning financiers, bankers, manufacturers—anyone and everyone he could corner—of the dangers of a Bryan victory. From the Standard Oil Company, he got $250,000, an amount that nearly equaled the entire budget for the Democratic canvass. John D. Rockefeller, Standard Oil's owner, also sent a personal check for $2,500, saying, "I can see nothing else for us to do, to serve the Country and our honor." Banker J. P. Morgan contributed $250,000, various railroad companies $174,000, and Chicago meatpacking companies $40,000.[24] John A. McCall, president of the New York Life Insurance Company and a lifelong donor to Democratic causes, put in $50,000 of his firm's money, saying, "I consented to a payment to defeat Free Silver, not to defeat the Democratic Party . . . and I thank God that I did."[25]

The Republican funds were unusually large, and they went to pay for something of a revolution in American politics, the Republican party's 1896 "campaign of education," a shore-changing shift from the old military style of campaign that had dominated political tactics since at least the 1850s.

The change had begun a few years before, in the late 1880s and early 1890s, when important elements of the electorate became more independent-minded and less prone to respond to the emotional military style. The change reflected the gradual passing of Civil War traditions, a more educated electorate, and a growing fatigue with familiar electoral styles. Sensing this, political leaders shifted their strategy to appeal more and more to voters through publicity, advertising, and reasoned discussion. A new style of campaign, the "educational" or "merchandizing" style, was born.[26]

The approach still aimed, of course, at turning out the party's faithful voters, but it placed greater emphasis on winning new supporters with thoughtful and persuasive argument. It looked, therefore, to literature, pamphlets, and advertising, and in the long run, it exploited smaller meetings, with even as few as several hundred people listening to expert speakers unravel the mysteries of the major issues of the day.[27]

The old mass meetings and bonfires began slowly to die away, as did the torchlight parades that the young Herbert Hoover had so much admired. Wisconsin Republicans concluded as early as 1892 that "they can put campaign funds to better uses than the purchase of uniforms, torches and banners, the hiring of brass bands and all the rest. They consider that not many votes are made in that way." In a telling moment, an Indiana reporter in

1916 came across an old kerosene torch, left over from the 1892 campaign, and wondered aloud why people had ever carried them in parades. All they did, he said, was to drip oil on the marchers' clothes.[28]

A torchlight parade, the *New York Times* remarked even more caustically in 1924, could appeal only in an era of drab farm or village life. "There are no villages now," the *Times* said smugly. "We are all urban, children of the movie and the radio, speeders of the car, 'fed up' with searchlights and colored lights."[29]

In 1896, the Republicans were not yet fed up with searchlights and colored lights—their campaign would soon demonstrate that—but they were ready to adjust to the clear currents of change. "This is a year for press and pen," McKinley said that year, signaling a movement to the newer ways. "The sword has been sheathed. The only force now needed is the force of reason and the only power to be invoked is that of intelligence and patriotism."[30]

The "force of reason"—they were powerful words, and the McKinley campaign turned them into a lasting memory. To do it, Dawes, with Hanna's instructions, dispensed almost $2 million, including nearly $500,000 on printing and another $150,000 on campaign speakers. Hanna was pleased, boasting soon after the campaign began, "Our workshop at Chicago is a great institution. Fifty or sixty employees are busy all day keeping up with the demand for literature and information and meeting the people who come there from all parts of the west for consultation."[31]

Inundating voters with educational materials, Dawes gathered a team of writers who turned out campaign pamphlets in a dozen languages, among them German, French, Spanish, Italian, Swedish, Norwegian, Danish, Dutch, and Hebrew, as well as English. In all, he and his colleagues sent out over 200 million pamphlets, ample reading matter for the country's 15 million voters. The New York headquarters added another 20 million pamphlets, distributed mostly in the Northeast. It was the equivalent of 14 pieces of reading material for each voter in the country, 28 pieces for each person who wound up voting Republican.[32]

The mailing room in Chicago employed 100 workers, and boxcars loaded with literature left the city daily. There were 275 different pamphlets, nearly all of them tailored to a specific voting group and locale. Pamphlets treated the impact of free silver and the tariff on coal miners, ranchers, iron- and steelworkers, wool growers, wheat farmers, and a host of other groups. From Chicago, they went to state Republican committees, which in turn sent them on to county and precinct workers for distribution among the voters.

Apparently, they were read and reread, discussed, and passed from hand to hand. By election day, the Republicans had distributed more literature than in all their presidential campaigns since the founding of the party in the 1850s put together. "The operation," one historian has said, "has never been rivaled in American politics."[33]

They also sent out millions of posters, including a popular five-color lithograph of McKinley, captioned "The Advance Agent of Prosperity." A crew of veteran newsmen daily scanned the nation's press for material to be reprinted in pamphlet form or cast as "boilerplate" mats—prepared plates for easy printing—to distribute to country newspapers that did not have the staff or facilities to get it themselves. Every week, boilerplate went out to small papers, often rural weeklies, with a total circulation of nearly 3 million readers.[34]

Dawes shrewdly targeted voting groups and assigned specific subordinates to work on them. Besides the Literary Bureau and Speakers' Bureau, his Chicago office had a "colored voters'" department, a woman's department (though women could not vote in the election except in Wyoming, Utah, and Colorado), and a German office. There were even departments to deal with bicyclers (cycling was a popular recent fad) and traveling salesmen. A group of old Union army generals, assembled in a "patriotic heroes battalion," toured in a flag-draped train to rally Civil War veterans to the polls: "1896 is as vitally important as 1861," the flags on the train proclaimed. Rounding out McKinley's closing strategy, Dawes sent out 1,400 orators during the last two weeks of the campaign to "talk tariff, think tariff, dream tariff."[35]

As that strategy indicated, McKinley and Hanna had decided on a "blanket" campaign, emphasizing the currency issue for the first month or so and then focusing on the tariff. Despite warnings that reached him almost daily, McKinley, who had shaped his career around the tariff, hoped in fact that the enthusiasm for silver would diminish even sooner. In July 1896, he told close friends at home in Canton: "I am a Tariff man, standing on a Tariff platform. This money matter is unduly prominent. In thirty days you won't hear anything about it." "In my opinion," one of the friends quickly answered, "in thirty days you won't hear of anything else."[36]

For a time, the friend was right—Bryan's ambitious campaign made sure of that—but McKinley had spent a lifetime in politics, and he soon found ways to blend the currency and tariff issues, with references to patriotism, social harmony, and returning prosperity all added in. Before long, "he slipped smoothly," as a biographer has said, "from sound money to high wages, from good dollars to good times, from free silver to free trade, from open mints to open mills."[37]

Shrewdly, he emphasized these issues in his letter of acceptance, released to the public on August 26. Replaced in modern times by the candidate's televised acceptance speech to the party's national convention, the letter was an important custom in the nineteenth century, a sign that the "office still sought the man" and the nominee then "accepted" the honor. It also framed the candidate's intentions in the campaign. In McKinley's case, he spent the first three dozen paragraphs on the currency question, a signal to his party that he understood the importance of the issue. Free silver, he wrote, "would not make labor easier, the hours of labor shorter or the pay better. It would not make farming less laborious or more profitable. It would not start a factory or make a demand for an additional day's labor." Instead, it would derange existing values and strike "a deadly blow" to trade and commerce.

That done, he turned his attention to his first love, the tariff, saying that his party was "wedded to the doctrine of protection," even more sure, after "the lesson and experience of the last three years," of its vital importance to economic well-being. If elected, he would make it the "first duty" of the Republican party to enact a new tariff law, a promise he kept once in office. Holding to another campaign theme, he closed his letter with an eloquent appeal for inclusiveness and sectional reconciliation.[38]

On his front porch in Canton, addressing his crowds of visitors, McKinley expanded on these issues, providing for each a thoughtful epigram or two that would stick in the minds of the millions of voters who were reading his speeches at home. First, he emphasized, free silver meant inflation and devalued dollars at home; economic isolation abroad, where most nations in fact traded in gold; and lower earnings for labor and the middle class. "That which we call money, my fellow citizens," he said again and again, " . . . must be as true as the bushel which measures the grain of the farmer, and as honest as the hours of labor which the man who toils is required to give. (Loud applause.)"[39]

Second, he stressed, the way to restore prosperity after the devastation of the 1890s lay in adopting a tariff policy that would defend American products from competition overseas, foster higher wages and crop prices at home, and put revenues back in the Treasury to support the nation's gold reserve.

Free silver will not cure over-production nor under-consumption. (Laughter.) Free silver will not remove the competition of Russia, India and [the]

Argentine Republic, [even if the country coined] all the silver of the world. Free silver will not increase the demand for your wheat or make a single new consumer. You don't get consumers through the mints. (Great laughter and cries of 'No, no.') You get them through the factories. (Cries of 'That's right.')[40]

And finally, he repeated over and over, the Republicans spoke for cultural unity, the Bryan Democrats for divisive class interests, at a time when the country cried out for inclusiveness.

> Every attempt to array class against class, "the classes against the masses," section against section, labor against capital, "the poor against the rich," or interest against interest in the United States, is in the highest degree reprehensible. It is opposed to the National instinct and interest, and should be resisted by every citizen. We are not a nation of classes, but of sturdy, independent and honorable people despising the demagogue, and never capitulating to dishonor.[41]

Other Republican campaigners quickly picked up on the theme. "The city for the country, and the country for the city, and all for the flag," was the way ex-president Harrison put it. "There never has been a time in the history of the republic when each one should be more willing to say to his neighbor, 'Come and let us reason together,'" the Republican candidate for governor in Michigan said. "We have always practiced the Golden Rule," McKinley himself said. "The best policy is to 'live and let live.'"[42]

Promising a warm and tolerant pluralism, McKinley made a point of welcoming each group of visitors to his home, his family, and his town, something Bryan could not do on tour. The Major's forum, as a Republican senator said, was "an American door-yard," his rostrum "the porch of an American cottage."[43]

"The sword has been sheathed," McKinley had said early in the campaign: "We are dependent upon each other, no matter what our occupations may be. All of us want good times, good wages, good prices, good markets, and then we want good money too."[44]

These were powerful and persuasive arguments, and by September, McKinley and Hanna sensed that they had begun to counter the silver issue in key areas, especially in the areas they wanted the most, the states of the Midwest. Voters there, particularly industrial workers and middle-class farmers, had begun to rethink the effect free silver might have on their lives. "The free silver sentiment in these states began to wane the latter part of July, and is still waning," a Gold Democrat wrote of the crucial Midwest that month. Once filled with alarm, John Hay, a shrewd though jittery observer who would later become McKinley's secretary of state, found new confidence. "I think we have got The Boy on the run," he wrote a leading New York Republican.[45]

Just as McKinley had planned, the time had come to focus on the tariff. "I am confident that the height of the silver agitation has been reached and that public sentiment is already traveling down the opposite side of the hill," he had happily written the head of the American Protective Tariff League as early as August. "Get your tariff army all ready for the battle. There will be work for them to do and they can get to work with full assurance of a sweeping victory." At the end of September, Hanna and Dawes, with growing confidence in the way the campaign was going, began to cut back on silver literature and send out more pamphlets on the tariff.[46]

Election results from Vermont and Maine, two New England states that traditionally voted early, confirmed the optimism. On September 1, Vermont Republicans won their biggest victory in twenty-four years. In elections for governor and the state legislature two weeks later, Maine ran up the largest Republican majorities in its history—and this in a state the Republicans had dominated for decades. State elections in Alabama, Arkansas, South Carolina, Georgia, and Florida went Democratic, as usual, but did so by smaller margins. McKinley and Hanna were jubilant, as were President Cleveland and his Gold Democratic friends, one of whom concluded happily that Vermont and Maine had "settled Bryan's hash."[47]

Bryan soon suffered another blow, this time from an unexpected spike in wheat prices, reflecting shortages in India, Russia, and Australia. He had spent his campaign tying low crop prices to the devaluation of silver and reliance on gold. If the country coined silver in the proper amounts, he had argued, the prices for American wheat—and other agricultural products—would begin to rise. McKinley, however, had said that, for better or worse, farm prices followed global market conditions. With crop failures abroad boosting wheat prices at home, McKinley suddenly seemed right.

It was good news for McKinley and a welcome windfall for wheat farmers. On October 19 and 20, just days before the election, the price of wheat at Chicago reached 79¾ cents a bushel, about 20 cents above its selling price when the 1896 campaign began. "What has happened to this 'law' under which silver and wheat must go arm in arm?" the Republican *Chicago Tribune* promptly inquired. "What has so abruptly sundered this agricultural-mineral alliance? What agency has dared to separate those whom Altgeld and Bryan have joined together in the unholy bonds of rotten money?"[48]

"Too busy down here following the rise in prices to bother with the silver theory," a wheat farmer said in central Illinois, a remark Republican newspapers happily quoted.[49]

If they sensed victory in September, McKinley and Hanna were sure of it by October. Shrewdly, they had varied their appeal to suit the tastes of particular regions. Everywhere, of course, the Republicans had stressed prosperity, the need, as Reed eloquently put it, to "re-build out of the ruins of the last four years the stately mansions of national happiness, prosperity and self-respect."[50]

In the Northeast, they emphasized sound money and stable policies, confident of a large turnout against Bryan. In the Midwest, they touted the homegrown McKinley—the Advance Agent of Prosperity—and the benefits of the tariff and a sound currency for the region's developing urban-industrial system. A similar strategy prevailed in the border states, where Republicans hoped to capitalize on widespread doubts about Bryan and silver. Farther west, campaigners mixed the tariff and currency, adroitly using the tariff issue to woo moderate silverites who feared Democratic low tariffs. Emphasizing McKinley's commitment to international bimetallism, many Republicans in the West campaigned openly for silver, a tactic that held some silverites in the McKinley fold and kept the western campaign from becoming a clear-cut contest between silver and gold.[51]

In the last weeks before the election, the Republicans grew openly confident, Hanna even returning a campaign contribution at the end of October, telling the donor it was no longer needed. "It is all over," he said. "Reports are satisfactory just where we wanted them most." "The outlook is generally encouraging," he wrote ex-president Harrison a few days before the election, "and I feel there is no doubt of our success."[52]

In a move that outraged Bryan, Hanna called for a national "flag day" on Saturday, October 31, urging voters to "unfurl your flags, show your colors, and vote for the protection of your family." The move may have angered Bryan, but it worked. On the chosen day, hundreds of thousands of marchers paraded through flag-filled streets in towns and cities across the country, demonstrating, among other things, that political transitions, even major ones, are rarely precisely clean: this first major campaign of education would end with a powerful display of the ongoing appeal of the military style.[53]

People turned out in enormous numbers. In Chicago, there were 100,000

HARPER'S WEEKLY
JOURNAL OF CIVILIZATION

Vol. XL.—No. 2071.
Copyright, 1896, by Harper & Brothers.
All Rights Reserved.

NEW YORK, SATURDAY, AUGUST 29, 1896.

TEN CENTS A COPY.
FOUR DOLLARS A YEAR.

THE DEADLY PARALLEL.

Entitled "The Deadly Parallel," this cartoon pointedly contrasted the ages and experiences of McKinley and Bryan, the two main candidates in the election. (Harper's Weekly, August 29, 1896; Library of Congress, Washington, D.C.)

marchers, and it took five hours for them to complete their route. In San Francisco, they took four hours. In New York City, there were 110,000 marchers in line, the largest demonstration since General William T. Sherman's famous March of the Veterans in Washington, D.C., in 1865, celebrating the end of the Civil War. The parade in New York took most of the day, and some 750,000 people lined the streets cheering the paraders along. Every marcher, newspapers said, carried a flag. "The flag was everywhere," the *New York Tribune,* which was not an impartial observer, reported. "It flaunted from every window; it waved from every portico; it flew from every roof; it floated over almost every street, and many times in every block."[54]

Canton hosted its own campaign-ending rally that day as well. Townspeople cheered, bands played, fireworks boomed, and flags flew everywhere. "Glorious old banner it is," McKinley said in ending his campaign, staying with the same theme on which he had conducted it. "So long as we carry it in our hands and have what it typifies in our hearts the Republic and our splendid free institutions will be forever secure." "It is a holy banner," he added. "No flag represents as much as it does. It represents liberty, it represents equality, it represents opportunity, it represents possibilities for American manhood attainable in no other land beneath the sun. (Cheers.)"[55]

"The election is going to be a tremendous landslide in our favor," Dawes, a cautious observer, had predicted as early as October 1. Thorough organization and a campaign of education had done the job. In the end, Bryan's single-minded silver crusade had faltered, as such crusades often do. It won some new voters but alienated many others, who preferred McKinley's platform and calm and inclusive pluralism.[56]

Bryan spoke of class, ethnic, and sectional divisions, but McKinley stressed broad, positive programs in which everyone could share. United, the nation could turn with renewed vigor to the critical tasks at hand, a process in which farmers, laborers, and manufacturers—city and country, East and West, natives and foreign-born—all had vital roles to play.[57]

On November 2, the day before the election, Hanna and Dawes reviewed final details and forecast overwhelming victory. At home, McKinley waited patiently, his porch and lawn a wreck, Ida ready for a rest, and he himself tired and confident, pleased that the taxing "battle of the standards" was nearly over.[58]

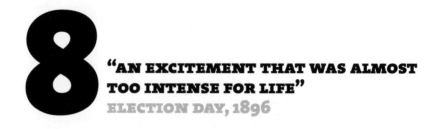

8

"AN EXCITEMENT THAT WAS ALMOST TOO INTENSE FOR LIFE"

ELECTION DAY, 1896

Election day. Went after dinner to vote for Wm. McKinley.
—John A. Sanborn, Nebraska farmer, diary entry, November 3, 1896 [1]

On election day, November 3, 1896, the Bryan Home Guards, a horse troop common in political campaigns in the nineteenth century, met the Bryans, who were finishing their last exhausting campaign day, at the train station and escorted the candidate to the city clerk's office to register to vote and then on to his polling place, a local fire station. Bryan walked through a row of tethered horses to the narrow stalls where voters were marking their ballots by lantern light. Reporters joked with the weary candidate, trying in pantomime to persuade him to vote for McKinley. His vote cast, the Guards rode with him to his home, "where," he reported, "I thanked them for the consideration they had shown, and the sacrifices which they had made during the campaign." Remarkably, he had lost only ten pounds during his tiring months on the stump, a measure, perhaps, of how much he had eaten along the way.[2]

In Canton, at 8:55 that same morning, William McKinley walked four blocks to his polling place, a small store, and waited in line to vote. He took his ballot—a sheet of paper with eight horizontal lines, the top line bearing his own name and the rest of his ticket—and entered a curtained booth in the rear of the store. Emerging one minute and eighteen seconds later, he handed the ballot to the officials in charge. "This is a solemn occasion for me," he remarked to a friend. "I am deeply impressed by it." As he left the store, people cheered.[3]

Those were the ways Americans voted in 1896 in small towns across the country, where most people still lived. In New York City, rapidly becoming one of the largest cities in the world, G. W. Steevens, a celebrated reporter for the *Daily Mail* (London), had been assigned to follow New Yorkers as they went to vote.

Steevens had been in New York the previous Saturday to witness the enormous McKinley flag day march, the like of which he had never seen before, and then he looked on as New Yorkers, anxious and tense, waited through Sunday and Monday for election day to arrive at last. "For [party workers]," he noted, "the suspense is little less than an agony. Their work is over, yet somehow they have had to put in twenty-four hours without seeing the fruit of it. It is like the breathless interval between the firing of a cannon and the hearing of the report, when every second seems a year."

Polls on election day opened at 6 a.m., and even at that hour, there were long lines at the polling booths. "Unbreakfasted, unwashed, unclothed, all hastened to get the momentous vote off their chests." Whereas Englishmen usually voted in public buildings, Americans, at least in New York City, often did not. As election day approached, dark-green wooden sheds, the official polling places, appeared in streets across the city. In poorer districts, polls opened in shops and cigar stores, sometimes, Steevens said, "with genial irony for the defeated candidate," even in undertakers' offices. The city's young "street Arabs," as he called them, made a full day of it, happily collecting barrels, planks, and boxes for the evening's bonfires. Nearly half the votes had been cast in New York by the time the city normally awakened.

After voting, a number of families headed for ferries and railway stations for a day in the country, but thousands of those who remained crowded into City Hall Park and Printing House Square, where most of the great newspapers had their headquarters. Enormous screens covered the outside of the *New York World, New York Tribune,* and other newspaper buildings, ready for the stereopticon (or magic lantern) bulletins that would bring election news to excited onlookers throughout the day. By chance, Steevens ran into Theodore Roosevelt, head of New York's police board, who told him that "this was the most peacefully conducted election in American history. Hardly an arrest was made all day."

As the returns began to come in, it became apparent that New York City was going for McKinley, the first time ever for a Republican presidential candidate. People watching the bulletins started to yell and whoop and cheer. The crowd, Steevens noted, became thicker and thicker, "almost terrifying in its unmeasureable and ungovernable force." Searchlights played across the

*In 1896, in a time well before radio and television, election-night news bulletins were relayed to the public by stereopticon (or magic lantern) slides shown on the sides of newspaper buildings, such as this one from New York City announcing McKinley's election in 1896. (*New York Journal, *November 4, 1896)*

sky. Soon, the stereopticons showed that Chicago had also gone for McKinley, and Illinois had defeated John P. Altgeld in his bid for a second term as governor. "That settles it," a man in Steevens's hearing snapped. When Kentucky joined the McKinley column, more cheers broke out. Many people carried tin horns, which they blew at each mention of a new Republican victory, leaving "no escape from the infernal din," as Steevens noted.

Paying a final visit to Republican headquarters, Steevens found "the worn, pale, sleepless heroes of the fight summoning their last energies to revel" in their victory. Democratic headquarters, in contrast, were quiet, "with the exception of a few unconquerable optimists, who were still vainly trying to demonstrate that maturer returns might retrieve all." Members of Tammany Hall, knowing they would remain in power this year or next, no matter who won, went home early.

Trains and cable cars began to leave for the suburbs. The urban poor disappeared into dingy apartments and tenements. "So New York began to empty," Steevens reported, "the vast assemblage falling asleep with the reaction from an excitement that was almost too intense for life. And through the crowd came pushing a man with matted hair crying the morning papers. . . . New York was her daily self again, with the most stirring night of her recent fate behind her."[4]

In Franklin, Nebraska, some 160 miles southwest of Bryan's home in Lincoln, farmer John A. Sanborn wrote in his diary: "Election day. Went after dinner to vote for Wm. McKinley." It was one of the most important remarks recorded that day.[5]

Across the nation, voter turnout was extraordinarily high, a measure of the intense interest in the issues and the candidates. Experts, noting the duel between deeply competing philosophies, called it the most important election since 1860, and many voters clearly agreed. In hotly contested Illinois, Indiana, Iowa, Michigan, and Ohio, turnout reached 95 percent of the eligible voters, a figure that would rarely be approached again. That evening, huge crowds gathered outside newspaper offices around the country to watch the returns. By nightfall, the outcome was clear. William McKinley, the Republican candidate, had won the largest presidential victory in twenty-four years.[6]

He won a great swath of states from Maine to North Dakota, took Oregon and California, and carried four border states: Maryland, Delaware, Kentucky, and West Virginia, the closest a Republican presidential candidate had come in twenty years to breaking into the Democratic South. Nationwide, McKinley won 271 electoral votes to 176 for Bryan. He took 7,105,144 votes (51 percent of the total) to Bryan's 6,307,897 (46 percent), the largest margin for either party since Ulysses S. Grant's victory in 1872. Palmer and the National Gold Democrats got only 132,718 votes, a dismal total, but they probably helped swing several close states into the McKinley column. Unknown thousands of Cleveland Democrats, of course, voted directly for McKinley.[7]

Reflecting the large turnout, both Bryan and McKinley received more votes than any previous candidate of their respective parties. Even in defeat, Bryan won 750,000 more votes than Cleveland had in his great triumph in 1892. But McKinley won nearly 2 million more votes than had Harrison the same year. Bryan carried twenty-six states and territories, most of them in the sparsely populated Rocky Mountain, Great Plains, and Deep South regions. He failed to hold all the border states, did not sweep the West, and carried no states at all in the crucial Midwest.[8]

Disgruntled, James K. Jones, Bryan's campaign manager, promptly charged that the outcome stemmed from "every kind of coercion and intimidation on the part of the money power, including threats of lockouts and dismissals, and impending starvation, by the employment of the largest corruption fund ever used in this country, and by the subornation of the American press." McKinley, Hanna, and the so-called money power, in short, had bribed and threatened their way to victory.[9]

That some Republicans had coerced and intimidated voters there was no doubt. Employers placed warnings in paychecks, whispered cautions on the factory floor: vote for Bryan, and orders might be canceled, perhaps even whole factories closed. Insurance companies, it was said, threatened to foreclose overdue mortgages if McKinley lost. Some employers, Bryan charged, paid their workers on the Saturday night before the election and told them that they could return to work on Wednesday if McKinley were elected but not if Bryan won. "Men, vote as you please, but if Bryan is elected tomorrow, the whistle will not blow Wednesday morning."[10]

There was ample evidence confirming the charge. William C. Beer, a key member of the McKinley campaign, wrote his wife in late October that he had been assigned to help businesses "keep their employees licked into shape for election." Beer and the Republicans licked everyone they could reach into shape. Employers moved workers from plant to plant to disqualify them from voting. A friend of Beer's reported that a Standard Oil executive in Ohio had transferred 100 Democrats from one refinery to another, thus disqualifying them by reason of residence on election day. In a more subtle move, New York bankers worked to maintain a gold reserve in the Treasury above $100 million to avoid a new bond issue by the Cleveland administration, "which it was feared would strengthen the silver party in the presidential campaign."[11]

"This is a very grave charge and it has now assumed a form that justifies giving it some attention," Hanna said in a public statement on behalf of the Republican National Committee on October 21. "It is an insult to both employer and employee. We do not believe that one is despotic enough to attempt to coerce, or that the other is so cringing as to be coerced." He and the Republicans offered a reward of $500—a handsome sum in those days—for evidence of voter coercion (significantly, they received none). "This committee will spare no pains to secure to every citizen whatever his politics, the right to cast his vote according to his convictions and to have his vote honestly counted."[12]

In Canton, McKinley also joined in. "They say, too, that coercion is going on," he said to a large delegation of railroad employees, who laughed at the remark. "The only coercion that is operating in the United States today is that of reason, conscience, and experience. (Immense applause and cries of 'That's right.')"[13]

Excuses of Chairman Jones's sort, understandably attractive to losing candidates, die hard. Suasion and coercion, it is clear, took place on both sides: among some employers who, as Jones charged, pressured workers in one way or another to support McKinley and among many Democrats who used fraud and intimidation in the cities and, even more criminally, against hundreds of thousands of African Americans in the South.

But coercion, despite the Democratic charges, did not determine the outcome in 1896, except by artificially inflating Democratic margins in the South. Bryan lost because in a campaign of education, he failed to lure the critical voters: the labor, farm, immigrant, middle-class, and other voters who were sure they had a stake in urban-industrial America. McKinley won precisely because he attracted those voters and seemed in step with a nation preparing to move into the twentieth century. That was one reason it was significant that John A. Sanborn, a farmer in Bryan's own Nebraska, "went after dinner to vote for Wm. McKinley."[14]

In 1896, McKinley swept the densely populated Northeast and Midwest, including the eight states—New York, New Jersey, Pennsylvania, Ohio, Indiana, Illinois, Michigan, and Wisconsin—in which one-half of the country's total vote was polled. In both the Northeast and the Midwest, he won a clear majority of the rural (presumably Bryan) vote and took the urban centers, which had generally gone for Cleveland in 1892.[15]

Crushing Bryan in the cities, McKinley extended the pattern of Republican gains that had emerged there two years before. Bryan carried only one midwestern city with more than 45,000 inhabitants; lost San Francisco, Philadelphia, Baltimore, St. Louis, and other cities; and won only seven of Boston's twenty-five wards. He lost both New York and Kings (Brooklyn) counties, the first Democratic candidate to do so since the 1840s. He also failed to carry Chicago, where McKinley piled up 58 percent of the vote. In Newark, New Jersey, McKinley won fourteen of the fifteen wards. In Trenton, he won a startling 68 percent of the vote. In eighty-five midwestern cities, where Cleveland's plurality in 1892 had been 162,000 votes, McKinley outpolled Bryan by 464,000.[16]

Dwelling almost always on free silver, Bryan had failed clearly to create a constituency among labor. In northern cities, he lost votes, significantly, in working-class as well as middle-class and silk-stocking districts.[17] In New England, as Republican strategists had suspected, he had attracted large and curious crowds to his rallies but few voters to the polls, garnering less than one-third of the vote, in fact, in the entire region. He carried only one county in all of New York State and none of the industrial cities of the South.

In a number of key states, Bryan also did more poorly than he had hoped among farmers. In Iowa, which Democratic strategists had counted on carrying, he won only seventeen out of ninety-nine counties, and the Republican majority came to over 65,000 votes, 20,000 more than Republican leaders in the state had predicted privately in September. McKinley took rural counties in Iowa such as Kossuth, Clay, and Sioux in the northern and northwestern part of the state by large majorities. James B. Weaver, the veteran Iowa politician, was so stunned by the outcome that he called the vote in the state "absurd and dishonest." It was neither.[18]

In Minnesota, another critical state for Bryan, McKinley carried sixty-four counties to only seventeen for the Nebraskan, and he won a popular majority of 53,768 votes. He easily won the urban vote in Hennepin and Ramsey counties (Minneapolis and St. Paul), by 44,308 votes to Bryan's 32,563. Republican victories in rural counties were even larger, with McKinley carrying two southern Minnesota counties (Faribault and Freeborn), among others, by a margin of three to one.

It was the same in the state of Illinois, where the Republican plurality amounted to 141,537. Cook County (including Chicago) alone provided 69,913 of that margin, another remarkable victory in one of the nation's largest cities. Bryan also failed to win the heavy downstate vote that might have enabled him to overcome this deficit. The Republicans won agricultural counties such as Champaign, Piatt, Vermillion, McLean, Livingston, and Ford by substantial majorities. In other crucial Bryan states, McKinley lost by only 13,565 votes in Kansas and by 11,943 votes in Bryan's home state of Nebraska. He carried North Dakota.[19]

Bryan tried to ally the South and West but lost crucial portions of each. He did well in the once-Republican plains and mountain states and fell just a few thousand votes short in California, Kentucky, Indiana, and other needed states. Besides Nebraska, his own state, McKinley also pressed him in Tennessee, Virginia, Kansas, South Dakota, and Wyoming, a sign of the effectiveness of the Republican campaign.

The rise in crop prices before the election, related to crop failures abroad, hurt Bryan in wheat- and corn-producing areas. He had linked wheat prices to the price of silver, a connection now disproven. In the Midwest, thousands of German Lutherans and Catholics, attracted by sound money and McKinley's inviting pluralism, helped tip the region to McKinley. Ironically, Bryan, the crusading moralist, lost votes for almost precisely the same reasons the Republican pietists had lost them earlier in the decade.[20]

In retrospect, the Republican victory in 1896, combined with the party's overwhelming triumphs in 1894, marked a "critical election" in American political history, paving the way for Republican victories in election after election until the 1930s. New voting patterns supplanted the old, a new majority party emerged to govern the country, and national policies adapted to the new realities.

The election was critical in other ways as well. Together with the results in 1894, it shifted power in the Democratic party to the South, and the party increasingly reflected the views of southern whites on race and other issues. McKinley's 1896 campaign also displayed the growing power of money and business in American political life, affirmed the success of Mark Hanna's new methods of party organization and centralized control, and through the use of advances in technology, it brought candidates in far closer contact than ever before with the voters they wooed.[21]

On election night, Bryan, exhausted, took to his bed. Reporters gathered in the library below to analyze the returns, and Mary Baird Bryan brought the important telegrams directly to him—"her face betraying their purport before I received them from her hand," he recalled in his memoir of the campaign. He sadly studied the returns, looking, said a newsman who was there, like "a general reading the reports of some great battle in which whole armies were swept away. His eye never changed. His countenance was unreadable." By 11 o'clock that night, he knew he had lost. He was relieved, he said, and "free from official responsibility, I fell asleep."[22]

Asked later by a reporter about the loss, he said, "I regard it in some respects as fortunate that I was not elected, considering the fact that for four years I would have been confronted by a gold congress. No free silver bill would have been passed. My hands would have been tied." It was a gracious thought but, for a man so ambitious, an unlikely one. On November 5, two days after the election, he telegraphed McKinley his congratulations, the first losing candidate ever to do so: "We have submitted the issue to the American people and their will is law," he said.[23]

A few days later, he issued a message to his fellow silverites, arguing that their issue, having come so close to victory, had emerged from the election in a stronger position than ever. "The fight is just begun," Josephus Daniels wired him. "We have enlisted for the war. We look for you to blaze the way." "Our cause is just and will prevail," Richard P. Bland, the revered silverite, said. "The battle is still on." Although greatly disappointed, Bryan was justifiably proud. At the age of thirty-six, he had taken control of a major political party and won more than 6 million votes. Despite numerous errors, he brought the Democrats closer to victory than any other candidate could likely have done.[24]

In part, his loss, of course, reflected a continuation of 1894's devastating anti-Democratic trend. Bryan's emotional crusade for silver capitalized on agrarian discontent, buoyed disheartened Democrats, and attracted voters who otherwise would not have supported the Democratic ticket. His terse explanation for his defeat—"I have borne the sins of Grover Cleveland"— oversimplified the outcome but made considerable sense. The nominee of a divided and discredited party, he had come remarkably close to winning. Bryan promptly called 1896 the "First Battle" and prepared for 1900.[25]

For the Populists, the election marked an end rather than a beginning. Nationwide, the straight Bryan-Watson ticket got only 222,583 votes (less than 2 percent of the popular vote), and Populist totals were down nearly everywhere. McKinley's victory dazed People's party leaders. Deeply embittered, Tom Watson left politics for law, saying: "Our party, as a party, does not exist any more." Ignatius Donnelly despaired. "Will the long lane never have a turning?" he wrote in his diary. "Will the sun of triumph never rise?"[26]

It never did. Vestiges of the party lingered into the new century but never as suns, only as shadows. The Populist heyday, transfixing though it was, had passed quickly, ending by the middle of the 1890s. The Bryan campaign served simply as a final flourish. In its time, the People's party won some important successes but not the ones that mattered most. It could not preserve the small independent farmer in an era of consolidation and complex growth. It could not restore agrarian power in a nation that hurried toward city and factory. In a political system that built on majorities, it never won a majority of the country's voters. It never even came close, and failing, it declined as swiftly as it had arisen.

Grover Cleveland spent election night with his cabinet at the White House, following the returns. Long after midnight, they parted, satisfied that McKinley had won. There was sadness in the occasion, and thoughts turned naturally to what might have been. At the start of the decade, Democratic hopes had been high. Successive elections in 1890 and 1892 repudiated the Republican party and, in the eyes of many observers, seemed to establish enduring Democratic rule. It was not to be. Within a few years, amid depression, internal dissension, and a glaring inability to govern, Cleveland and the Democrats had squandered their hard-won gains.

Cleveland himself never understood what had happened. He left office in March 1897, the most unpopular president since Andrew Johnson. A few old friends gathered at the ceremony marking the inauguration of his successor. McKinley had the presidency; Bryan had the party; and for Cleveland, there was only bitter retirement. William L. Wilson, himself a sad victim in the decade's drama, caught the mood that inaugural day. "I felt very much like I had been to a funeral," he said.[27]

In Canton, election night brought giant celebrations. Workers tied down the switches on factory steam whistles, boys yelled through megaphones, and crowds shouted around the McKinley house. The din mounted through the early night. "Pandemonium is let loose," a reporter said. "Canton is beside itself with joy."

In his study, McKinley was already turning his attention to devising a cabinet and policy for the new administration. The prospects seemed exciting. Cementing the voter revolution of 1894, the election of 1896 closed a distinct era in American political history. It terminated the politics of equilibrium and laid the foundation for a generation of Republican rule. The Republicans had won the decade's crucial battle for party mastery, and now, at last, they could govern.[28]

A blend of piety and pragmatism, the president-elect prayed for guidance, yet he did not neglect to consult key Republican leaders. Fashioning his administration, he planned to move vigorously on the tariff and international bimetallism, work to restore relations with Congress that had been so badly damaged under Cleveland, and hope for prosperity. Building again on 1894's outcome, the Republicans remained in control of Congress. Foreign affairs required sensitive attention. There were troubles in Cuba, which threatened war with Spain.

In the aftermath of the election, the country relaxed, hoping to leave behind the tart divisiveness of the mid-1890s. People thronged to see the president-elect, who once again was a symbol of national unity. The decade of the 1890s so far seemed a kaleidoscope of depression, divisiveness, and flashing movement, with little opportunity for planning or reflection. Perhaps now the pace of change could slow and tempers mellow. If all went well, the next four years would carry McKinley and the nation triumphantly into the twentieth century. The presidential election of 1896 at last was over, "an excitement," the reporter from the *Daily Mail* had said, "that was almost too intense for life."[29]

9
MCKINLEY'S AMERICA
THE ELECTION'S AFTERMATH

On this auspicious day, the sky is blue, the birds sing and joy is
unconfined. It is the last day of the Cleveland administration.
—San Francisco Examiner, *March 4, 1897*[1]

Following recent tradition, McKinley had dinner with Grover Cleveland, the outgoing president, in the White House
the evening before the inauguration. Ida, as was often the
case, was too tired to join them. The meeting was cordial.
The two men talked about the election, about Cleveland's recent agreement with Great Britain over a dispute involving
Venezuela, and about serious current troubles over Spain's
role in Cuba. Cleveland told McKinley what he had done to
try to keep the peace. Later, McKinley recalled the "settled
sadness and sincerity" of the conversation.[2]

The next morning, a large crowd waited in the park to the east
of the Capitol. On one side, cameramen had set up Thomas A.
Edison's new "kinetoscope"—symbol of a rapidly changing
America—to film the event, the first inaugural in history to
be filmed. In another first, a woman voted in the Electoral
College that year for the office of president of the United
States. Sarah Malloy of Cheyenne, Wyoming, had the honor,
though newspapers quickly reassured readers that, as one
paper put it, "while Mrs. Malloy takes extreme interest in politics, she is a good housewife and a kind mother."[3] In many
homes across the country, there was relief in simply having a
new occupant in the White House. "On this auspicious day,"
the *San Francisco Examiner,* a Democratic newspaper, said,
"the sky is blue, the birds sing and joy is unconfined. It is the
last day of the Cleveland administration."[4]

A photograph of William McKinley on Inauguration Day in March 1897, with outgoing president Grover Cleveland to his left. (Library of Congress, Washington, D.C.)

In office, McKinley profited from his own skillful policies, the newly won dominance of his party, and the return of prosperity after the hardships of the 1890s. At his request, Congress quickly passed the Dingley Tariff, which raised tariff rates and brought new revenues into the Treasury to protect the gold reserve. In April, as promised, he named a three-member commission to work with European powers on an international agreement for silver, an effort that foundered several months later over British and French opposition.[5]

The new president himself was open and accessible, a pleasant contrast to Cleveland's self-imposed isolation. McKinley rode the Washington streetcars, walked the streets around the White House, and enjoyed looking in department store windows. Children lay in wait for him on his walks, anticipating his smile, handshake, and ready greeting. In the afternoons, he walked with aides in "the yard," as the homespun administration called the White House grounds. In the evenings, he relaxed on the back piazza of the mansion, puffing contentedly on a cigar and chatting with congressional and party leaders as the evening traffic flowed by. During his term, McKinley became the first president to ride in an automobile, reaching the handsome speed of eighteen miles an hour.[6]

In the 1900 campaign, McKinley and the Republicans again used many of the educational methods they had tapped so skillfully in 1896. He drubbed William Jennings Bryan, once more the nominee of the Democratic party, carrying six states (including Bryan's own state of Nebraska) that had voted for the Democrat in 1896. Embarrassingly, McKinley also carried Bryan's county, city, and precinct. His plurality of 860,000 votes was the greatest for any presidential candidate since 1824, and the election confirmed the Republicans as the nation's majority party.[7] At Bryan's home, the mood was somber. "At the close of another presidential campaign it is my lot to congratulate you on a second victory," he wired McKinley.[8]

The last president who had served in the Civil War, McKinley became an important transitional figure in the nation's presidential history. He put together a staff to do the business of an active presidency, including a press office to distribute news of presidential decisionmaking. He consulted often with congressional leaders, many of whom admired him greatly, and along with them shaped the legislation he wanted. He traveled and spoke widely, creating a bully pulpit for the White House that his vice-president and successor in the office, Theodore Roosevelt, would greatly enlarge. He adopted views and approaches that carried into the twentieth and twenty-first centuries. He became, as one of his leading biographers has said, "the first modern president."[9]

Grover Cleveland watched these events with a baleful eye. Leaving office, he retired to Princeton, New Jersey, where he settled in comfortably with his family and the circle of friends he developed on Princeton University's faculty. He fathered two sons and spent much of his time fishing and entertaining old colleagues. Princeton gave him an honorary degree in 1897, and he delivered a series of lectures at the university on matters related to his administration. He continued to rally the gold Democrats, hoping for their return to power within his old party. "I am drifting along, doing no work and yet puttering at something all day long," he wrote an old cabinet colleague.[10]

He also watched with dismay as the administration he had helped elect promptly passed the Dingley Tariff, raising tariff rates to new levels. McKinley's efforts to annex Hawaii upset him, as did his policies toward the troubles in Cuba. He detested McKinley's decision to keep the Philippine Islands after the war with Spain. Bryan's support for the peace treaty with Spain, which Bryan helped save from defeat, angered him.[11]

Cleveland lamented the nomination of the Nebraskan again in 1900, still "cursing the animals who have burglarized and befouled the Democratic home." He prayed for Bryan's defeat. "My feeling is that the safety of the country is in the rehabilitation of the old Democratic party," he wrote a friend in July 1900. To his dismay, some of his sound money friends decided to back Bryan that year. Olney, Carlisle, and Morton all voted for Bryan, Morton writing Cleveland that "it is a choice between evils, and I am going to shut my eyes, hold my nose, vote, go home, and disinfect myself." That kind of thinking never appealed to Grover Cleveland.[12]

With serious diseases of the heart and kidneys, Cleveland spent parts of his last years confined to bed. He also experienced something of a revival in respect for his political courage, a contrast to earlier feelings against him that had amounted almost to hatred. Stricken at a favorite retreat on the New Jersey shore, he was taken back to Princeton, where he died on the morning of June 24, 1908. His last words were emblematic of the man: "I have tried so hard to do right."[13]

He had done that, indeed, but he never grasped that the time for him and "the old Democratic party," as he liked to call it, was vanishing quickly into an outmoded past. Like some Democratic presidents before him, Cleveland on occasion had exerted presidential power—for him, most notably, in his signature fight for silver repeal—and he had won the victory he wanted. But the victory amounted to just that, repeal, getting rid of a "bad" law, an action very much in the Democratic party's late nineteenth-century tradition.[14]

Cleveland did not recognize it, but that outlook was already changing, fostering a party dramatically different in policies and methods, which was one of the reasons the elections of 1894 and 1896 together formed a critical election. Bryan himself had a hand in it, and even more so, of course, did Woodrow Wilson, elected in 1912. Using aggressive presidential power, Wilson pushed through Congress in his first term the Underwood Tariff, the Clayton antitrust law, and the Federal Reserve Act, the latter still important in American life today. In doing so, he laid the way for Franklin D. Roosevelt and later Democratic presidents. A new day and a new Democratic party had begun to emerge.[15]

Within hours of learning the 1896 election results, the Bryans had begun planning for 1900. "Will does not feel discouraged—he is working very hard—getting material together for our book about the campaign," Mary Bryan wrote a friend. *The First Battle,* a compilation of a few memories and a lot of speeches, sold 200,000 copies in its first nine months at $3.75 a copy, a nice income that Bryan contributed to free silver organizations. In farm homes across the South and West, it soon occupied a place alongside the Bible. Its title alone made it clear that Bryan would continue the fight. "If we are right," he promised, "we shall yet triumph."[16]

Many in the country admired what he had done, even people such as Nannie Lodge, the smart and talented wife of the staunch Massachusetts Republican Henry Cabot Lodge, who reflected after the election that

> "the great fight is won . . . a fight conducted by trained and experienced and organized forces, with both hands full of money, with the power of the press—and of prestige—on one side; on the other, a disorganized mob at first, out of which burst into sight, hearing, and force—one man, but such a man! Alone, penniless, without backing, without money, with scarce a paper, without speakers, that man fought such a fight that even those in the East can call him a Crusader, an inspired fanatic—a prophet! It has been marvellous. Hampered by such a following, such a platform . . . he almost won."[17]

In the weeks after the election, Bryan received 186,000 letters and telegrams, a testimony to his remarkable appeal to many Americans. The years from 1897 to 1900 he spent on the stump for silver. He also joined the Chautauqua lecture circuit, which gave him the chance to spread his message even more widely. "The contest for financial independence will go on," he wrote in an article in the *North American Review* in December 1896. "We entered the contest with a disorganized army; we emerge from it a united and disciplined force without the loss of a soldier. We are ready for another contest."[18]

Like Grover Cleveland, he was sorely disappointed with McKinley, whose first six months in office he called "the most disastrous in the history of the country." Running against McKinley again in 1900, Bryan insisted on a free silver plank in the platform, though many Democrats, even some of his most fervent allies, wanted to stress newer issues such as imperialism and the expanding trusts, to lure back those who had left the party four years before. But Bryan demanded another free silver plank, foreshadowing a second defeat. "Bryan," Thomas B. Reed was happy to quip, "had rather be wrong than president."[19]

In later years, he ran for president a third time, in 1908, and between 1913 and 1915 served as Woodrow Wilson's secretary of state, a position he courageously resigned in protest against Wilson's growing steps toward war.[20] His last years brought mounting criticism. He worked with a Washington, D.C., law firm that helped companies such as Standard Oil invest in Latin America; he became the front man for sales of Florida real estate; he took the floor at the 1924 Democratic national convention to oppose a resolution denouncing the Ku Klux Klan. In 1925, he argued against the teaching of evolution in the legendary Scopes Monkey Trial, since commemorated in the play and film *Inherit the Wind*.

By then, time and constant travel had taken their toll on the passionate Nebraskan. The waistline had expanded; hips and legs had stiffened. A reporter who had seen Bryan's famous speech at Chicago in 1896 saw him again in 1924. This was not the same Bryan, he said: "A word man, eyes dimmed, shoulders stooped, the old spirit glowing faintly like the thin flame from a burnt out log, voice no longer resonant, many of the delegates and spectators hostile to his pleading, scarcely tolerant of the leader they had followed so many years."[21] His energy spent, Bryan died in his sleep on July 26, 1925, five days after the Scopes trial ended.

The poet Vachel Lindsay, sixteen years old in 1896, celebrated his cause and lamented his defeat, in a poem that gained fame as the years went on:

> In a nation of one hundred five, mob-hearted, lynching,
> relenting, repenting millions,
> There are plenty of sweeping, swinging, stinging, gorgeous

things to shout about,
And knock your old blue devils out.
I brag and chant of Bryan, Bryan, Bryan,
Candidate for president who sketched a silver Zion

Election night at midnight:
Boy Bryan's defeat.
Defeat of western silver.
Defeat of the wheat.

Where is that boy, that Heaven-born Bryan,
That Homer Bryan, who sang from the West?
Gone to join the shadows with Altgeld the Eagle,
Where the kings and the slaves and the troubadours rest.[22]

To everyone's relief, the economy soon showed signs of recovery, after the heartbreaking depression of the 1890s. By midsummer 1897, just a few months after McKinley's inauguration, there were already favorable indications: factories were running again, employment was up, crop prices were at last on the rise. "Wheat sold at $1 per bushel today—the highest price since 1891," Charles G. Dawes noted in his diary on August 21. "Prosperity seems to be dawning at last."[23]

One of the stimulants, ironically, was gold, whose scarcity Bryan and the silverites had lamented again and again during the 1890s. Almost overnight, it seemed, supplies of gold became more plentiful. The cyanide process of extraction, first introduced in 1890, allowed the use of ores that had previously been cast aside. New goldfields opened up—in Australia, South Africa, and the famed Klondike mines in Alaska. The result was an inflation of the currency, exactly what Bryan had called for, but it rode a swelling tide of gold rather than silver.[24]

Other tides helped as well. After 1897, the triumph of McKinley and the Republican party fostered political stability, assured industry of tariff protection, and guaranteed a monetary system that helped renew business confidence. Between 1897 and World War I, farmers themselves experienced a new golden age, thanks in part to global demand. Prices for wheat, cotton, and other crops shot up. The average value of farms also rose, and farmers began to expand their holdings and purchase washing machines, water pumps, and tractors that made life easier. By 1920, one-third of all American farmers owned a car or truck, and rural free delivery, begun in 1893, cut down on rural isolation, bringing mail, catalogs, and newspapers to the farmer's door.[25]

"The hum of industry has drowned the voice of calamity, and the voice of despair is no longer heard in the United States," McKinley told an audience in Kewanee, Illinois, in October 1897. McKinley and the Republican party prospered under that hum. The decade between 1898 and 1907 brought one of the highest rates of economic growth in the nation's history—and, along with it, repeated Republican victories.[26]

The People's party, by contrast, continued to wither. The party was a tiny remnant of its earlier self, and its adherents found it harder and harder after 1896 to attract support for Populist reforms in a nation reunited by war and returning prosperity.

"To-morrow is the 4th of March," Ignatius Donnelly wrote sardonically in his newspaper the day before McKinley's first inauguration. "McKinley will move into the White House. The reign of Confidence will begin. The Advance Agent of Prosperity will advance. Every man and woman will have plenty to eat and drink and wear. Hunger will depart forever from the land. Wheat will be worth a dollar a bushel, oats fifty cents, barley seventy-five cents. The workingman will have steady employment at big wages."[27]

Though bitter, Donnelly came closer to the truth than he knew. Wheat did sell for a dollar a bushel, and other crops and manufactured goods found better markets and prices as well. Every American did not have enough to eat and drink and wear, and hunger never did depart from the land, but many in the society had fresh reasons for confidence and renewed faith in a brighter future.

Not the Populists, however. "For the last year," an Arizona Populist wrote in mid-1897, "everything seems to have gone wrong with the organization, and we have become almost discouraged and sick at heart, and if there is a rift in the clouds that seem to have settled down about us that is visible from any point of view we want to know it." Sadly, no rift in the clouds ever appeared. Returning prosperity, the "splendid little war" of 1898, and changing views about politics rewarded the Republicans, punished the Democrats, and robbed the Populists of support. "Should there be war with Spain the Pops would stand no more show in the election this fall than an armless man at a hugging match," a shrewd observer had predicted in April 1898.[28]

Somehow, it was even worse than that. The Populists lost badly in those 1898 elections, both in the South and in the West. Party leadership fractured again, in ever more surprising ways. A few Populists, William A. Peffer and

Mary E. Lease among them, supported the Spanish-American War and the acquisition of colonies. Most Populists, especially in the West, bitterly opposed McKinley's foreign policy. They wanted nothing to do with colonies and empire, knowing, too, that war would divert attention from problems at home. "The Spanish War finished us," Tom Watson famously said. "The blare of the bugle drowned the voice of the Reformer."[29]

It was a nice phrase, which historians often repeat, but it was in fact well off the mark: the voice of that reformer had begun fading long before 1898, and it died out almost completely after 1900. Scarcely 200 delegates attended the Populist national convention in 1904, which named Watson for president. In 1908, another sparsely attended convention nominated Watson again, though everyone who was there knew it was the party's last convention. Delegates shed tears of joy and despair and shared memories of the promising movement of the early 1890s. Watson won only 28,862 votes in the entire country that year, most of them in his own state of Georgia.[30]

The most important Populists—Lease, Allen, Watson, Simpson, and others—soon moved on, following their own unusual paths. After the 1896 election, Mary E. Lease retired from People's party politics. She and her husband divorced, and she took her four children to New York City, where she spent her last thirty years writing for Joseph Pulitzer and the *New York World*, lecturing for the New York City Board of Education, and presiding over national and international birth control societies. Her most popular lecture had nothing to do with urging farmers to raise less corn and more hell. "An Evening with Tennyson," it was named.[31]

In 1900, Lease went back to Kansas and Nebraska to campaign for William McKinley, not for William Jennings Bryan, whom she had come to detest for his single-minded devotion to silver. At home in New York, she became a fervent supporter of Theodore Roosevelt, a "man of destiny," she said, "an instrument in God's hands, to send the gift of human liberty to the far off islands of the sea and to give America the proud place of the foremost of the nations that inhabit the face of the earth." She backed TR in the election of 1912.[32]

In 1900, Pulitzer sent her to report on the Democratic national convention, where Bryan once again became the nominee. Her reports to the *World* were scathing: "The old Populist circus is here," she wrote, "or rather some of its remains." James B. Weaver, her longtime ally, "tired of the world and the world tired of him, is here to lift his cracked and aged voice." Bryan, for whom she had campaigned four years before, was "a failure as a lawyer, a failure as a newspaperman," she wrote. He "is a selfish demagogue. I was his friend, but now I would not make another speech for him if it would save his neck. . . . He was afraid to defend the government ownership of railroads. He has no other cry, no other purpose, than 'sixteen to one.'" "Give this message to those in the West who still remember me," she told a reporter from Kansas in 1931. "I used to be radical and vindictive. I am still radical; but I am not vindictive. . . . Time has mellowed me." Mary E. Lease died October 29, 1933, in the first year of the New Deal.[33]

A remarkable individual, Thomas E. Watson revived his law practice after 1896; wrote, among other things, a two-volume history of France that retold the French Revolution in Populist terms, as part of "the long-continued struggle of the many to throw off the yoke of the few"; and by 1904 owned 9,000 acres of Georgia land, on which sat Hickory Hill, his white-pillared mansion. "My political career has forever ended," Watson said after the 1896 campaign, though it had not. He ran twice more for the presidency on the Populist ticket, in 1904 and 1908. "I am a political non-entity," he declared during an election speech in 1908.[34]

In July 1910, Watson announced his return to the Democratic party. Betraying the cause of racial unity he had sometimes defended during the 1890s, he became a bitter racist and anti-Semite, helping to pass new laws that made it virtually impossible for African Americans to vote in Georgia. In an editorial about Booker T. Washington in his newspaper, Watson wrote: "What does Civilization owe to the negro? Nothing! *Nothing!!* NOTHING!!!"[35]

Tom Watson died September 26, 1922, two years after his election to the U.S. Senate from Georgia. "He was a great man," Eugene Debs wrote his widow, "a heroic soul who fought the power of evil his whole life long in the interest of the common people, and they loved and honored him." Not all the common people: a cross of roses eight feet high, a gift from the Ku Klux Klan, stood at his funeral.[36]

Arthur Sewall, Watson's nemesis in 1896, had gone quietly back to running his Maine businesses and died suddenly of apoplexy in September 1900.

McKinley celebrated his second inauguration in March 1901, praising in a brief inaugural address the nation's special destiny. In April, he and Ida were off on a transcontinental trip that brought out cheering crowds through the South, the Southwest, and California. In San Francisco, he christened the new steel battleship *Ohio,* named after his home state. The McKinleys then returned to Washington, where the president, overwhelmingly popular, dispelled rumors that he might run for a third term. "I not only am not and will not be a candidate for a third term, but would not accept a nomination for it if it were tendered me."[37]

After a summer's rest at home in Canton, the McKinleys entrained for Buffalo, New York, where McKinley was to give an important address in honor of President's Day at the Pan-American Exposition. On the morning of September 5, he spoke to a crowd of nearly 50,000 people, surrounded, as he told them, by the many new machines and inventions that had changed their world. "Expositions," he said, "are the timekeepers of progress. They record the world's advancement."

McKinley's remarks that day reflected both his changing ideas and his growing assurance. The United States, he said, had to adjust to a transformed world in which it would play a leading role. "Isolation," he declared, "is no longer possible or desirable." The country's expanding economy demanded larger markets abroad, which in turn called for lower tariffs—a dramatic change in outlook from the author of the McKinley Act—and the aggressive use of tariff reciprocity: "We must not repose in the fancied security that we can forever sell everything and buy little or nothing." Free trade, however, was also not the answer but rather "sensible trade arrangements which will not interrupt our home production. . . . The period of exclusiveness is past. The expansion of trade and commerce is the pressing problem."

The next morning, he and Ida took a special train to see the famous Niagara Falls, one of the country's most popular tourist attractions, and then returned to Buffalo, where he planned to meet the public that afternoon at a special reception in the exposition's Temple of Music. Fearful for his safety, some of his staff urged him to cancel this part of the schedule. "Why should I?" he asked in reply. "No one would wish to hurt me." Besides, he would shake hands for only ten minutes, and reception lines always gave him pleasure, as he had earlier told a reporter: "Everyone in that line has a smile and a cheery word. They bring no problems with them; only good will. I feel better after the contact."[38]

Not this time. In the receiving line waited an anarchist named Leon Czolgosz who concealed a revolver under bandages on his right hand. McKinley, in his thoughtful way, reached to shake Czolgosz's left hand and was shot. He was shot twice, one bullet grazing his sternum and dropping harmlessly into his clothing, the other cutting into his abdomen.[39]

Guards wrestled Czolgosz to the floor. McKinley, though dangerously wounded, said, "Don't let them hurt him."[40] As usual, his thoughts went immediately to his beloved Ida. "My wife," he told an aide, "be careful how you tell her—oh, be careful." An ambulance took him to the exposition's small hospital, where doctors tried to probe and clean the wound. "It must have been some poor misguided fellow," McKinley said calmly.[41]

For several days, hopes remained high, but the doctors had failed to find the bullet. A new contraption called the X-ray, one of "the timekeepers of progress," was among the new inventions on display at the exposition, but it was not used. Gangrene soon set in, and McKinley lost consciousness. His old friend Mark Hanna limped into the sickroom on his cane, stood by the bed, and broke out, a reporter said, "with a horrible sob: 'William—William—don't you know me?'"[42]

Reviving briefly, McKinley said to his doctors, "It is useless, gentlemen, I think we ought to have prayer." Ida held his hands and kissed him. "Good-bye—good-bye, all," he said in a weak voice, then, "It is God's way. His will, not ours, be done." Early in the morning of September 14, 1901, McKinley died, murmuring the words to his favorite hymn, "Nearer My God to Thee, Nearer to Thee."[43] "The great life was ended," Charles G. Dawes, who was there, wrote in his diary.[44] McKinley, John Hay, his eloquent secretary of state, said in his eulogy, "showed in his life how a citizen should live, and in his last hours taught us how a gentleman could die."[45]

Ida McKinley lived until 1907. Calling on her a few years earlier, a visitor found her seated limply in a chair, a frail figure in a plain black gown. "Over and over she moaned: 'Why should I linger? Please, God, if it is Thy will, let me go. I want to be with him. I am so tired.'"[46]

As Americans and their political leaders looked back, they could take pride in introducing the new educational style of campaign in the 1896 election. It had seemed to work well that year, especially in educating and drawing out the voters. Nearly 80 percent of eligible voters across the nation cast ballots in 1896, and in some states, especially in the Midwest, turnouts ran far higher than that.

That was all well and good—it was hard to argue, after all, against campaigns that stressed education, literature, and reasoned argument. But for the country's political parties and political system, there was a penalty, at first unrecognized, to the educational style—an erosion of partisan loyalty that over decades resulted in a drastic drop in voter turnout. Politics stirred and involved fewer voters; emphasized the personalities of candidates; and in the absence of mass involvement, promoted the participation of pressure groups.[47] In some sense, the result was unfortunate. Something important had been lost, a feeling of involvement, a point of vital contact between voter and the system, an assurance that democratic politics could work.[48]

During the late 1890s, it became clear, the third party system began to give way to the fourth, a time when interest in politics fell sharply, fewer people took an active role in their parties, and fewer people took the trouble to vote. In the last five presidential elections of the nineteenth century, turnout averaged 79.2 percent of eligible voters; in the first five presidential elections of the new century, it averaged only 65 percent, a dramatic drop. Thanks to extreme measures in the South designed to take the vote away from African Americans and poor whites, the falloff was most severe there, but it occurred in every area of the country.

"The drop in voting," one historian has noted, "was nationwide, substantial, and cumulative." It also had never occurred before, neither in the nation's own history—for more than a hundred years, the United States had consistently broadened suffrage and boosted turnout—nor in what was going on in other Western democracies. And it was enduring. Turnout rates, to be sure, fluctuated during the twentieth century—dropping in the 1920s, rising somewhat in the 1930s, stabilizing after World War II, and then falling again after 1960—but they remained fairly close to the levels seen before World War I.[49]

The change stemmed from several considerations. For one thing, the massive Republican realignment of the 1890s, inaugurating more than three decades of Republican party dominance, reduced partisan competition in most parts of the country. With minor exceptions, Republicans took charge in the North, Midwest, and West, and Democrats prevailed in the South. In many areas, party competition dwindled, which reduced voter enthusiasm and in turn, of course, reduced turnout.[50]

Nationwide, the Republicans went on to victory after victory, losing in 1912 to Woodrow Wilson only because of a split in their own ranks—between TR, who ran as an insurgent on the Progressive party ticket, and William Howard Taft, the Republican nominee. The Democrats bumbled, confined to their southern stronghold and voters in some northern cities. In 1924, the Democratic national convention took an embarrassing 103 ballots to choose its presidential nominee, and party members wondered what had happened to the great party of Andrew Jackson. As Will Rogers, the famed humorist of the 1920s and 1930s, put it, "I am not a member of any organized political party—I am a Democrat."[51]

The Australian secret ballot, which spread rapidly across the country during the 1880s and 1890s, also dampened party spirit. The secret ballot had the compelling advantage of reducing the power of party bosses and cleaning up politics, but it also weakened the political party. No longer could parties print their own ballots, which allowed cheating and encouraged people to vote a straight ticket; no longer could party workers at the polls watch how people voted. The secret ballot, in short, worked well for political honesty but not so well for political involvement.[52]

Finally, during the fourth party system, people consciously worked—as the Populists had once urged—to weaken the power of politicians and parties through measures such as direct primaries, direct election of U.S. senators, and the initiative, referendum, and recall, all designed to bring voters more closely into the political process. At the same time, Americans turned more and more to their growing professional associations to get things done. Lawyers, doctors, and teachers formed professional societies; farmers joined cooperatives; businesspeople banded together in trade associations—and they all relied increasingly on lobbyists, not politicians, to satisfy their desires.[53]

The old array of campaign activities—parades, rallies, and bonfires—began to disappear. Campaign buttons were still produced but more rarely worn. Campaign managers relied on media, advertising, and sophisticated voter polls rather than on the older forms of mass voter mobilization. A growing range of leisure-time activities—automobiles, professional baseball, amusement parks, and circuses—diverted Americans from politics in new ways. Political campaigns, once one of a handful of important occasions around which Americans organized their lives, became listless and dull.[54]

Later campaigns, remembering the genius of the McKinley-Bryan contest, tried often to recapture it. In 1920, hoping to evoke the old feeling of the Front Porch Campaign, Warren G. Harding even took the flagpole from McKinley's front yard and erected it in his own.[55] In 2000, George W. Bush and political adviser Karl Rove reportedly looked to William McKinley for a model of presidential and party leadership, missing the fact that the Republican party—and the Democrats as well—had changed greatly over the years. McKinley was a moderate Republican of the party's nineteenth-century tradition: protective of democratic institutions; attuned to the appropriate uses of government power; respectful of the country's role in the world; and grounded in a pluralistic, inclusive outlook toward the varying elements within American society. Modern-day Republicans for the most part have moved in a different direction.[56]

Still, the 1896 presidential election continues to fascinate and instruct—and no wonder. Bryan's dramatic address to the Chicago convention and his even more dramatic whistle-stop tour changed politics and set patterns for later campaigns. McKinley's remarkable Front Porch Campaign used modern technology to bring 750,000 visitors to his small hometown and dispatched his message nationwide. A new approach to campaigning, the educational or merchandising style, continues to mold campaigns today, as does McKinley's focus on message, Hanna's use of money, and Dawes's reliance on efficiency and education. The elections of 1894 and 1896 together established a new majority party that governed and legislated in lasting ways.

These were hard-fought and meaningful contests, the elections and party battles between 1888 and 1896. The issues were important, the outcomes unknown. Acting decisively in 1894 and 1896, voters responded to parties, leaders, and outlooks in ways that seemed suited to the needs of an emerging urban-industrial society. More than a century later, Americans and their political leaders can still learn from the events of the 1890s, whose lessons echo down the years today.

BALLOT TOTALS, REPUBLICAN NATIONAL CONVENTION, JUNE 18, 1896

	McKinley	Reed	Morton	Allison	Quay
Alabama	19	2	1	—	—
Arkansas	16	—	—	—	—
California	18	—	—	—	—
Colorado*	—	—	—	—	—
Connecticut	7	5	—	—	—
Delaware	6	—	—	—	—
Florida	6	—	2	—	—
Georgia	22	2	—	—	2
Idaho*	—	—	—	—	—
Illinois	46	2	—	—	—
Indiana	30	—	—	—	—
Iowa	—	—	—	26	—
Kansas	20	—	—	—	—
Kentucky	26	—	—	—	—
Louisiana	11	4	—	1/2	1/2
Maine	—	12	—	—	—
Maryland	15	1	—	—	—
Massachusetts	1	29	—	—	—
Michigan	28	—	—	—	—
Minnesota	18	—	—	—	—
Mississippi	17	—	—	—	1
Missouri	34	—	—	—	—
Montana†	1	—	—	—	—
Nebraska	16	—	—	—	—
Nevada†	3	—	—	—	—
New Hampshire	—	8	—	—	—
New Jersey	19	1	—	—	—
New York‡	17	—	55	—	—
North Carolina	19 1/2	2 1/2	—	—	—
North Dakota	6	—	—	—	—
Ohio	46	—	—	—	—
Oregon	8	—	—	—	—
Pennsylvania	6	—	—	—	58
Rhode Island	—	8	—	—	—
South Carolina	18	—	—	—	—
South Dakota	8	—	—	—	—
Tennessee	24	—	—	—	—
Texas	21	5	—	3	—

	McKinley	Reed	Morton	Allison	Quay
Utah	3	—	—	3	—
Vermont	8	—	—	—	—
Virginia	23	1	—	—	—
Washington	8	—	—	—	—
West Virginia	12	—	—	—	—
Wisconsin	24	—	—	—	—
Wyoming	6	—	—	—	—
District of Columbia	—	1	—	1	—
Arizona	6	—	—	—	—
New Mexico	5	—	—	1	—
Oklahoma	4	1	—	1	—
Alaska	4	—	—	—	—
Indian Territory	6	—	—	—	—
TOTAL	661 1/2	84 1/2	58	35 1/2	61 1/2

Source: *Official Proceedings of the Eleventh National Republican Convention* (n.p.: C. W. Johnson, 1896), 123.

*Bolted convention.

†Four blank, one for J. Donald Cameron.

‡One vote passed.

BALLOT TOTALS, DEMOCRATIC NATIONAL CONVENTION, JULY 10, 1896

FIRST BALLOT

	Bryan	Bland	Boies	Matthews	McLean	Pattison	Blackburn	Stevenson	Teller	Russell	Tillman	Campbell	Pennoyer	Hill	Not Voting
Alabama	—	—	22	—	—	—	—	—	—	—	—	—	—	—	—
Arkansas	—	16	—	—	—	—	—	—	—	—	—	—	—	—	—
California	4	—	2	2	—	—	9	—	—	—	—	1	—	—	—
Colorado	—	—	—	—	—	—	—	—	8	—	—	—	—	—	—
Connecticut	—	—	—	—	—	—	—	—	—	2	—	—	—	—	10
Delaware	1	—	—	—	—	3	—	—	—	—	—	—	—	—	2
Florida	1	2	1	2	—	1	1	—	—	—	—	—	—	—	—
Georgia	26	—	—	—	—	—	—	—	—	—	—	—	—	—	—
Idaho	—	6	—	—	—	—	—	—	—	—	—	—	—	—	—
Illinois	—	48	—	—	—	—	—	—	—	—	—	—	—	—	—
Indiana	—	—	—	30	—	—	—	—	—	—	—	—	—	—	—
Iowa	—	—	26	—	—	—	—	—	—	—	—	—	—	—	—
Kansas	—	20	—	—	—	—	—	—	—	—	—	—	—	—	—
Kentucky	—	—	—	—	—	—	26	—	—	—	—	—	—	—	—
Louisiana	16	—	—	—	—	—	—	—	—	—	—	—	—	—	—
Maine	2	2	—	—	—	5	—	—	—	—	—	—	—	—	3
Maryland	4	—	·	—	—	11	—	—	—	—	—	—	—	—	1
Massachusetts	1	2	—	—	—	3	—	5	—	—	—	—	—	1	18
Michigan	9	4	5	—	—	—	—	—	—	—	—	—	—	—	10
Minnesota	2	—	4	—	—	2	1	1	—	—	—	—	—	—	8
Mississippi	18	—	—	—	—	—	—	—	—	—	—	—	—	—	—

FIRST BALLOT, *continued*

	Bryan	Bland	Boies	Matthews	McLean	Pattison	Blackburn	Stevenson	Teller	Russell	Tillman	Campbell	Pennoyer	Hill	Not Voting
Missouri	—	34	—	—	—	—	—	—	—	—	—	—	—	—	—
Montana	—	4	—	—	—	—	2	—	—	—	—	—	—	—	—
Nebraska	16	—	—	—	—	—	—	—	—	—	—	—	—	—	—
Nevada	—	—	—	3	3	—	—	—	—	—	—	—	—	—	—
New Hampshire	—	—	—	—	—	1	—	—	—	—	—	—	—	—	7
New Jersey	—	—	—	—	—	—	—	—	—	—	—	—	—	—	20
New York	—	—	—	—	—	—	—	—	—	—	—	—	—	—	72
North Carolina	22	—	—	—	—	—	—	—	—	—	—	—	—	—	—
North Dakota	—	—	6	—	—	—	—	—	—	—	—	—	—	—	—
Ohio	—	—	—	—	46	—	—	—	—	—	—	—	—	—	—
Oregon	—	—	—	—	—	—	—	—	—	—	—	—	8	—	—
Pennsylvania	—	—	—	—	—	64	—	—	—	—	—	—	—	—	—
Rhode Island	—	—	—	—	—	6	—	—	—	—	—	—	—	—	2
South Carolina	—	—	—	—	—	—	—	—	—	—	17	—	—	—	1
South Dakota	6	—	—	—	—	1	—	—	—	—	—	—	—	—	1
Tennessee	—	24	—	—	—	—	—	—	—	—	—	—	—	—	—
Texas	—	30	—	—	—	—	—	—	—	—	—	—	—	—	—
Utah	—	6	—	—	—	—	—	—	—	—	—	—	—	—	—
Vermont	4	—	—	—	—	—	—	—	—	—	—	—	—	—	4
Virginia	—	—	—	—	—	—	24	—	—	—	—	—	—	—	—
Washington	1	7	—	—	—	—	—	—	—	—	—	—	—	—	—
West Virginia	—	—	—	—	—	—	12	—	—	—	—	—	—	—	—
Wisconsin	4	—	—	—	—	—	1	—	—	—	—	—	—	—	19
Wyoming	—	—	—	—	—	—	6	—	—	—	—	—	—	—	—

	Bryan	Bland	Boies	Matthews	McLean	Pattison	Blackburn	Stevenson						Not Voting
Alaska	—	6	—	—	—	—	—	—	—	—	—	—	—	—
Arizona	—	6	—	—	—	—	—	—	—	—	—	—	—	—
District of Columbia	—	—	1	5	—	—	—	—	—	—	—	—	—	—
Oklahoma	—	6	—	—	—	—	—	—	—	—	—	—	—	—
Indian Territory	—	6	—	—	—	—	—	—	—	—	—	—	—	—
New Mexico	—	6	—	—	—	—	—	—	—	—	—	—	—	—
TOTAL	137	235	67	37	54	97	82	6	8	2	17	8	1	178

SECOND BALLOT

	Bryan	Bland	Boies	Matthews	McLean	Pattison	Blackburn	Stevenson	Teller	Pennoyer	Hill	Not Voting
Alabama	—	22	—	—	—	—	—	—	—	—	—	—
Arkansas	—	16	—	—	—	—	—	—	—	—	—	—
California	14	2	1	1	—	—	—	—	—	—	—	—
Colorado	—	—	—	—	—	—	—	—	8	—	—	10
Connecticut	—	—	—	—	—	2	—	—	—	—	—	2
Delaware	1	—	—	—	—	3	—	—	—	—	—	—
Florida	2	1	1	2	—	1	—	1	—	—	—	—
Georgia	26	—	—	—	—	—	—	—	—	—	—	—
Idaho	—	6	—	—	—	—	—	—	—	—	—	—
Illinois	—	48	—	—	—	—	—	—	—	—	—	—
Indiana	—	—	—	30	—	—	—	—	—	—	—	—
Iowa	—	—	26	—	—	—	—	—	—	—	—	—
Kansas	—	20	—	—	—	—	—	—	—	—	—	—

	Bryan	Bland	Boies	Matthews	McLean	Pattison	Blackburn	Stevenson	Teller	Pennoyer	Hill	Not Voting
Kentucky	—	—	—	—	—	—	26	—	—	—	—	—
Louisiana	16	—	—	—	—	—	—	—	—	—	—	—
Maine	2	2	—	—	—	5	—	—	—	—	—	3
Maryland	4	—	—	—	—	11	—	—	—	—	—	1
Massachusetts	1	2	—	1	—	3	—	5	—	—	1	17
Michigan	28	—	—	—	—	—	—	—	—	—	—	—
Minnesota	4	—	2	—	—	1	2	4	—	—	—	5
Mississippi	18	—	—	—	—	—	—	—	—	—	—	—
Missouri	—	34	—	—	—	—	—	—	—	—	—	—
Montana	—	6	—	—	—	—	—	—	—	—	—	—
Nebraska	16	—	—	—	—	—	—	—	—	—	—	—
Nevada	—	—	—	—	6	—	—	—	—	—	—	—
New Hampshire	—	—	—	—	—	1	—	—	—	—	—	7
New Jersey	—	—	—	—	—	2	—	—	—	—	—	18
New York	—	—	—	—	—	—	—	—	—	—	—	72
North Carolina	22	—	—	—	—	—	—	—	—	—	—	—
North Dakota	—	—	6	—	—	—	—	—	—	—	—	—
Ohio	—	—	—	—	46	—	—	—	—	—	—	—
Oregon	—	—	—	—	—	—	—	—	—	8	—	—
Pennsylvania	—	—	—	—	—	64	—	—	—	—	—	—
Rhode Island	—	—	—	—	—	6	—	—	—	—	—	2
South Carolina	18	—	—	—	—	—	—	—	—	—	—	—
South Dakota	7	—	—	—	—	1	—	—	—	—	—	—
Tennessee	—	24	—	—	—	—	—	—	—	—	—	—

	Bryan	Bland	Boies	Matthews	McLean	Pattison	Blackburn			Stevenson	Hill	Not Voting
Texas	—	30	—	—	—	—	—	—	—	—	—	—
Utah	—	6	—	—	—	—	—	—	—	—	—	—
Vermont	4	—	—	—	—	—	—	—	—	—	—	4
Virginia	—	24	—	—	—	—	—	—	—	—	—	—
Washington	1	7	—	—	—	—	—	—	—	—	—	—
West Virginia	—	—	—	—	—	12	—	—	—	—	—	—
Wisconsin	4	—	—	—	—	1	—	—	—	—	—	19
Wyoming	6	—	—	—	—	—	—	—	—	—	—	—
Alaska	—	6	—	—	—	—	—	—	—	—	—	—
Arizona	—	6	—	—	—	—	—	—	—	—	—	—
District of Columbia	3	1	1	—	—	—	1	—	—	—	—	—
New Mexico	—	6	—	—	—	—	—	—	—	—	—	—
Oklahoma	—	6	—	—	—	—	—	—	—	—	—	—
Indian Territory	—	6	—	—	—	—	—	—	—	—	—	—
TOTAL	197	281	37	34	53	100	41	10	8	8	1	160

THIRD BALLOT

	Bryan	Bland	Boies	Matthews	McLean	Pattison	Blackburn	Stevenson	Hill	Not Voting
Alabama	—	22	—	—	—	—	—	—	—	—
Arkansas	—	16	—	—	—	—	—	—	—	—
California	13	2	1	1	—	—	1	—	—	—
Colorado	8	—	—	—	—	—	—	—	—	—
Connecticut	—	—	—	—	—	2	—	—	—	10
Delaware	1	—	—	—	—	3	—	—	—	2

THIRD BALLOT, *continued*

	Bryan	Bland	Boies	Matthews	McLean	Pattison	Blackburn	Stevenson	Hill	Not Voting
Florida	5	—	—	3	—	—	—	—	—	—
Georgia	26	—	—	—	—	—	—	—	—	—
Idaho	—	6	—	—	—	—	—	—	—	—
Illinois	—	48	—	—	—	—	—	—	—	—
Indiana	—	—	—	30	—	—	—	—	—	—
Iowa	—	—	26	—	—	—	—	—	—	—
Kansas	—	20	—	—	—	—	—	—	—	—
Kentucky	—	—	—	—	—	—	26	—	—	—
Louisiana	16	—	—	—	—	—	—	—	—	—
Maine	2	2	—	—	—	5	—	—	—	3
Maryland	5	—	—	—	—	10	—	—	—	1
Massachusetts	1	2	—	—	—	3	—	5	1	18
Michigan	28	—	—	—	—	—	—	—	—	6
Minnesota	9	1	—	—	—	—	—	2	—	—
Mississippi	18	—	—	—	—	—	—	—	—	—
Missouri	—	34	—	—	—	—	—	—	—	—
Montana	—	6	—	—	—	—	—	—	—	—
Nebraska	16	—	—	—	—	—	—	—	—	—
Nevada	—	—	—	—	6	—	—	—	—	—
New Hampshire	—	—	—	—	—	1	—	—	—	7
New Jersey	—	—	—	—	—	2	—	—	—	18
New York	—	—	—	—	—	—	—	—	—	72
North Carolina	22	—	—	—	—	—	—	—	—	—
North Dakota	—	—	6	—	—	—	—	—	—	—

Ohio	—	—	—	—	46	—	—	—	—	—
Oregon	5	2	—	—	1	64	—	—	—	—
Pennsylvania	—	—	—	—	—	—	—	—	—	—
Rhode Island	18	—	—	—	—	6	—	—	—	2
South Carolina	7	—	—	—	—	1	—	—	—	—
South Dakota	—	—	—	—	—	—	—	—	—	—
Tennessee	—	24	—	—	—	—	—	—	—	—
Texas	—	30	—	—	—	—	—	—	—	—
Utah	—	6	—	—	—	—	—	—	—	—
Vermont	4	—	—	—	—	—	—	—	—	4
Virginia	—	24	—	—	—	—	—	—	—	—
Washington	1	7	—	—	—	—	—	—	—	—
West Virginia	1	7	2	—	—	—	—	2	—	—
Wisconsin	3	2	—	—	—	—	—	—	—	19
Wyoming	6	—	—	—	—	—	—	—	—	—
Alaska	—	6	—	—	—	—	—	—	—	—
Arizona	—	6	—	—	—	—	—	—	—	—
District of Columbia	4	—	1	—	1	—	—	—	—	—
New Mexico	—	6	—	—	—	—	—	—	—	—
Oklahoma	—	6	—	—	—	—	—	—	—	—
Indian Territory	—	6	—	—	—	—	—	—	—	—
TOTAL	219	291	36	34	54	97	27	9	1	162

FOURTH BALLOT

	Bland	Boies	Bryan	Matthews	Blackburn	Pattison	McLean	Stevenson	Hill	Not Voting or Absent
Alabama	—	—	22	—	—	—	—	—	—	—
Arkansas	16	—	—	—	—	—	—	—	—	—
California	2	1	12	2	1	—	—	—	—	—
Colorado	—	—	8	—	—	—	—	—	—	—
Connecticut	—	—	—	—	—	2	—	—	—	10
Delaware	—	—	1	3	—	3	—	—	—	2
Florida	—	—	5	3	—	—	—	—	—	—
Georgia	—	—	26	—	—	—	—	—	—	—
Idaho	—	—	6	—	—	—	—	—	—	—
Illinois	48	—	—	—	—	—	—	—	—	—
Indiana	—	—	—	30	—	—	—	—	—	—
Iowa	—	26	—	—	—	—	—	—	—	—
Kansas	—	—	20	—	—	—	—	—	—	—
Kentucky	—	—	—	—	26	—	—	—	—	—
Louisiana	—	—	16	—	—	—	—	—	—	—
Maine	2	—	2	—	—	5	—	—	—	3
Maryland	—	—	5	—	—	10	—	—	—	1
Massachusetts	2	—	1	—	—	3	—	5	1	18
Michigan	—	—	28	—	—	—	—	—	—	—
Minnesota	1	—	10	—	—	—	—	2	—	5
Mississippi	—	—	18	—	—	—	—	—	—	—
Missouri	34	—	—	—	—	—	—	—	—	—
Montana	6	—	—	—	—	—	—	—	—	—
Nebraska	—	—	16	—	—	—	—	—	—	—
Nevada	—	—	6	—	—	—	—	—	—	—
New Hampshire	—	—	—	—	—	1	—	—	—	7

State										
New Jersey	—	—	—	—	—	2	—	—	—	18
New York	—	—	—	—	—	—	—	—	—	72
North Carolina	—	6	22	—	—	—	—	—	—	—
North Dakota	—	—	—	—	—	—	—	—	—	—
Ohio	—	—	—	—	—	—	46	—	—	—
Oregon	—	—	8	—	—	—	—	—	—	—
Pennsylvania	—	—	—	—	—	64	—	—	—	—
Rhode Island	—	—	—	—	—	6	—	—	—	2
South Carolina	—	—	18	—	—	1	—	—	—	—
South Dakota	—	—	7	—	—	—	—	—	—	—
Tennessee	24	—	—	—	—	—	—	—	—	—
Texas	30	—	—	—	—	—	—	—	—	—
Utah	6	—	—	—	—	—	—	—	—	—
Vermont	—	—	4	—	—	—	—	—	—	4
Virginia	24	—	—	—	—	—	—	—	—	—
Washington	6	—	2	—	—	—	—	—	—	—
West Virginia	10	—	1	—	—	—	—	1	—	—
Wisconsin	—	—	5	—	—	—	—	—	—	19
Wyoming	—	—	6	—	—	—	—	—	—	—
Alaska	6	—	—	—	—	—	—	—	—	—
Arizona	6	—	—	—	—	—	—	—	—	—
District of Columbia	—	—	5	1	—	—	—	—	—	—
New Mexico	6	—	—	—	—	—	—	—	—	—
Oklahoma	6	—	—	—	—	—	—	—	—	—
Indian Territory	6	—	—	—	—	—	—	—	—	—
TOTAL	241	33	280	36	27	97	46	8	1	161

FIFTH BALLOT

	Bryan	Bland	Pattison	Stevenson	Hill	Turpie	Not Voting
Alabama	22	—	—	—	—	—	—
Arkansas	16	—	—	—	—	—	—
California	18	—	—	—	—	—	—
Colorado	8	—	—	—	—	—	—
Connecticut	—	—	2	—	—	—	10
Delaware	1	—	3	—	—	—	2
Florida	8	—	—	—	—	—	—
Georgia	26	—	—	—	—	—	—
Idaho	6	—	—	—	—	—	—
Illinois	48	—	—	—	—	—	—
Indiana	30	—	—	—	—	—	—
Iowa	26	—	—	—	—	—	—
Kansas	20	—	—	—	—	—	—
Kentucky	26	—	—	—	—	—	—
Louisiana	16	—	—	—	—	—	—
Maine	4	—	4	—	—	—	4
Maryland	5	—	10	—	—	—	1
Massachusetts	6	—	3	2	1	—	18
Michigan	28	—	—	—	—	—	—
Minnesota	11	—	—	2	—	—	5
Mississippi	18	—	—	—	—	—	—
Missouri	34	—	—	—	—	—	—
Montana	6	—	—	—	—	—	—
Nebraska	16	—	—	—	—	—	—
Nevada	6	—	—	—	—	—	—
New Hampshire	—	—	1	—	—	—	7

New Jersey	—	—	2	—	—	18
New York	—	—	—	—	—	72
North Carolina	22	—	—	—	—	—
North Dakota	4	—	—	2	—	—
Ohio	46	—	—	—	—	—
Oregon	8	—	—	—	—	—
Pennsylvania	—	—	64	—	—	—
Rhode Island	—	—	6	—	—	2
South Carolina	18	—	—	—	—	—
South Dakota	8	—	—	—	—	—
Tennessee	24	—	—	—	—	—
Texas	30	—	—	—	—	—
Utah	6	—	—	—	—	—
Vermont	4	—	—	—	—	4
Virginia	24	—	—	—	—	—
Washington	4	4	—	—	—	—
West Virginia	2	7	—	2	1	—
Wisconsin	5	—	—	—	—	19
Wyoming	6	—	—	—	—	—
Alaska	6	—	—	—	—	—
Arizona	6	—	—	—	—	—
District of Columbia	6	—	—	—	—	—
New Mexico	6	—	—	—	—	—
Oklahoma	6	—	—	—	—	—
Indian Territory	6	—	—	—	—	—
TOTAL	652	11	95	8	1	162

Source: *Official Proceedings of the Democratic National Convention* (Logansport, Ind.: Humphries, 1896), 311–326.

GENERAL ELECTION VOTING TOTALS, NOVEMBER 3, 1896

	William McKinley Republican	William Jennings Bryan Democrat	John M. Palmer National Democrat	Joshua Levering Prohibition	Other
Alabama	55,673	130,298	6,375	2,234	—
Arkansas	37,512	110,103	—	889	892
California	146,688	123,143	2,006	2,573	24,285
Colorado	26,271	161,005	1	1,717	545
Connecticut	110,285	56,740	4,336	1,806	1,227
Delaware	16,883	13,425	877	355	—
Florida	11,298	30,683	1,778	656	2,053
Georgia	60,107	94,733	2,809	5,613	47
Idaho	6,324	23,135	—	172	—
Illinois	607,130	465,593	6,307	9,796	1,940
Indiana	323,754	305,538	2,145	3,061	2,591
Iowa	289,293	223,744	4,516	3,192	805
Kansas	159,484	173,049	1,209	1,723	620
Kentucky	218,171	217,894	5,084	4,779	—
Louisiana	22,037	77,175	1,834	—	—
Maine	80,403	34,587	1,867	1,562	—
Maryland	136,959	104,150	2,499	5,918	723
Massachusetts	278,976	105,414	11,749	2,998	2,132
Michigan	293,336	237,164	6,923	4,978	3,182
Minnesota	193,503	139,735	3,222	4,348	954
Mississippi	4,819	63,355	1,021	396	—
Missouri	304,940	363,667	2,365	2,169	891
Montana	10,509	42,628	—	193	—
Nebraska	103,064	115,007	2,885	1,242	983

State					
Nevada	1,938	7,802	—	—	574
New Hampshire	57,444	21,271	3,520	779	656
New Jersey	221,367	133,675	6,373	—	9,599
New York	819,838	551,369	18,950	16,052	17,667
North Carolina	155,122	174,408	578	635	594
North Dakota	26,335	20,686	—	358	12
Ohio	525,991	474,882	1,858	5,068	6,496
Oregon	48,700	46,739	977	919	—
Pennsylvania	728,300	427,125	11,000	19,274	8,656
Rhode Island	37,437	14,459	1,166	1,160	563
South Carolina	9,313	58,801	824	—	—
South Dakota	41,040	41,225	—	672	—
Tennessee	148,683	167,168	1,953	3,099	—
Texas	163,413	267,803	4,989	1,797	77,985
Utah	13,491	64,607	—	—	—
Vermont	51,127	10,179	1,331	733	461
Virginia	135,379	154,708	2,129	2,350	108
Washington	39,153	51,646	—	968	1,668
West Virginia	105,379	94,480	678	1,220	—
Wisconsin	268,135	165,523	4,584	7,507	1,660
Wyoming	10,072	10,376	—	159	486
TOTAL	7,105,144	6,370,897	132,718	125,118	171,814

Source: Congressional Quarterly, *Presidential Elections, 1789–2004* (Washington, D.C.: Congressional Quarterly Press, 2005), 136.

Note: *Congressional Quarterly*'s guidelines: "Bryan was nominated by both the Democrats and the Populists but with different running mates. In several states different slates of electors were entered by each party. It is legally incorrect to combine the vote. The separate vote for Bryan usually under the Populist ticket is listed under 'Other.' In other states it appears that the two slates of electors were the same and it is correct to combine the vote."

WILLIAM MCKINLEY'S
FIRST INAUGURAL ADDRESS, MARCH 4, 1897

Fellow-Citizens:

In obedience to the will of the people, and in their presence, by the authority vested in me by this oath, I assume the arduous and responsible duties of President of the United States, relying upon the support of my countrymen and invoking the guidance of Almighty God. Our faith teaches that there is no safer reliance than upon the God of our fathers, who has so singularly favored the American people in every national trial, and who will not forsake us so long as we obey His commandments and walk humbly in His footsteps.

The responsibilities of the high trust to which I have been called—always of grave importance—are augmented by the prevailing business conditions entailing idleness upon willing labor and loss to useful enterprises. The country is suffering from industrial disturbances from which speedy relief must be had. Our financial system needs some revision; our money is all good now, but its value must not further be threatened. It should all be put upon an enduring basis, not subject to easy attack, nor its stability to doubt or dispute. Our currency should continue under the supervision of the Government. The several forms of our paper money offer, in my judgment, a constant embarrassment to the Government and a safe balance in the Treasury. Therefore I believe it necessary to devise a system which, without diminishing the circulating medium or offering a premium for its contraction, will present a remedy to those arrangements which, temporary in their nature, might well in the years of our prosperity have been displaced by wiser provisions. With adequate revenue secured, but not until then, we can enter upon such changes in our fiscal laws as will, while insuring safety and volume to our money, no longer impose upon the Government the necessity of maintaining so large a gold reserve, with its attendant and inevitable temptations to speculation. Most of our financial laws are the outgrowth of experience and trial, and should not be amended without investigation and demonstration of the wisdom of the proposed changes. We must be both "sure we are right" and "make haste slowly." If, therefore, Congress, in its wisdom, shall deem it expedient to create a commission to take under early consideration the revision of our coinage, banking and currency laws, and give them that exhaustive, careful and dispassionate examination that their importance demands, I shall cordially concur in such action. If such power is vested in the President, it is my purpose to appoint a commission of prominent, well-informed citizens of different parties, who will command public confidence, both on account of their ability and special fitness for the work. Business experience and public training may thus be combined, and the patriotic zeal of the friends of the country be so directed that such a report will be made as to receive the support of all parties, and our finances cease to be the subject of mere partisan contention. The experiment is, at all events, worth a trial, and, in my opinion, it can but prove beneficial to the entire country.

The question of international bimetallism will have early and earnest attention. It will be my constant endeavor to secure it by co-operation with the other great commercial powers of the world. Until that condition is realized when the parity between our gold and silver money springs from and is supported by the relative value of the two metals, the value of the silver already coined and of that which may hereafter be coined, must be kept constantly at par with gold by every resource at our command. The credit of the Government, the integrity of its currency, and the inviolability of its obligations must be preserved. This was the commanding verdict of the people, and it will not be unheeded.

Economy is demanded in every branch of the Government at all times, but especially in periods, like the present, of depression in business and distress among the people. The severest economy must be observed in all public expenditures, and extravagance stopped wherever it is found, and prevented wherever in the future it may be developed. If the revenues are to remain as now, the only relief that can come must be from decreased expenditures. But the present must not become the permanent condition of the Government. It has been our uniform practice to retire, not increase our outstanding obligations, and this policy must again be resumed and vigorously enforced. Our revenues should always be large enough to meet with ease and promptness not only our current needs and the principal and interest of the public debt, but to make proper and liberal provision for that most deserving body of public creditors, the soldiers and sailors and the widows and orphans who are the pensioners of the United States.

The Government should not be permitted to run behind or increase its debt in times like the present. Suitably to provide against this is the mandate of duty—the certain and easy remedy for most of our financial difficulties. A deficiency is inevitable so long as the expenditures of the Government exceed its receipts. It can only be met by loans or an increased revenue. While a large annual surplus of revenue may invite waste and extravagance, inadequate revenue creates distrust and undermines public and private credit. Neither should be encouraged. Between more loans and more revenue there ought to be but one opinion. We should have more revenue, and that without delay, hindrance, or postponement. A surplus in the Treasury created by loans is not a permanent or safe reliance. It will suffice while it lasts, but it can not last long while the outlays of the Government are greater than its receipts, as has been the case during the past two years. Nor must it be forgotten that however much such loans may temporarily relieve the situation, the Government is still indebted for the amount of the surplus thus accrued, which it must ultimately pay, while its ability to pay is not strengthened, but weakened by a continued deficit. Loans are imperative in great emergencies to preserve the Government or its credit, but a failure to supply needed revenue in time of peace for the maintenance of either has no justification.

The best way for the Government to maintain its credit is to pay as it goes—not by resorting to loans, but by keeping out of debt—through an adequate income secured by a system of taxation, external or internal, or both. It is the settled policy of the Government, pursued from the beginning and practiced by all parties and Administrations, to raise the bulk of our revenue from taxes upon foreign productions entering the United States for sale and consumption, and avoiding, for the most part, every form of direct taxation, except in time of war. The country is clearly opposed to any needless additions to the subject of internal taxation, and is committed by its latest popular utterance to the system of tariff taxation. There can be no misunderstanding, either, about the principle upon which this tariff taxation shall be levied. Nothing has ever been made plainer at a general election than that the controlling principle in the raising of revenue from duties on imports is zealous care for American interests and American labor. The people have declared that such legislation should be had as will give ample protection and encouragement to the industries and the development of our country. It is, therefore, earnestly hoped and expected that Congress will, at the earliest practicable moment, enact revenue legislation that shall be fair, reasonable, conservative, and just, and which, while supplying sufficient revenue for public purposes, will still be signally beneficial and helpful to every section and every enterprise of the people. To this policy we are all, of whatever party, firmly bound by the voice of the people—a power vastly more potential than the expression of any political platform. The paramount duty of Congress is to stop deficiencies by the restoration of that protective legislation which has always been the firmest prop of the Treasury. The passage of such a law or laws would strengthen the credit of the Government both at home and abroad, and go far toward stopping the drain upon the gold reserve held for the redemption of our currency, which has been heavy and well-nigh constant for several years.

In the revision of the tariff especial attention should be given to the re-enactment and extension of the reciprocity principle of the law of 1890, under which so great a stimulus was given to our foreign trade in new and advantageous markets for our surplus agricultural and manufactured products. The brief trial given this legislation amply justifies a further experiment and additional discretionary power in the making of commercial treaties, the end in view always to be the opening up of new markets for the products of our country, by granting concessions to the products of other lands that we need and cannot produce ourselves, and which do not involve any loss of labor to our own people, but tend to increase their employment.

The depression of the past four years has fallen with especial severity upon the great body of toilers of the country, and upon none more than the holders of small farms. Agriculture has languished and labor suffered. The revival of manufacturing will be a relief to both. No portion of our population is more devoted to the institution of free government nor more loyal in their support, while none bears more cheerfully or fully its proper share in the maintenance of the Government or is better entitled to its wise and liberal care and protection. Legislation helpful to producers is beneficial to all. The depressed condition of industry on the farm and in the mine and factory has lessened the ability of the people to meet the demands upon them, and they rightfully expect that not only a system of revenue shall be established that will secure the largest income with the least burden, but that every means will be taken to decrease, rather than increase, our public expenditures. Business conditions are not the most promising. It will take time to restore the prosperity of former years. If we cannot promptly attain it, we can resolutely turn our faces in that direction and aid its return by friendly legislation. However troublesome the situation may appear, Congress will not, I am sure, be found lacking in disposition or ability to relieve it as far as legislation can do so. The restoration of confidence and the revival of business, which men of all parties so much desire, depend more largely upon the prompt, energetic, and intelligent action of Congress than upon any other single agency affecting the situation.

It is inspiring, too, to remember that no great emergency in the one hundred and eight years of our eventful national life has ever arisen that has not been met with wisdom and courage by the American people, with fidelity to their best interests and highest destiny, and to the honor of the American name. These years of glorious history have exalted mankind and advanced the cause of freedom throughout the world, and immeasurably strengthened the precious free institutions which we enjoy. The people love and will sustain these institutions. The great essential to our happiness and prosperity is that we adhere to the principles upon which the Government was established and insist upon their faithful observance. Equality of rights must prevail, and our laws be always and everywhere respected and obeyed. We may have failed in the discharge of our full duty as citizens of the great Republic, but it is consoling and encouraging to realize that free speech, a free press, free thought, free schools, the free and unmolested right of religious liberty and worship, and free and fair elections are dearer and more universally enjoyed to-day than ever before. These guaranties must be sacredly preserved and wisely strengthened. The constituted authorities must be cheerfully and vigorously upheld. Lynchings must not be tolerated in a great and civilized country like the United States; courts, not mobs, must execute the penalties of the law. The preservation of public order, the right of discussion, the integrity of courts, and the orderly administration of justice must continue forever the rock of safety upon which our Government securely rests.

One of the lessons taught by the late election, which all can rejoice in, is that the citizens of the United States are both law-respecting and law-abiding people, not easily swerved from the path of patriotism and honor. This is in entire accord with the genius of our institutions, and but emphasizes the advantages of inculcating even a greater love for law and order in the future. Immunity should be granted to none who violate the laws, whether individuals, corporations, or communities; and as the Constitution imposes upon the President the duty of both its own execution, and of the statutes enacted in pursuance of its provisions, I shall endeavor carefully to carry them into effect. The declaration of the party now restored to power has been in the past that of "opposition to all combinations of capital organized in trusts, or otherwise, to control arbitrarily the condition of trade among our citizens," and it has supported "such legislation as will prevent the execution of all schemes to oppress the people by undue charges on their supplies, or by unjust rates for the transportation of their products to the market." This purpose will be steadily pursued, both by the enforcement of the laws now in existence and the recommendation and support of such new statutes as may be necessary to carry it into effect.

Our naturalization and immigration laws should be further improved to the constant promotion of a safer, a better, and a higher citizenship. A grave peril to the Republic would be a citizenship too ignorant to understand or too vicious to appreciate the great value and beneficence of our institutions and laws, and against all who come here to make war upon them our gates must be promptly and tightly closed. Nor must we be unmindful of the need of improvement among our own citizens, but with the zeal of our forefathers encourage the spread of knowledge and free education. Illiteracy must be banished from the land if we shall attain that high destiny as the foremost of the enlightened nations of the world which, under Providence, we ought to achieve.

Reforms in the civil service must go on; but the changes should be real and genuine, not perfunctory, or prompted by a zeal in behalf of any party simply because it happens to be in power. As a member of Congress I voted and spoke in favor of the present law, and I shall attempt its enforcement in the spirit in which it was enacted. The purpose in view was to secure the most efficient service of the best men who would accept appointment under the Government, retaining faithful and devoted public servants in office, but shielding none, under the authority of any rule or custom, who are inefficient, incompetent, or unworthy. The best interests of the country demand this, and the people heartily approve the law wherever and whenever it has been thus administrated.

Congress should give prompt attention to the restoration of our American merchant marine, once the pride of the seas in all the great ocean highways of commerce. To my mind, few more important subjects so imperatively demand its intelligent consideration. The United States has progressed with marvelous rapidity in every field of enterprise and endeavor until we have become foremost in nearly all the great lines of inland trade, commerce, and industry. Yet, while this is true, our American merchant marine has been steadily declining until it is now lower, both in the percentage of tonnage and the number of vessels employed, than it was prior to the Civil War. Commendable progress has been made of late years in the upbuilding of the American Navy, but we must supplement these efforts by providing as a proper consort for it a merchant marine amply sufficient for our own carrying trade to foreign countries. The question is one that appeals both to our business necessities and the patriotic aspirations of a great people.

It has been the policy of the United States since the foundation of the Government to cultivate relations of peace and amity with all the nations of the world, and this accords with my conception of our duty now. We have cherished the policy of non-interference with the affairs of foreign governments wisely inaugurated by Washington, keeping ourselves free from entanglement, either as allies or foes, content to leave undisturbed with them the settlement of their own domestic concerns. It will be our aim to pursue a firm and dignified foreign policy, which shall be just, impartial, ever watchful of our national honor, and always insisting upon the enforcement of the lawful rights of American citizens everywhere. Our diplomacy should seek nothing more and accept nothing less than is due us. We want no wars of conquest; we must avoid the temptation of territorial aggression. War should never be entered upon until every agency of peace has failed; peace is preferable to war in almost every contingency. Arbitration is the true method of settlement of international as well as local or individual differences. It was recognized as the best means of adjustment of differences between employers and employees by the Forty-ninth Congress, in 1886, and its application was extended to our diplomatic relations by the unanimous concurrence of the Senate and House of the Fifty-first Congress in 1890. The latter resolution was accepted as the basis of negotiations with us by the British House of Commons in 1893, and upon our invitation a treaty of arbitration between the United States and Great Britain was signed at Washington and transmitted to the Senate for its ratification in January last. Since this treaty is clearly the result of our own initiative; since it has been recognized as the leading feature of our foreign policy throughout our entire national history—the adjustment of difficulties by judicial methods rather than force of arms—and since it presents to the world the glorious example of reason and peace, not passion and war, controlling the relations between two of the greatest nations in the world, an example certain to be followed by others, I respectfully urge the early action of the Senate thereon, not merely as a matter of policy, but as a duty to mankind. The importance and moral influence of the ratification of such a treaty can hardly be overestimated in the cause of advancing civilization. It may well engage the best thought of the statesmen and people of every country, and I cannot but consider it fortunate that it was reserved to the United States to have the leadership in so grand a work.

It has been the uniform practice of each President to avoid, as far as possible, the convening of Congress in extraordinary session. It is an example which, under ordinary circumstances and in the absence of a public necessity, is to be commended. But a failure to convene the representatives of the people in Congress in extra session when it involves neglect of a public duty places the responsibility of such neglect upon the Executive himself. The condition of the public Treasury, as has been indicated, demands the immediate consideration of Congress. It alone has the power to provide revenues for the Government. Not to convene it under such circumstances I can view in no other sense than the neglect of a plain duty. I do not sympathize with the sentiment that Congress in session is dangerous to our general business interests. Its members are the agents of the people, and their presence at the seat of Government in the execution of the sovereign will should not operate as an injury, but a benefit. There could be no better time to put the Government upon a sound financial and economic basis than now. The people have only recently voted that this should be done, and nothing is more binding upon the agents of their will than the obligation of immediate action. It has always seemed to me that the postponement of the meeting of Congress until more than a year after it has been chosen deprived Congress too often of the inspiration of the popular will and the country of the corresponding benefits. It is evident, therefore, that to postpone action in the presence of so great a necessity would be unwise on the part of the Executive because unjust to the interests of the people. Our action now will be freer from mere partisan consideration than if the question of tariff revision was postponed until the regular session of Congress. We are nearly two years from a Congressional election, and politics cannot so greatly distract us as if such contest was immediately pending. We can approach the problem calmly and patriotically, without fearing its effect upon an early election.

Our fellow-citizens who may disagree with us upon the character of this legislation prefer to have the question settled now, even against their preconceived views, and perhaps settled so reasonably, as I trust and believe it will be, as to insure great permanence, than to have further uncertainty menacing the vast and varied business interests of the United States. Again, whatever action Congress may take will be given a fair opportunity for trial before the people are called to pass judgment upon it, and this I consider a great essential to the rightful and lasting settlement of the question. In view of these considerations, I shall deem it my duty as President to convene Congress in extraordinary session on Monday, the 15th day of March, 1897.

In conclusion, I congratulate the country upon the fraternal spirit of the people and the manifestations of good will everywhere so apparent. The recent election not only most fortunately demonstrated the obliteration of sectional or geographical lines, but to some extent also the prejudices which for years have distracted our councils and marred our true greatness as a nation. The triumph of the people, whose verdict is carried into effect to-day, is not the triumph of one section, nor wholly of one party, but of all sections and all the people. The North and the South no longer divide on the old lines, but upon principles and policies; and in this fact surely every lover of the country can find cause for true felicitation. Let us rejoice in and cultivate this spirit; it is ennobling and will be both a gain and a blessing to our beloved country. It will be my constant aim to do nothing, and permit nothing to be done, that will arrest or disturb this growing sentiment of unity and co-operation, this revival of esteem and affiliation which now animates so many thousands in both the old antagonistic sections, but I shall cheerfully do everything possible to promote and increase it.

Let me again repeat the words of the oath administered by the Chief Justice which, in their respective spheres, so far as applicable, I would have all my countrymen observe: "I will faithfully execute the office of President of the United States, and will, to the best of my ability, preserve, protect, and defend the Constitution of the United States." This is the obligation I have reverently taken before the Lord Most High. To keep it will be my single purpose, my constant prayer; and I shall confidently rely upon the forbearance and assistance of all the people in the discharge of my solemn responsibilities.

Source: James D. Richardson, ed., *A Compilation of the Messages and Papers of the Presidents* (New York: Bureau of National Literature, 1897), 14:6236–6244.

NOTES

AUTHOR'S PREFACE

1 The "battle of the standards" referred to the struggle between those who favored the use of the silver standard in the nation's currency and those backing the gold standard.

2 For the long-standing literature on the theory of critical elections, see, among others, V. O. Key Jr., "A Theory of Critical Elections," *Journal of Politics* 17 (February 1955): 3–18; Charles Sellars, "The Equilibrium Cycle in Two-Party Politics," *Public Opinion Quarterly* 29 (Spring 1965): 16–37; Samuel Lubell, *The Future of American Politics* (New York: Harper, 1952): 1–7, 28–57, 198–226; Gerald Pomper, "A Classification of Presidential Elections," *Journal of Politics* 29 (August 1967): 535–566; Michael Rogin, "California Populism and the 'System of 1896,'" *Western Political Quarterly* 22 (March 1969): 179–196. David R. Mayhew, in *Electoral Realignments: A Critique of an American Genre* (New Haven, Conn.: Yale University Press, 2002), argues that the election of 1896 was not a critical election. For my reflections, see chapter 8.

3 Walter Dean Burnham, *Critical Elections and the Mainsprings of American Politics* (New York: Norton, 1970), 1–33, 71–90.

4 Arthur Meier Schlesinger, *The Rise of the City, 1878–1898* (New York: Macmillan, 1933), 1–2, 53–77; Edward C. Kirkland, *Industry Comes of Age: Business, Labor, and Public Policy, 1860–1897* (New York: Holt, Rinehart and Winston, 1961), 163–180, 280–285; Fred A. Shannon, *The Farmer's Last Frontier: Agriculture, 1860–1897* (New York: Farrar and Rinehart, 1945), 125–267.

5 Maury Klein, *The Genesis of Industrial America, 1870–1920* (Cambridge: Cambridge University Press, 2007); *Milwaukee Sentinel*, October 22, 1892, in David P. Thelen, *The New Citizenship: Origins of Progressivism in Wisconsin, 1885–1900* (Columbia: University of Missouri Press, 1972), 43; Thomas G. Shearman, "The Owners of the United States," *Forum* 8 (November 1889): 269–273; C. B. Spahr, *An Essay on the Present Distribution of Wealth in the United States* (New York: Thomas Y. Crowell, 1896).

6 Charles Postel, *The Populist Vision* (Chicago: Oxford University Press, 2007), 3, has pointed out that as early as the mid-1890s, a person in New York City could wire a dozen American Beauty roses to a woman in Paris, France, and have them arrive in time for dinner.

7 The eligible electorate comprised those who were entitled to vote under state and local laws.

CHAPTER 1 1896: THE PARTY BACKGROUND

1 Robert Dallek, *Hail to the Chief: The Making and Unmaking of American Presidents* (New York: Hyperion, 1996), xii.

2 Arthur M. Schlesinger Jr., "Introduction," in his *History of U.S. Political Parties*, 4 vols. (New York: Chelsea House Publishers, 1973), 1:xxxiv; Robert H. Wiebe, *Self-Rule: A Cultural History of American Democracy* (Chicago: University of Chicago Press, 1995), 1; G. Scott Thomas, *The Pursuit of the White House: A Handbook of Presidential Election Statistics and History* (Westport, Conn.: Greenwood Press, 1987), 3.

3 Jane Addams, *Twenty Years at Hull-House with Autobiographical Notes* (New York: Macmillan, 1912), 417.

4 Wiebe, *Self-Rule*, 10.

5 Charles Dickens, *American Notes for General Circulation* (New York: D. Appleton, 1868), 29.

6 Morton Keller, *Affairs of State: Public Life in Late Nineteenth Century America* (Cambridge, Mass.: Belknap Press of Harvard University, 1977), 241; Mark Lawrence Kornbluh, *Why America Stopped Voting: The Decline of Participatory Democracy and the Emergence of Modern American Politics* (New York: New York University Press, 2000), 23–25.

7 Alexis de Tocqueville, *Democracy in America*, 2 vols. (New York: Knopf, 1994), 1:249.

8 Angus Campbell, Philip E. Converse, Warren E. Miller, and Donald E. Stokes, *The American Voter* (New York: Wiley, 1960), 3.

9 Joel H. Silbey, *Political Ideology and Voting Behavior in the Age of Jackson* (Englewood Cliffs, N.J.: Prentice-Hall, 1974), 216; Jean H. Baker, "The Ceremonies of Politics: Nineteenth-Century Rituals of National Affirmation," in William J. Cooper Jr., Michael F. Holt, and John McCardell, eds., *A Master's Due: Essays in Honor of David Herbert Donald* (Baton Rouge: Louisiana State University Press, 1985), 168–175; Michael McGerr, "Political Style and Women's Power, 1830–1930," *Journal of American History* 77 (December 1990): 865.

10 Michael McGerr, *The Decline of Popular Politics: The American North, 1865–1928* (New York: Oxford University Press, 1988), 5–6. Based on a study of contested House election cases, Richard Franklin Bensel has concluded that many midcentury voters actually knew little about their party's position on issues, a conclusion that likely says more about the issues in contested election cases than about what was actually going on in politics: *The American Ballot Box in the Mid-nineteenth Century* (Cambridge: Cambridge University Press, 2004).

11 Osborne H. Oldroyd, *Lincoln's Campaign: or, The Political Revolution of 1860* (Chicago: Laird and Lee, Publishers, 1896), 104–109; Edmund B. Sullivan, *Collecting Political Americana* (New York: Crown, 1980), 144–146; McGerr, *Decline of Popular Politics*, 24.

12 McGerr, *Decline of Popular Politics*, 28; *Springfield (Mass.) Republican*, October 15, 1860.

13 R. Hal Williams, "The Politics of the Gilded Age," in John F. Marszalek and Wilson D. Miscamble, eds., *American Political History: Essays on the State of the*

Discipline (Notre Dame, Ind.: University of Notre Dame Press, 1997), 108. Italics in the original.

14   Kornbluh, *Why America Stopped Voting*, 29–31; Robert Kelley, "Ideology and Political Culture from Jefferson to Nixon," *American Historical Review* 82 (June 1977): 547.

15   Dale Baum, *The Civil War Party System: The Case of Massachusetts, 1848–1876* (Chapel Hill: University of North Carolina Press, 1984), 8.

16   Richard J. Jensen, *Grass Roots Politics: Parties, Issues, and Voters, 1854–1983* (Westport, Conn.: Greenwood Press, 1983), 31.

17   Roger A. Fischer and Edmund B. Sullivan, *American Political Ribbons and Ribbon Badges, 1825–1981* (Lincoln, Mass.: Quarterman Publications, 1985), 264; Roger A. Fischer, *Tippecanoe and Trinkets Too: The Material Culture of Presidential Campaigns, 1828–1984* (Urbana: University of Illinois Press, 1988), 144–145; John Doyle DeWitt, *A Century of Campaign Buttons, 1789–1889* (Hartford, Conn., 1959), i; Edmund B. Sullivan, *American Political Badges and Medalets, 1789–1892* (Lincoln, Mass.: Quarterman Publications, 1981), vii. Another new invention, first used in the 1896 campaign, was the megaphone.

18   Keith Melder, *Hail to the Candidate: Presidential Campaigns from Banners to Broadcasts* (Washington, D.C.: Smithsonian Institution Press, 1992), 38–39; Sullivan, *Collecting Political Americana*, 32–36.

19   Fischer, *Tippecanoe and Trinkets Too*, 155, 157.

20   The secret ballot spread so quickly because of the example of neighboring states that had adopted it, its success in organizing and cleaning up the messy American voting process, and the fact that even within its careful rules, skilled politicians could find ways to manipulate its requirements to their advantage.

21   Tracy Campbell, *Deliver the Vote: A History of Election Fraud, an American Political Tradition—1742–2004* (New York: Carroll & Graff Publishers, 2005), 97–102; Jamie L. Carson and Jason M. Roberts, "Strategic Politicians and U.S. House Elections, 1874–1914," *Journal of Politics* 67 (May 2005): 477; Samuel Kernell, "Toward Understanding 19th Century Congressional Careers: Ambition, Competition, and Rotation," *American Journal of Political Science* 21 (November 1977): 669–693; Jonathan N. Katz and Brian R. Sala, "Careerism, Committee Assignments, and the Electoral Connection," *American Political Science Review* 90 (March 1996): 21–33.

22   Peter Argersinger, "'A Place on the Ballot': Fusion Politics and Antifusion Laws," *American Historical Review* 85 (April 1980): 287–306, offers a superb analysis of the effect of the secret ballot laws. Also, Jerrold G. Rusk, "The Effect of the Australian Ballot Reform on Split Ticket Voting: 1876–1908," *American Political Science Review* 64 (December 1970): 1220–1238.

23   The first party system lasted from 1789 to the early 1820s and witnessed the initial steps toward the establishment of lasting party organizations. Running from about 1828 to the great realignment of the 1850s, the second party system saw the shift from strong local alignments into full two-party competition across the entire country, mainly between the Democrats and the Whigs.

24 For an excellent analysis of Gilded Age elections, see Samuel T. McSeveney, *The Politics of Depression: Political Behavior in the Northeast, 1893–1896* (New York: Oxford University Press, 1972), 3–31; "Electoral and Popular Vote Cast for President, by Political Party: 1789–1968," in U.S. Bureau of the Census, *Historical Statistics of the United States from Colonial Times to 1970, Bicentennial Edition* (Washington, D.C.: U.S. Department of Commerce, 1975), 2:1073; Peter F. Nardulli, "A Normal Vote Approach to Electoral Change: Presidential Elections, 1828–1984," *Political Behavior* 16 (December 1994): 483–484. For Benjamin Harrison and Grover Cleveland, see Charles W. Calhoun, *Minority Victory: Gilded Age Politics and the Front Porch Campaign of 1888* (Lawrence: University Press of Kansas, 2008); Mark Wahlgren Summers, *Rum, Romanism, and Rebellion: The Making of a President, 1884* (Chapel Hill: University of North Carolina Press, 2000).

25 Robert J. Steinfeld, "Property and Suffrage in the Early American Republic," *Stanford Law Review* 41 (January 1989): 335–376; Chilton Williamson, *American Suffrage: From Property to Democracy* (Princeton, N.J.: Princeton University Press, 1960); Keller, *Affairs of State*, 522–523.

26 Keller, *Affairs of State*, 442; Paula Baker, "The Domestication of Politics: Women in American Political Society, 1780–1920," *American Historical Review* 89 (June 1984): 634n. Poll tax laws and similar measures were used to keep African Americans, Asian Americans, and other minorities from the polls.

27 Donald W. Rogers, ed., *Voting and the Spirit of American Democracy: Essays on the History of Voting and Voting Rights in America* (Urbana: University of Illinois Press, 1992), 11. In a significant—and disturbing—contrast to today's trends, the young, those just coming of voting age in the mid-1890s, had a turnout rate of 79.6 percent, a measure of the strong forces leading people to vote: Paul Kleppner, *Who Voted? The Dynamics of Electoral Turnout, 1870–1980* (Westport, Conn.: Greenwood Publishing Group, 1981), 48.

28 "Voter Participation in Presidential Elections by State: 1824 to 1968," in U.S. Bureau of the Census, *Historical Statistics of the United States from Colonial Times to 1970, Bicentennial Edition* (Washington, D.C.: U.S. Department of Commerce, 1975), 2:1071–1072; Walter Dean Burnham, "Those High Nineteenth-Century American Voting Turnouts: Fact or Fiction?" *Journal of Interdisciplinary History* 16 (Spring 1985): 613–644; Walter Dean Burnham, *Critical Elections and the Mainsprings of American Politics* (New York: Norton, 1970), 18–21, 71–91; McSeveney, *Politics of Depression*, 3–31.

29 Richard Jensen, "Armies, Admen, and Crusaders: Types of Presidential Election Campaigns," *History Teacher* 2 (January 1969): 34.

30 Richard Jensen, *The Winning of the Midwest: Social and Political Conflict, 1888–1896* (Chicago: University of Chicago Press, 1971), 11–12.

31 Ibid., 164–165.

32 John M. Taylor, *Garfield of Ohio: The Available Man* (New York: Norton, 1970), 200.

33 Jensen, *Winning of the Midwest*, 13–14; Harry J. Sievers, *Benjamin Harrison*, vol. 2, *Hoosier Statesman: From the Civil War to the White House, 1865–1888* (New

York: University Publishers, 1959), 371, 423–425; *Hell-Bent for the White House,* exhibition catalog (N.p., n.d.), Museum of American Political Life, University of Hartford, Hartford, Conn.

34 W. Dean Burnham, *Presidential Ballots, 1836–1892* (Baltimore, Md.: Johns Hopkins University Press, 1955), 118–158; Walter Dean Burnham, "The Changing Shape of the American Political Universe," *American Political Science Review* 59 (March 1965): 7–28.

35 Samuel J. Tilden, in Robert Kelley, *The Transatlantic Persuasion: The Liberal-Democratic Mind in the Age of Gladstone* (New York: Knopf, 1969), 270.

36 *New York Evening Post,* August 9, 1892. Also, Geoffrey Blodgett, *The Gentle Reformers: Massachusetts Democrats in the Cleveland Era* (Cambridge, Mass.: Harvard University Press, 1966), 91, 147; R. Hal Williams, "'Dry Bones and Dead Language': The Democratic Party," in H. Wayne Morgan, ed., *The Gilded Age: Revised and Enlarged Edition* (Syracuse, N.Y.: Syracuse University Press, 1970), 129–148; John Gerring, *Party Ideologies in America, 1828–1996* (Cambridge: Cambridge University Press, 1998), 163–171.

37 William L. Wilson, *The National Democratic Party: Its History, Principles, Achievements, and Aims* (Baltimore, Md.: H. L. Harvey, 1888), 222–236; *New York Times,* October 4, 1888; *Chicago Tribune,* March 4, 1889.

38 C. Vann Woodward, *Origins of the New South, 1877–1913* (Baton Rouge: Louisiana State University Press, 1951), 65; Dewey W. Grantham Jr., *The Democratic South* (Athens: University of Georgia Press, 1963), 23; William J. Cooper, *The Conservative Regime: South Carolina, 1877–1890* (Baltimore, Md.: Johns Hopkins University Press, 1968), 105–106.

39 Alexander Clarence Flick, *Samuel Jones Tilden: A Study in Political Sagacity* (New York: Dodd, Mead, 1939), 169; Paul Kleppner, *The Cross of Culture: A Social Analysis of Midwestern Politics, 1850–1900* (New York: Free Press, 1970), 35–91. Also, Melvyn Hammarberg, "Indiana Farmers and the Group Basis of the Late Nineteenth-Century Political Parties," *Journal of American History* 61 (June 1974): 91–115.

40 Julia B. Foraker, *I Would Live It Again: Memories of a Vivid Life* (New York: Harper & Bros., 1932), 140; George Frisbie Hoar, "Are the Republicans In to Stay?" *North American Review* 149 (November 1889): 619–629.

41 Charles Hedges, *Speeches of Benjamin Harrison, Twenty-third President of the United States* (New York: United States Book, 1892), 59; *New York Weekly Mail and Express,* April 30, 1890, in scrapbooks in the Papers of Benjamin Harrison, Manuscript Division, Library of Congress, Washington, D.C. For a superb analysis of Republican party structure and outlook, see Lewis L. Gould, "The Republican Search for a National Majority," in Morgan, *Gilded Age,* 171–187.

42 *New York Tribune,* October 25, 1890; *Beatrice Webb's American Diary, 1898* (Madison: University of Wisconsin Press, 1963), 54–55.

43 For a detailed and insightful study of the 1888 campaign, see Charles W. Calhoun, *Minority Victory: Gilded Age Politics and the Front Porch Campaign of 1888* (Lawrence: University Press of Kansas, 2008).

44 R. Hal Williams, *Years of Decision: American Politics in the 1890s* (New York:

John Wiley & Sons, 1973), 19–41; *Congressional Record* [hereafter *CR*], 51st Cong., 1st sess. (April 16, 1890), 4253, 51st Cong., 1st sess. (September 27, 1890), 10575–10641, 51st Cong., 1st sess. (September 30, 1890), 10740; *New York Tribune*, October 1, 1890; *Chicago Tribune*, September 27, October 1–2, 1890. Both of the Sherman acts were named after their author, the influential Senator John Sherman of Ohio.

45 *CR*, 51st Cong., 1st sess. (May 19, 1890), 4506, 51st Cong., 1st sess. (June 23, 1890), 6385.

46 *Baltimore American and Commercial Advertiser*, June 2, 1890, in scrapbooks in Harrison Papers; William A. Robinson, *Thomas B. Reed: Parliamentarian* (New York: Dodd, Mead, 1930), 241–249; *New York Tribune*, September 4–5, 1890.

47 James S. Clarkson to E. W. Halford, December 5, 1891, Harrison Papers; Richard Harmond, "Troubles of Massachusetts Republicans during the 1880s," *Mid-America* 56 (April 1974): 85–99; Lois Bannister Merk, "Boston's Historic Public School Crisis," *New England Quarterly* 31 (June 1958): 172–199.

48 For an analysis of ethnocultural interpretations of voting, see Richard L. McCormick, "Ethno-cultural Interpretations of Nineteenth-Century Voting Behavior," *Political Science Quarterly* 89 (June 1974): 351–377. For other examples, see Michael F. Holt, *Forging a Majority: The Formation of the Republican Party in Pittsburgh, 1848–1860* (New Haven, Conn.: Yale University Press, 1969); Jensen, *Winning of the Midwest*; Kleppner, *Cross of Culture*; McSeveney, *Politics of Depression*; Richard Jensen, "The Religious and Occupational Roots of Party Identification: Illinois and Indiana in the 1870s," *Civil War History* 16 (December 1970): 325–343; Frederick C. Luebke, "German Immigrants and the Churches in Nebraska, 1889–1915," *Mid-America* 50 (April 1968): 121–130; Roger E. Wyman, "Wisconsin Ethnic Groups and the Election of 1890," *Wisconsin Magazine of History* 51 (Summer 1968): 269–293.

49 Cyrenus Cole, *Iowa through the Years* (Iowa City: State Historical Society of Iowa, 1940), 363–379; *New York Times*, November 7, 1889.

50 *Chicago Tribune*, September 23, 1890; Louise Phelps Kellogg, "The Bennett Law in Wisconsin," *Wisconsin Magazine of History* 2 (September 1918): 3–25; J. J. Mapel, "The Repeal of the Compulsory Education Laws in Wisconsin and Illinois," *Educational Review* 1 (January 1891): 53–55.

51 H. C. Payne to Jeremiah Rusk, December 2, 1890, in Richard N. Current, *Pine Logs and Politics: A Life of Philetus Sawyer, 1816–1900* (Madison: State Historical Society of Wisconsin, 1950), 253–254; William F. Whyte, "The Bennett Law Campaign in Wisconsin," *Wisconsin Magazine of History* 10 (June 1927): 377–390.

52 Thomas Richard Ross, *Jonathan Prentiss Dolliver: A Study in Political Integrity and Independence* (Iowa City: State Historical Society of Iowa, 1940), 65; Jean B. Kern, "The Political Career of Horace Boies," *Iowa Journal of History* 47 (July 1949): 215–246.

53 *St. Louis Republic*, November 5, 1890; Harrison to Howard Cale, November 17, 1890, Harrison Papers; *Brooklyn Standard-Union*, November 5, 1890; *New York Tribune*, November 5, 1890.

54 Blodgett, *Gentle Reformers*, 98–99; Gerald W. McFarland, "The Breakdown of Deadlock: The Cleveland Democracy in Connecticut, 1884–1894," *Historian* 31 (May 1969): 394–395; Wyman, "Wisconsin Ethnic Groups," 269–293.

55 *Philadelphia Bulletin*, November 18, 1890; Stuart Noblin, *Leonidas LaFayette Polk: Agrarian Crusader* (Chapel Hill: University of North Carolina Press, 1949), 227; Frank M. Drew, "The Present Farmers' Movement," *Political Science Quarterly* 6 (June 1891): 308–309.

56 C. Vann Woodward, *Tom Watson: Agrarian Rebel* (New York: Macmillan, 1938), 143; Washington Gladden, "The Embattled Farmers," *Forum* 10 (November 1890): 315–322.

57 Steven Hahn, *The Roots of Southern Populism: Yeoman Farmers and the Transformation of the Georgia Upcountry, 1850–1890* (New York: Oxford University Press, 2006), 201–202.

58 *New York Tribune*, August 3, 1890; J. L. Lockhart to Arthur C. Mellette, July 13, 1890, in Howard R. Lamar, *Dakota Territory, 1861–1889: A Study of Frontier Politics* (New Haven, Conn.: Yale University Press, 1956), 274; *Washington Post*, October 29, 1890.

59 O. Gene Clanton, *Kansas Populism: Ideas and Men* (Lawrence: University Press of Kansas, 1969), 87–90; Stanley B. Parsons, *The Populist Context: Rural versus Urban Power on a Great Plains Frontier* (Westport, Conn.: Greenwood Press, 1973), 75–90.

60 Woodward, *Origins of the New South*, 203–204, 235; *Washington Post*, November 6, 1890.

61 Victor Murdock, *"Folks"* (New York: Macmillan, 1921), 102; Woodward, *Watson*, 129–166; Elizabeth N. Barr, "The Populist Uprising," in William E. Connelley, ed., *A Standard History of Kansas and Kansans*, 2 vols. (Chicago: Lewis, 1918), 2:67–68.

62 Annie L. Diggs, "The Women in the Alliance Movement," *Arena* 6 (July 1892): 166–167.

63 Clanton, *Kansas Populism*, 37–39, 74–84; Lawrence Goodwyn, *Democratic Promise: The Populist Moment in America* (New York: Oxford University Press, 1976), 157–159; MaryJo Wagner, "Farms, Families, and Reform: Women in the Farmers' Alliance and Populist Party" (Ph.D. diss., University of Oregon, 1986); Marion K. Barthelme, ed., *Women in the Texas Populist Movement: Letters to the Southern Mercury* (College Station: Texas A&M University Press, 1997). See also O. Gene Clanton, *Populism: The Humane Preference in America, 1890–1900* (Boston: Twayne Publishers, 1991); Charles Postel, *The Populist Vision* (New York: Oxford University Press, 2007).

64 Noblin, *Leonidas LaFayette Polk*, 227; *Brooklyn Standard-Union*, December 11, 1890, in scrapbooks in Harrison Papers; *New York Herald*, December 9, 1890; Frank B. Tracy, "Menacing Socialism in the Western States," *Forum* 15 (May 1893): 332–342.

65 Entry for December 20, 1890, Lodge Diary, in John A. Garraty, *Henry Cabot Lodge: A Biography* (New York: Knopf, 1965), 122.

CHAPTER 2 THE DEMOCRATS IN POWER, 1893–1896

1   *Brooklyn Standard-Union,* November 19, 1892.

2   James D. Richardson, *A Compilation of Messages and Papers of the Presidents,* 20 vols. (New York: Bureau of National Literature, 1917), 8:5821–5825; *New York Tribune,* March 3–5, 1893; *San Francisco Examiner,* March 5, 1893.

3   Allan Nevins, *Grover Cleveland: A Study in Courage* (New York: Dodd, Mead, 1932), 505–509; Joseph H. Manley to Harrison, November 9, 1892, Papers of Benjamin Harrison, Manuscript Division, Library of Congress, Washington, D.C.; Carl N. Degler, "American Political Parties and the Rise of the City: An Interpretation," *Journal of American History* 51 (June 1964): 46–47; John M. Allswang, *A House for All Peoples: Ethnic Politics in Chicago, 1890–1936* (Lexington: University Press of Kentucky, 1971), 23–24.

4   Throughout the 1890s, the terms *People's party* and *Populists* were used interchangeably, referring to the same movement.

5   Stuart Noblin, *Leonidas LaFayette Polk: Agrarian Crusader* (Chapel Hill: University of North Carolina Press, 1949), 286–291; *People's Party Paper,* January 7, 1892, July 8, 1892; *New York Tribune,* July 2–6, 1892; Thomas E. Watson, "Why the People's Party Should Elect the Next President," *Arena* 6 (July 1892): 203–204.

6   H. Wayne Morgan, *From Hayes to McKinley: National Party Politics, 1877–1896* (Syracuse, N.Y.: Syracuse University Press, 1969), 431; Daniel M. Robinson, "Tennessee Politics and the Agrarian Revolt, 1888–1896," *Mississippi Valley Historical Review* 20 (December 1933): 377.

7   O. Gene Clanton, *Populism: The Humane Preference in America, 1890–1900* (Boston: Twayne Publishers, 1991), 42; Elizabeth N. Barr, "The Populist Uprising," in William E. Connelley, ed., *A Standard History of Kansas and Kansans,* 2 vols. (Chicago: Lewis, 1918), 2:11–83; James E. Wright, *The Politics of Populism: Dissent in Colorado* (New Haven, Conn.: Yale University Press, 1974), 151; *People's Party Paper,* September 30, 1892.

8   Wright, *Politics of Populism,* 151–158; Richard Jensen, *The Winning of the Midwest: Social and Political Conflict, 1888–1896* (Chicago: University of Chicago Press, 1971), 170; Samuel Gompers, "Organized Labor in the Campaign," *North American Review* 155 (July 1892): 93; Theodore Saloutos, "The Professors and the Populists," *Agricultural History* 40 (October 1966): 238.

9   Entry for November 10, 1892, Donnelly Diary, in Martin Ridge, *Ignatius Donnelly: The Portrait of a Politician* (Chicago: University of Chicago Press, 1962), 309; William Warren Rogers, *The One-Gallused Rebellion: Agrarianism in Alabama, 1865–1896* (Baton Rouge: Louisiana State University Press, 1970), 188–235.

10 *People's Party Paper,* November 25, 1892; *Washington Post,* November 11, 1892.

11 Richard E. Welch Jr., *The Presidencies of Grover Cleveland* (Lawrence: University Press of Kansas, 1988), 111. The record was exceeded afterward only by Franklin D. Roosevelt, four decades later.

12 "The Progress of the World," *Review of Reviews* 7 (April 1893): 260.

13 Woodrow Wilson, "Mr. Cleveland's Cabinet," *Review of Reviews* 7 (April 1893): 289.

14 *Brooklyn Standard-Union*, November 19, 1892.

15 *Chicago Tribune*, May 1–2, 1893; *New York Tribune*, May 2, 1893; *Spectator* 70 (May 6, 1893): 590, 594–595; Larzer Ziff, *The American 1890s: Life and Times of a Lost Generation* (New York: Viking Press, 1966), 3–23.

16 Richardson, *Compilation of Messages and Papers*, 8:5741–5744; R. G. Dun & Co., quoted in *Boston Journal*, December 31, 1892.

17 Charles Hoffman, *The Depression of the Nineties: An Economic History* (Westport, Conn.: Greenwood Press, 1970), 47–141; *New York Tribune*, February 18–19, 1893.

18 W. Jett Lauck, *The Causes of the Panic of 1893* (Boston: Houghton Mifflin, 1907), 65–94; *New York Tribune*, February 2–10, 14–15, 1893; *Brooklyn Daily Eagle*, February 4, 1893; George R. Gibson, "The Financial Excitement and Its Causes," *Forum* 15 (June 1893): 483–493.

19 Henry Lee Higginson to Olney, April 19, 1893, Papers of Richard Olney, Manuscript Division, Library of Congress, Washington, D.C.

20 *New York Tribune*, May 3–7, 1893; *Washington Post*, May 6, 1893; Jonathan W. Macartney to Reed, May 4, 1893, Thomas Brackett Reed Papers, George J. Mitchell Department of Special Collections and Archives, Bowdoin College Library, Brunswick, Maine.

21 Entry for May 14, 1893, in Charles G. Dawes, *A Journal of the McKinley Years* (Chicago: Lakeside Press, 1950), 28; Albert C. Stevens, "Analysis of the Phenomena of the Panic in the United States in 1893," *Quarterly Journal of Economics* 8 (January 1894): 126–144.

22 Samuel Rezneck, "Unemployment, Unrest, and Relief in the United States during the Depression of 1893–1897," *Journal of Political Economy* 61 (August 1953): 325–327; *New York Tribune*, August 2, 1893.

23 *New York Tribune*, August 16, October 14, December 24, 1893; American Federation of Labor, *Report of Proceedings of the Annual Convention* (New York, 1893), 11. See R. G. Dun & Co.'s review of business for 1893, in Charles S. Olcott, *The Life of William McKinley*, 2 vols. (Boston: Houghton Mifflin, 1916), 1:294.

24 Ray Stannard Baker to J. S. Baker, December 15, 1893, in Robert C. Bannister Jr., *Ray Stannard Baker: The Mind and Thought of a Progressive* (New Haven, Conn.: Yale University Press, 1966), 43; Carlos C. Closson Jr., "The Unemployed in American Cities," *Quarterly Journal of Economics* 8 (January 1894): 192.

25 Karel D. Bicha, "The Conservative Populists: A Hypothesis," *Agricultural History* 47 (April 1973): 9–24; Henry Markham Page, *Pasadena: Its Early Years* (Los Angeles: Privately printed by L. L. Morrison, 1964), 182–183.

26 Charles Francis Adams, *Charles Francis Adams, 1835–1915: An Autobiography* (Boston: Houghton Mifflin, 1916), 200.

27 *Superior Evening Telegram*, March 21, 1896, in David P. Thelen, *The New Citizenship: Origins of Progressivism in Wisconsin, 1885–1900* (Columbia: University of Missouri Press, 1972), 55; Grover Cleveland, *Presidential Problems* (New York: Century, 1904), 80.

28 Cleveland to Carlisle, January 22, 1893, in Allan Nevins, ed., *Letters of Grover Cleveland* (Boston: Houghton Mifflin, 1933), 314–315; Olney Autobiography, in Olney Papers; *Washington Post,* January 22, 1893; Henry Clews, *The Wall Street Point of View* (New York: Silver, Burdett, 1900), 71–73.

29 *Washington Post,* June 27–July 1, 1893; *Atlanta Constitution,* June 29, July 1, 1893.

30 Richardson, *Compilation of Messages and Papers,* 8:5828; Cleveland to Henry T. Thurber, August 20, 1893, Papers of Grover Cleveland, Manuscript Division, Library of Congress, Washington, D.C.

31 Nevins, *Grover Cleveland,* 532.

32 *People's Party Paper,* July 14, 1893; *New York Tribune,* July 2–5, 1893; *Philadelphia Press,* August 29, 1893.

33 Stephen M. White to W. M. Eddy, August 22, 1893, Stephen M. White Papers, Stanford University Library, Stanford, Calif.

34 *New York Tribune,* June 28, 1893; William M. Stewart, *The Reminiscences of Senator William M. Stewart of Nevada* (New York: Neale Publishing, 1908), 313; "The Business Outlook," *North American Review* 157 (October 1893): 385–398.

35 Leon W. Fuller, "Colorado's Revolt against Capitalism," *Mississippi Valley Historical Review* 21 (December 1934): 343.

36 *New York Tribune,* July 12–13, August 2–4, 1893; *People's Party Paper,* July 7, 21, 1893.

37 *CR,* 53d Cong., 1st sess. (August 7, 1893), 197; Richardson, *Compilation of Messages and Papers,* 8:5833–5837; James J. Hill to Cleveland, August 9, 1893, Cleveland Papers; *New York Tribune,* August 6–9, 1893.

38 *CR,* 53d Cong., 1st sess. (August 16, 1893), 410–411, 53d Cong., 1st sess. (August 26, 1893), Appendix, 552; *CR,* 53d Cong., 2d sess. (March 7, 1894), 2673; *New Orleans Daily Picayune,* August 7–9, 1893; Arthur Wallace Dunn, *From Harrison to Harding: A Personal Narrative, Covering a Third of a Century, 1888–1921,* 2 vols. (New York: G. P. Putnam's Sons, 1932), 1:123.

39 Thomas Richard Ross, *Jonathan Prentiss Dolliver: A Study in Political Integrity and Independence* (Iowa City: State Historical Society of Iowa, 1960), 104.

40 *CR,* 53d Cong., 1st sess. (August 28, 1893), 1004–1008; William E. Curtis to Elizabeth Curtis, August 28, 1893, William E. Curtis Papers, Manuscript Division, Library of Congress, Washington, D.C.

41 *CR,* 52d Cong., 2d sess. (February 17, 1893), 1734; entry for August 18, 1893, Charles S. Hamlin Diary, Charles S. Hamlin Papers, Manuscript Division, Library of Congress, Washington, D.C.; White to W. M. Eddy, August 22, 1893, White Papers.

42 Seigniorage is the government's profit when it purchases bullion at a price below the value placed on the metal when coined; it is the difference between intrinsic value and face value.

43 *New York Tribune,* October 17–23, 1893; *Washington Post,* September 8, 1893; *CR,* 53d Cong., 1st sess. (October 4, 1893), 2106–2119; John Q. Lambert, *Arthur Pue Gorman* (Baton Rouge: Louisiana State University Press, 1953), 187–199.

44 Josephus Daniels, *Editor in Politics* (Chapel Hill: University of North Carolina Press, 1941), 54.

45 Morton to Olney, October 22, 1893, Olney Papers; J. R. McPherson to Cleveland, October 23, 1893, Voorhees to Cleveland, October 24, 1893, Cleveland
Papers; *Washington Post,* October 25–27, 1893.

46 *Washington Post,* October 25, 29, 1893; *CR,* 53d Cong., 1st sess. (October 28,
1893), 2917–2926, *CR,* 53d Cong., 1st sess. (October 30, 1893), 2958; *New
York Tribune,* November 2, 1893; Paul W. Glad, *McKinley, Bryan, and the People*
(Philadelphia: J. B. Lippincott, 1964), 83.

47 *Raleigh News and Observer,* November 2, 1893; Andrew Carnegie, "A Word to
Wage-Earners," *North American Review* 157 (September 1893): 365; *New York
Tribune,* November 1–3, 1893; F. W. Taussig, "The United States Treasury in
1894–1896," *Quarterly Journal of Economics* 13 (January 1899): 204–205.

48 *Louisville Courier-Journal,* July 10, 1904, in Arthur Krock, ed., *The Editorials of
Henry Watterson* (New York: George H. Doran, 1923), 98–99.

49 J. B. Romans to Dolliver, February 1, 1896, in Ross, *Jonathan Prentiss Dolliver,*
120–121. For the spread of enthusiasm for silver, see James A. Barnes, "Myths
of the Bryan Campaign," *Mississippi Valley Historical Review* 34 (December
1947): 370–374.

50 William H. Harvey, *Coin's Financial School Up to Date* (Chicago: Coin Publishing, 1895), 43–44; J. Laurence Laughlin, *Facts about Money* (Chicago:
E. A. Weeks, 1895); Willard Fisher, "'Coin' and His Critics," *Quarterly Journal
of Economics* 10 (January 1896): 187–208.

51 See, e.g., Ignatius Donnelly, *The American People's Money* (Chicago: Laird &
Lee, 1895); Mrs. S. E. V. Emery, *Seven Financial Conspiracies Which Have En-
slaved the American People* (Lansing, Mich.: L. Thompson, 1894); Wharton
Barker, *Bimetallism* (Philadelphia, 1897), 321–323. For a sampling of the pam-
phlet literature, see L. J. Powers, *Farmer Hayseed in Town; or, The Closing Days
of Coin's Financial School* (St. Paul, Minn.: Industrial Publishing, 1895); Major
Otis G. Gunn, *Bullion Versus Coin: A Full Verbatim Discussion upon the Free and
Unlimited Coinage of Silver* (Kansas City, Mo.: Hailman & Bowes, 1895); Silas
Honest Money, *Base "Coin" Exposed, Being the Arrest, Exposure and Confession
of W. H. H. Money, and the Dismissal of the So-Called "Coin's Financial School"*
(Chicago: E. A. Weeks, 1895); Leo Stanton Rowe, *The Mistakes of Coin* (Chi-
cago: Sound Printing, 1895); Horace White, *Coin's Financial Fool; or, The Artful
Dodger Exposed* (New York: J. S. Ogilvie, 1895).

52 William H. Harvey, *Coin's Financial School* (Chicago: Coin Publishing, 1894), 82.

53 David W. Brady, *Congressional Voting in a Partisan Era: A Study of the McKinley
Houses and a Comparison to the Modern House of Representatives* (Lawrence:
University Press of Kansas, 1973), 2.

54 O. O. Stealey, *Twenty Years in the Press Gallery: A Concise History of Important
Legislation* (New York: Publishers Printing, 1906), 28.

55 *Washington Post,* November 8–9, 1893; *New York Tribune,* November 8–9,
1893; Morton to John P. Irish, November 8, 1893, J. Sterling Morton Papers,
Nebraska Historical Society, Lincoln.

56 E. M. Ross to Jackson A. Graves, November 10, 1893, Jackson A. Graves Papers,

Henry E. Huntington Library, San Marino, Calif.; *Washington Post,* November 8–9, 1893; *Chicago Tribune,* December 21, 1893, April 3–5, 1894.

57 *CR,* 53d Cong., 2d sess. (March 1, 1894), 2524–2525, *CR,* 53d Cong., 2d sess. (March 7, 1894), 2673–2675, *CR,* 53d Cong., 2d sess. (March 15, 1894), 2981; *Chicago Times,* March 20–30, 1894; *Washington Post,* March 16, 28–30, 1894. The bill proposed to add about $55 million in silver currency to a money stock of nearly $2 billion.

58 *Washington Star,* March 17, 1894; George Gray to Cleveland, undated, 1894, Cleveland Papers; *Raleigh News-Observer-Chronicle,* March 31, 1894; *Atlanta Constitution,* March 30–31, 1894; *Washington Post,* March 30, 1894. Even some of Cleveland's cabinet members hoped he would sign it: Dewey W. Grantham Jr., *Hoke Smith and the Politics of the New South* (Baton Rouge: Louisiana State University Press, 1958), 95.

59 *San Francisco Examiner,* March 30, 1894; Cleveland to Everett P. Wheeler, April 16, 1894, in Nevins, *Letters of Grover Cleveland,* 351, italics in the original; John Hay to C. S. H., August 5, 1894, in John Hay, *Letters of John Hay and Extracts from Diary,* 3 vols. (New York: Gordian Press, 1969), 2:318.

60 Stanley Buder, *Pullman: An Experiment in Industrial Order and Community Planning, 1880–1930* (New York: Oxford University Press, 1967), 147–201; *San Francisco Chronicle,* July 7, 1894; Harrison Gray Otis to Thomas R. Bard, July 18, 1894, Thomas R. Bard Papers, Henry E. Huntington Library, San Marino, Calif.

61 Altgeld to Cleveland, July 5, 1894, Cleveland Papers; Grover Cleveland, "The Government in the Chicago Strike of 1894," *McClure's Magazine* 23 (July 1904): 227–240.

62 Morton to John P. Irish, July 21, 1894, Levi P. Morton Papers, New York Public Library, New York; Joseph H. Call to Olney, July 18, 1894, in appendix to the *Annual Report of the Attorney-General of the United States for the Year 1896* (Washington, D.C.: Government Printing House, 1896), 34; *Chicago Times,* July 21, 1894.

63 *CR,* 53d Cong., 2d sess. (July 19, 1894), 7710—7713, *CR,* 53d Cong., 2d sess. (July 20, 1894), 7730–7737, *CR,* 53d Cong., 2d sess. (July 23, 1894), 7801–7809; *Washington Post,* July 20–21, 24, 1894; Lambert, *Arthur Pue Gorman,* 231–235.

64 *New York Tribune,* October 14, 1894; Cleveland to Wilson, August 13, 1894, Cleveland to Thomas C. Catchings, August 27, 1894, in Nevins, *Letters of Grover Cleveland,* 363–366; *Washington Post,* August 30, 1894.

65 Roosevelt to Anna Roosevelt, June 24, 1894, in Elting E. Morison, ed., *Letters of Theodore Roosevelt* (Boston: Harvard University Press, 1954) 1:385; William Alexander Robinson, *Thomas B. Reed Parliamentarian* (New York: Dodd, Mead, 1930), 294–304; David W. Brady and Phillip Althoff, "Party Voting in the U.S. House of Representatives, 1890–1910: Elements of a Responsible Party System," *Journal of Politics* 36 (August 1974): 753–775.

66 George R. Peck to Reed, August 29, 1894, Reed Papers.

67 Roscoe C. Martin, *The People's Party in Texas: A Study in Third Party Politics* (Austin: University of Texas Press, 1933), 67n; J. Wesley Boynton to Chauncey

Depew, March 9, 1894, Chauncey Depew Papers, Yale University Library, New Haven, Conn.

68 *New York Tribune,* October 20, 1894; John P. Altgeld, *Live Questions* (Chicago: Donohue and Henneberry, 1899), 440; Benjamin Harrison, *Views of an Ex-President* (Indianapolis, Ind.: Bowen-Merrill, 1901), 401; Olcott, *Life of McKinley,* 1:298.

69 Festus P. Summers, *William L. Wilson and Tariff Reform: A Biography* (New Brunswick, N.J.: Rutgers University Press, 1953), 221; *Washington Post,* November 7–8, 1894; *New York Tribune,* November 8, 1894; *Chicago Tribune,* November 7–8, 1894.

70 V. O. Key, "A Theory of Critical Elections," *Journal of Politics* 17 (February 1955): 3–15.

71 Chester McArthur Destler, *Henry Demarest Lloyd and the Empire of Reform* (Philadelphia: University of Pennsylvania Press, 1963), 272; Willis J. Abbot, "The Chicago Populist Campaign," *Arena* 11 (February 1895): 330–337; Alexander Saxton, "San Francisco Labor and the Populist and Progressive Insurgencies," *Pacific Historical Review* 34 (1965): 425–427; Roger E. Wyman, "Agrarian or Working-Class Radicalism? The Electoral Basis of Populism in Wisconsin," *Political Science Quarterly* 89 (Winter 1974–1975): 825–826.

72 Paul Kleppner, *The Cross of Culture: A Social Analysis of Midwestern Politics, 1850–1900* (New York: Free Press, 1970), 179–268; O. Gene Clanton, *Kansas Populism: Ideas and Men* (Lawrence: University Press of Kansas, 1969), 168–169; Wright, *Politics of Populism,* 186–201.

73 Altgeld to John W. Ela, March 27, 1895, in Altgeld, *Live Questions,* 467–468; John P. Irish to Morton, November 8, 1894, Morton Papers.

74 Cleveland to Thomas F. Bayard, February 13, 1895, Cleveland Papers; Joseph L. Morrison, *Josephus Daniels: The Small-d Democrat* (Chapel Hill: University of North Carolina Press, 1966), 24; *New York Tribune,* December 12, 1895.

CHAPTER 3 "THE PEOPLE AGAINST THE BOSSES": THE REPUBLICAN NOMINATION OF WILLIAM MCKINLEY

1 *Official Proceedings of the Eleventh Republican National Convention* (n.p.: C. W. Johnson, 1896), 84–85.

2 Harrison to Stephen B. Elkins, February 3, 1896, Harrison to Elkins, April 28, 1896, Papers of Benjamin Harrison, Manuscript Division, Library of Congress, Washington, D.C. "There has never been an hour since I left the White House that I have felt a wish to return to it": typewritten statement, February 3, 1896, Harrison Papers, in Stanley L. Jones, *The Presidential Election of 1896* (Madison: University of Wisconsin Press, 1964), 116–117.

3 Charles S. Olcott, *The Life of William McKinley,* 2 vols. (Boston: Houghton Mifflin, 1916), 1:307–308.

4 Leland L. Sage, *William Boyd Allison: A Study in Practical Politics* (Iowa City: State Historical Society of Iowa, 1956), 261–264.

5 Eugene H. Roseboom, *A History of Presidential Elections* (New York: Macmillan, 1957), 304.

6 James A. Kehl, *Boss Rule in the Gilded Age: Matt Quay of Pennsylvania* (Pittsburgh, Pa.: University of Pittsburgh Press, 1981), xiii–xv.

7 Ibid., xix.

8 Harry J. Sievers, *Benjamin Harrison: Hoosier Statesman—From the Civil War to the White House, 1865–1888* (New York: University Publishers, 1959), 426–427.

9 A. K. McClure, *Old Time Notes of Pennsylvania*, 2 vols. (Philadelphia: John C. Winton, 1905), 2:572–573.

10 Lemuel Ely Quigg, "Thomas Platt," *North American Review* 191 (May 1910): 668–674.

11 Harold F. Gosnell, *Boss Platt and His New York Machine* (Chicago: University of Chicago Press, 1924), 348; Quigg, "Thomas Platt," 668–677; Matthew Josephson, *The Politicos, 1865–1896* (New York: Harcourt, Brace, 1938), 244.

12 Frank A. Flower to Platt, March 6, 1896, Thomas C. Platt Papers, Yale University, New Haven, Conn. See also the letters from James S. Clarkson to Platt, dated in March and May 1896, in Platt Papers.

13 *New York Tribune*, October 31, November 18, 1895.

14 *Chicago Tribune*, December 2–3, 1895; Joseph H. Manley to Reed, September 6, 1894, Manley to Reed, September 14, 1894, Thomas Brackett Reed Papers, George J. Mitchell Department of Special Collections and Archives, Bowdoin College Library, Brunswick, Maine; Morris M. Estee to James S. Clarkson, January 11, 1896, James S. Clarkson Papers, Iowa State Historical Library, Des Moines.

15 H. Wayne Morgan, *William McKinley and His America* (Syracuse, N.Y.: Syracuse University Press, 1963), 203.

16 William A. Robinson, *Thomas B. Reed: Parliamentarian* (New York: Dodd, Mead, 1930), 327; Benjamin Butterworth to Reed, October 19, 1894, Reed Papers; "Silver and the Tariff at Washington," *Fortnightly Review* 55 (June 1894): 837–838.

17 Hayes to his wife, December 14, 1862, in Charles Richard Williams, ed., *Diary and Letters of Rutherford Birchard Hayes: Nineteenth President of the United States*, 4 vols. (Columbus: Ohio State Archaeological and Historical Society, 1922), 2:374; Margaret Leech, *In the Days of McKinley* (New York: Harper, 1959), 6–7; Ari Hoogenboom, *Rutherford B. Hayes: Warrior and President* (Lawrence: University Press of Kansas, 1995), 153–154.

18 Leech, *In the Days of McKinley*, 7–8; A. K. McClure, *Colonel Alexander K. McClure's Recollections of Half a Century* (Salem, Mass.: Salem Press, 1902), 148.

19 *New York Tribune*, November 1, 1892.

20 Hanna to McKinley, January 8, 1896, William McKinley Papers, Manuscript Division, Library of Congress, Washington, D.C.

21 H. Wayne Morgan, "William McKinley," in Phillip Weeks, *Buckeye Presidents: Ohioans in the White House* (Kent, Ohio: Kent State University Press, 2003), 186; Arthur Wallace Dunn, *From Harrison to Harding: A Personal Narrative, Covering a Third of a Century, 1888–1921*, 2 vols. (New York: G. P. Putnam's Sons, 1932), 1:300–302.

22 Julia B. Foraker, *I Would Live It Again: Memories of a Vivid Life* (New York: Harper & Bros., 1932), 238.

23 H. Wayne Morgan, "Governor McKinley's Misfortune: The Walker-McKinley Feud of 1893," *Ohio History Quarterly* 69 (April 1960): 103–120; Olcott, *Life of McKinley*, 1:290–291; Morgan, *William McKinley and His America*, 169–174; Leech, *In the Days of McKinley*, 58–60; Lewis L. Gould, *The Presidency of William McKinley* (Lawrence: Regents Press of Kansas, 1980), 7.

24 McKinley to James McKinley, November 1, 1898, McKinley Papers.

25 Leech, *In the Days of McKinley*, 28–29.

26 William Allen White, *The Autobiography of William Allen White* (New York: Macmillan, 1946), 251; Foraker, *I Would Live It Again*, 238.

27 *Canton Repository*, February 15, 1894.

28 Foraker, *I Would Live It Again*, 99; Roosevelt to Lodge, July 30, 1896, in Elting E. Morison, ed., *Letters of Theodore Roosevelt* (Boston: Harvard University Press, 1954), 1:552; *San Francisco Examiner*, August 11, 1896. There were widespread reports that Hanna had privately urged George W. Pullman to settle the Pullman Strike.

29 Hanna to Hapley, June 29, 1892, in Morgan, *William McKinley and His America*, 185.

30 Olcott, *Life of McKinley*, 1:303–304.

31 Leech, *In the Days of McKinley*, 68; entries for March 14 and March 29, 1896, in Charles G. Dawes, *A Journal of the McKinley Years* (Chicago: Lakeside Press, 1950), 72–74; Whitelaw Reid to Hanna, May 4, 1896, Whitelaw Reid Papers, Manuscript Division, Library of Congress, Washington, D.C.

32 Leon Burr Richardson, *William E. Chandler, Republican* (New York: Dodd, Mead, 1940), 513–517; Richard Stanley Offenberg, "The Political Career of Thomas Brackett Reed" (Ph.D. diss., New York University, 1963), 153–155.

33 Lyman to Lodge, April 30, 1896, Henry Cabot Lodge Papers, Massachusetts Historical Society, Boston.

34 *New York Times*, June 11, 1896; Manley to Reed, June 12, 1896, in Samuel W. McCall, *Life of Thomas Brackett Reed* (Boston: Houghton Mifflin, 1914), 224; Reed to Lodge, June 10, 1896, Lodge Papers; *St. Louis Post-Dispatch*, June 10–11, 1896; *Brooklyn Daily Eagle*, May 1, 1896; *New York Tribune*, June 11–12, 1896; *Chicago Chronicle*, June 13, 1896.

35 Morgan, *William McKinley and His America*, 196.

36 For analysis of the efforts to disfranchise African Americans in the South, see C. Vann Woodward, *The Strange Career of Jim Crow* (New York: Oxford University Press, 1955); J. Morgan Kousser, *The Shaping of Southern Politics: Suffrage Restriction and the Establishment of the One-Party South, 1880–1910* (New Haven, Conn.: Yale University Press, 1974); Douglas A. Blackmon, *Slavery by Another Name: The Re-enslavement of Black Americans from the Civil War to World War II* (New York: Doubleday, 2008).

37 McKinley to Reid, February 19, 1896, Reid to McKinley, April 2, 1896, Reid Papers. Once in office, McKinley adopted a number of initiatives favorable to sectional reconciliation, including pledging, in a major and well-received

speech in Atlanta, to provide federal care for the graves of Confederate veterans as well as those who died for the Union. Leech, *In the Days of McKinley*, 348–349, 455–456.

38 Morgan, *William McKinley and His America*, 193.

39 Lewis J. Lang, ed., *The Autobiography of Thomas Collier Platt* (New York: B. W. Dodge, 1910), 331.

40 Jones, *Presidential Election of 1896*, 118–119; Morgan, *William McKinley and His America*, 206; Frank A. Flower to Platt, March 6, 1896, Platt Papers; William Youngblood to Joseph H. Manley, March 6, 1895, Reed Papers; Hanna to McKinley, April 8, 1896, James A. Waymire to McKinley, April 13, 1896, McKinley Papers; *Brooklyn Daily Eagle*, May 7, 1896.

41 Paul W. Glad, *McKinley, Bryan, and the People* (Philadelphia: J. B. Lippincott, 1964), 104–105.

42 S. P. Peabody to McKinley, May 1, 1896, McKinley Papers; James W. Neilson, *Shelby M. Cullom: Prairie State Republican* (Urbana: University of Illinois Press, 1962), 168–170.

43 Quoted in Glad, *McKinley, Bryan, and the People*, 105–106; *New York World*, June 13, 1896.

44 *Cincinnati Commercial Gazette*, June 14, 1896, in Jones, *Presidential Election of 1896*, 158; *New York Times*, June 17, 1896.

45 *New York Sun*, May 15, 1896, in Robinson, *Thomas B. Reed*, 343n; J. Sloat Fassett to Platt, May 30, 1896, Platt Papers; *New York Tribune*, June 17, 1896; Hamilton Disston to Quay, April 1, 1896, Matthew S. Quay Papers, Manuscript Division, Library of Congress, Washington, D.C.; Amos L. Allen to Reed, June 17, 1896, Reed Papers.

46 Morgan, *William McKinley and His America*, 191; *Nation* 62 (June 4, 1896): 426.

47 E. L. Godkin, "The Political Situation," *Forum* 21 (May 1896): 268–270.

48 *Review of Reviews* 14 (July 1896): 3.

49 Hanna to A. K. McClure, June 28, 1900, in Herbert Croly, *Marcus Alonzo Hanna: His Life and Work* (New York: Macmillan, 1912), 198–199.

50 Olcott, *Life of McKinley*, 1:312; Lang, *Autobiography of Thomas Collier Platt*, 310; entry for June 15, 1896, Dawes, *Journal of the McKinley Years*, 85; *New York Times*, June 15, 1896.

51 *Official Proceedings of the Eleventh Republican National Convention*, 81–85; Joseph Benson Foraker, *Notes of a Busy Life*, 2 vols. (Cincinnati, Ohio: Kidd, 1916), 1:463–478.

52 *Official Proceedings of the Eleventh Republican National Convention*, 86–87.

53 Ibid., 89.

54 Ibid., 91. In a separate vote on the financial plank, the convention adopted it, 812½ to 110½. Ibid., 96.

55 White, *Autobiography of William Allen White*, 276–277.

56 *Official Proceedings of the Eleventh Republican National Convention*, 86–87; *Washington Evening Star*, June 18, 1896; *Chicago Tribune*, June 19, 1896; *New York Tribune*, June 19, 1896.

57 *Nation* 62 (June 25, 1896): 484; *St. Louis Post-Dispatch,* June 18, 1896; *New York World,* June 19, 1896.

58 Bryan later wrote that he was also there to encourage the silver Republicans in the fight they were making: *The Memoirs of William Jennings Bryan, by Himself and His Wife Mary Baird Bryan* (Philadelphia: United Publishers of America, 1925), 100. Also, William Jennings Bryan, *The First Battle: A Story of the Campaign of 1896* (Chicago: W. B. Conkey, 1896), 175; *Chicago Tribune,* June 19, 1896; Elmer Ellis, *Henry Moore Teller: Defender of the West* (Caldwell, Idaho: Caxton Printers, 1941), 257–262.

59 *People's Party Paper,* June 26, 1896; *New York Tribune,* June 19, 1896; *Washington Post,* June 18–19, 1896; *Raleigh (N.C.) Caucasian,* June 25, 1896.

60 Leech, *In the Days of McKinley,* 81.

61 *Official Proceedings of the Eleventh Republican National Convention,* 117.

62 Morgan, *William McKinley and His America,* 217–218.

63 Ibid., 218; *New York Times,* June 19, 1896; *New York Tribune,* June 19, 1896.

64 Leech, *In the Days of McKinley,* 82.

65 *Official Proceedings of the Eleventh Republican National Convention,* 118.

66 *Canton Repository,* June 21, 1896.

67 *New York Times,* June 19, 1896.

68 Leech, *In the Days of McKinley,* 82.

69 *Canton Repository,* June 21, 1896.

70 *Official Proceedings of the Eleventh Republican National Convention,* 123; *Nation* 62 (June 25, 1896): 481–482.

71 *Canton Repository,* June 21, 1896.

72 Joseph Smith, ed., *McKinley, the People's Choice: The Congratulations of the Country, the Calls of Delegations at Canton, the Addresses by Them—His Eloquent and Effective Responses; Full Text of Each Speech or Address Made by Him from June 18 to August 1, 1896* (Canton, Ohio: Repository Press, 1896), 13; *Canton Repository,* June 21, 1896.

73 *Canton Repository,* June 21, 1896; Smith, *McKinley, the People's Choice,* 6.

74 Foraker, *Notes of a Busy Life,* 1:487–488.

CHAPTER 4 DEMOCRATS DIVIDED: THE DEMOCRATIC CONVENTION AT CHICAGO

1 William Jennings Bryan, *The First Battle: A Story of the Campaign of 1896* (Chicago: W. B. Conkey, 1896), 206.

2 Cleveland to E. C. Benedict, May 9, 1895, Grover Cleveland Papers, Manuscript Division, Library of Congress, Washington, D.C.; entry for March 2, 1896, in Festus P. Summers, ed., *Cabinet Diary of William L. Wilson, 1896–1897* (Chapel Hill: University of North Carolina Press, 1957), 38.

3 Susan Orcutt to Governor Lorenzo Lewelling, June 29, 1894, Governor's Records, Lorenzo Dow Lewelling, Kansas Historical Society, http://www.kansasmemory.org/item/214162, accessed on August 25, 2009.

4 Alexander Keyssar, *Out of Work: The First Century of Unemployment in Massachusetts* (Cambridge: Cambridge University Press, 1986), 171–172.

5 Altgeld to William J. Stone, June 20, 1895, in John P. Altgeld, *Live Questions* (Chicago: Donohue and Henneberry, 1899), 486–488; Harvey Wish, "John Peter Altgeld and the Background of the Campaign of 1896," *Mississippi Valley Historical Review* 24 (March 1938): 503–518.

6 *New York Tribune*, June 6, 1895; *Chicago Tribune*, June 5–7, 1895; Bryan to T. O. Towles, April 9, 1896, William Jennings Bryan Papers, Manuscript Division, Library of Congress, Washington, D.C.

7 Charles M. Rosser, *The Crusading Commoner: A Close-Up of William Jennings Bryan and His Times* (Dallas, Tex.: Mathis, Van Nort, 1937), 37–38; Rosser to Bryan, November 23, 1895, Bryan Papers; Louis W. Koenig, *Bryan: A Political Biography of William Jennings Bryan* (New York: Putnam, 1971), 170.

8 Paolo E. Coletta, *William Jennings Bryan*, vol. 1, *Political Evangelist, 1860–1908* (Lincoln: University of Nebraska Press, 1964), 21–48; George R. Poage, "College Career of William Jennings Bryan," *Mississippi Valley Historical Review* 15 (September 1928): 165–182; Boyce House, "Bryan the Orator," *Illinois State Historical Society Journal* 53 (Autumn 1960): 266–282.

9 CR, 53d Cong., 2d sess., Appendix (December 22, 1894), 153; Michael Kazin, *A Godly Hero: The Life of William Jennings Bryan* (New York: Knopf, 2006), 47. In 1894, Bryan ran one more time in Nebraska, for a U.S. Senate seat, but he lost.

10 CR, 53d Cong., 1st sess. (August 16, 1893), 410–411; Robert Kelley, "Ideology and Political Culture from Jefferson to Nixon," *American Historical Review* 82 (June 1977): 541–548.

11 *Washington Post*, June 2, 1896.

12 Entry for May 27, 1896, in Summers, *Cabinet Diary of William L. Wilson*, 91; *San Francisco Examiner*, June 17, 1896; *Chicago Tribune*, May 17, 1896; Cleveland to Don M. Dickinson, June 10, 1896, Cleveland Papers.

13 *New York Tribune*, February 25, 1895, in Marian Silveus, "Antecedents of the Campaign of 1896" (Ph.D. diss., University of Wisconsin, 1932), 75; Stanley L. Jones, *The Presidential Election of 1896* (Madison: University of Wisconsin Press, 1964), 178–179. For a detailed and suggestive analysis of the convention and the events that preceded it, see Richard Franklin Bensel, *Passion and Preferences: William Jennings Bryan and the 1896 Democratic National Convention* (Cambridge: Cambridge University Press, 2008).

14 Silveus, "Antecedents of the Campaign of 1896," 185.

15 Tillman got his colorful nickname by once urging South Carolinians to re-elect him to the Senate so that he could "tickle Cleveland's fat ribs with [a] pitchfork."

16 Dickinson to Cleveland, June 12, 1896, in Allan Nevins, ed., *Letters of Grover Cleveland* (Boston: Houghton Mifflin, 1933), 440.

17 Entries for April 29, 30, 1896, in Summers, *Cabinet Diary of William L. Wilson*, 73–74; James A. Barnes, "Myths of the Bryan Campaign," *Mississippi Valley Historical Review* 34 (December 1947): 374–375.

18 Entries for April 29 and May 26, 1896, in Summers, *Cabinet Diary of William L. Wilson*, 73, 90.

19 Entry for May 27, 1896, in Summers, *Cabinet Diary of William L. Wilson*, 91.

20 Coletta, *William Jennings Bryan*, 1:115; Jones, *Presidential Election of 1896*, 195.

21 Cleveland to the Democratic Voters, June 16, 1896, in Nevins, *Letters of Grover Cleveland*, 440–441; Allan Nevins, *Grover Cleveland: A Study in Courage* (New York: Dodd, Mead, 1932), 694.

22 Entry for May 7, 1896, in Summers, *Cabinet Diary of William L. Wilson*, 78.

23 Nevins, *Grover Cleveland*, 690–691; *Nation* 63 (July 2, 1896): 1; James A. Barnes, "Illinois and the Gold-Silver Controversy, 1890–1896," *Transactions of the Illinois State Historical Society* 33 (1931): 35–59.

24 *Chicago Tribune*, June 25, 1896; *Washington Post*, May 31–June 5, 1896.

25 Jones, *Presidential Election of 1896*, 198; Bensel, *Passion and Preferences*, 30–31.

26 Coletta, *William Jennings Bryan*, 1:121–122.

27 Arthur Wallace Dunn, *From Harrison to Harding: A Personal Narrative, Covering a Third of a Century, 1888–1921*, 2 vols. (New York: G. P. Putnam's Sons, 1932), 1:183.

28 Jean B. Kern, "The Political Career of Horace Boies," *Iowa Journal of History* 47 (July 1949): 215–216, 234, 241. He was the only Democratic governor of Iowa between 1856 and 1932.

29 "The Progress of the World," *Review of Reviews* 14 (July 1896): 11; Silveus, "Antecedents of the Campaign of 1896," 78.

30 Henry Luther Stoddard, *As I Knew Them: Presidents and Politics from Grant to Coolidge* (New York: Harper & Bros., 1927), 275; Jones, *Presidential Election of 1896*, 179–180; Silveus, "Antecedents of the Campaign of 1896," 77.

31 *New York World*, June 30, 1896.

32 Kazin, *Godly Hero*, 53; William Vincent Byars, ed., *An American Commoner: The Life and Times of Richard Parks Bland* (Columbia, Mo.: E. W. Stephens, 1900), 296.

33 Champ Clark, *My Quarter Century of American Politics*, 2 vols. (New York: Harper & Bros., 1920), 2:66; Silveus, "Antecedents of the Campaign of 1896," 77–78; *New York Tribune*, July 7, 1896; *New York Times*, July 7, 1896. In Chicago, Bland's opponents passed around a circular saying, "If you want to see a confessional box in the White House, vote for Bland." *St. Louis Post-Dispatch*, July 9, 1896.

34 Clark, *My Quarter Century of American Politics*, 2:401–402.

35 William Jennings Bryan, *The Memoirs of William Jennings Bryan, by Himself and His Wife Mary Baird Bryan* (Philadelphia: United Publishers of America, 1925), 102. Also, Bryan to Charles S. Thomas, April 16, 1896, Thomas to Bryan, April 18, 1896, Josephus Daniels to Bryan, June 1, 1895, Bryan Papers; Kazin, *Godly Hero*, 47–48; William Allen White, *Masks in a Pageant* (New York: Macmillan, 1930), 243; James A. Barnes, "The Gold-Standard Democrats and the Party Conflict," *Mississippi Valley Historical Review* 17 (December 1930): 433.

36 Rosser, *Crusading Commoner*, 34–35.

37 For Bryan's lack of standing in the polls, see, e.g., *Review of Reviews* 14 (July 1896): 11; *New York Tribune*, July 4–5, 1896; *Chicago Tribune*, July 5, 1896; *Chicago Chronicle*, July 5, 1896; *Raleigh (N.C.) Caucasian*, July 9, 1896.

38 Entry for July 7, 1896, in Charles G. Dawes, *A Journal of the McKinley Years* (Chicago: Lakeside Press, 1950), 88–89.

39 Kazin, *Godly Hero*, 53.

40 Coletta, *William Jennings Bryan*, 1:120.

41 *New York Times*, June 19, 1896; Bensel, *Passion and Preferences*, 15.

42 Whitney to Russell, June 18, 1896, William E. Russell Papers, Harvard University, Cambridge, Mass.; *New York World*, June 13, 18, 1896.

43 *Canton Repository*, July 2, 1896; *New York World*, July 2, 1896.

44 Nevins, *Grover Cleveland*, 700.

45 Koenig, *Bryan*, 174. The two-thirds rule, long a staple of Democratic party convention politics, required that a candidate for president or vice-president receive at least two-thirds of the votes to win the nomination. Democrats abolished the rule in 1936.

46 Dunn, *From Harrison to Harding*, 1:150.

47 Kazin, *Godly Hero*, 56; Coletta, *William Jennings Bryan*, 1:127; *Nation* 63 (July 16, 1896): 39.

48 *New York Times*, July 4, 1896; *Chicago Chronicle*, July 3, 1896.

49 Thomas V. Cator to E. M. Wardell, July 9, 1896, Thomas V. Cator Papers, Stanford University, Stanford, Calif.; *New York World*, July 12, 1896; *New York Times*, July 4–5, 1896; *New York Tribune*, July 4–5, 1896; Jones, *Presidential Election of 1896*, 218.

50 Bryan, *First Battle*, 188; *New York Tribune*, July 7, 1896.

51 *Official Proceedings of the Democratic National Convention* (Logansport, Ind.: Wilson, Humphries, 1896), 191–196.

52 Ibid.; entry for July 9, 1896, Charles S. Hamlin Diary, Charles S. Hamlin Papers, Manuscript Division, Library of Congress, Washington, D.C.; *New Orleans Daily Picayune*, July 11, 1896; "Memorandum of a Meeting of Sound Money Men," July 7, 1896, William C. Whitney Papers, Manuscript Division, Library of Congress, Washington, D.C.

53 Bryan, *First Battle*, 614–615.

54 Rosser, *Crusading Commoner*, 34.

55 Bryan, *Memoirs of William Jennings Bryan*, 110–111.

56 Silveus, "Antecedents of the Campaign of 1896," 218.

57 Ibid., 193; *New York World*, July 7, 1896.

58 Rosser, *Crusading Commoner*, 37–38.

59 Francis E. Leupp, "The Dark Horse Convention," *Outlook* 101 (June 8, 1912): 298–299.

60 Dunn, *From Harrison to Harding*, 1:168–169; *Official Proceedings of the Democratic National Convention*, 199; Coletta, *William Jennings Bryan*, 1:135.

61 Bryan, *Memoirs of William Jennings Bryan*, 112; Morris Robert Werner, *Bryan* (New York: Harcourt, Brace, 1929), 68; Kazin, *Godly Hero*, 58.

62 *Official Proceedings of the Democratic National Convention*, 218; Bensel, *Passion and Preferences*, 218; Jones, *Presidential Election of 1896*, 226.

63 Jones, *Presidential Election of 1896*, 227.

64 Paxton Hibben, *The Peerless Leader, William Jennings Bryan* (New York: Farrar and Rinehart, 1929), 184.

65 Bryan, *Memoirs of William Jennings Bryan*, 112–113.

66 A. B. Macdonald, "Bryan, the Darkest of All Dark Horses," *Dallas Morning News*, June 24, 1928, in Rosser, *Crusading Commoner*, 40; Bryan, *Memoirs of William Jennings Bryan*, 112.

67 Josephus Daniels, *Editor in Politics* (Chapel Hill: University of North Carolina Press, 1941), 163.

68 Edgar Lee Masters, "The Christian Statesman," *American Mercury* 3 (December 1924): 387.

69 *New York World*, July 10, 1896, in Matthew Josephson, *The Politicos, 1865–1896* (New York: Harcourt, Brace, 1938), 674; Stoddard, *As I Knew Them*, 273.

70 Bryan, *Memoirs of William Jennings Bryan*, 103; Koenig, *Bryan*, 199.

71 Kazin, *Godly Hero*, 59; Bryan, *First Battle*, 615.

72 Bensel, *Passion and Preferences*, 226–227.

73 Bryan, *Memoirs of William Jennings Bryan*, 104; Coletta, *William Jennings Bryan*, 1:121.

74 Rosser, *Crusading Commoner*, 48–49.

75 Bryan, *First Battle*, 199–206.

76 Bryan, *Memoirs of William Jennings Bryan*, 114–116.

77 *New York Tribune*, July 10, 1896; Willis J. Abbot, *Watching the World Go By* (Boston: Little, Brown, 1933), 165; Clarence Darrow, *The Story of My Life* (New York: Charles Scribner's Sons, 1932), 91–92; *Chicago Chronicle*, July 10, 1896; *Atlanta Constitution*, July 10, 1896, in Bensel, *Passion and Preferences*, 1; *Review of Reviews* 14 (August 1896): 136.

78 *New York Times*, July 10, 1896.

79 Paul W. Glad, *McKinley, Bryan, and the People* (Philadelphia: J. B. Lippincott, 1964), 139.

80 Coletta, *William Jennings Bryan*, 1:143.

81 *New York Herald*, July 10, 1896.

82 Various delegations had nominated Bland, Boies, Blackburn, Bryan, John R. McLane of Ohio, Robert E. Pattison of Pennsylvania, Claude Matthews of Indiana, and Sylvester Pennoyer of Oregon. The delegations from New York, Massachusetts, and Wisconsin refused to name anyone at all on a free silver platform.

83 Coletta, *William Jennings Bryan*, 1:144.

84 Bryan, *First Battle*, 214; Coletta, *William Jennings Bryan*, 1:145; Bensel, *Passion and Preferences*, 101. These early votes may seem unexpected in light of the enthusiasm for Bryan's speech, but a large number of delegates, it should be remembered, were pledged by their state conventions to vote for a particular candidate. They could switch votes only if the candidate himself released them or if he had clearly begun to lose any chance at the nomination.

85 Bryan, *First Battle*, 217; *New York Times*, July 11, 1896.

86 Hibben, *Peerless Leader*, 187; Bensel, *Passion and Preferences*, 296; J. Rogers

Hollingsworth, *The Whirligig of Politics: The Democracy of Cleveland and Bryan* (Chicago: University of Chicago Press, 1963), 60–61; Jones, *Presidential Election of 1896*, 235. The unit rule dictated that the majority of the delegation could cast the vote of the entire delegation. It was finally abolished by the 1968 Democratic National Convention.

87 *New York Times*, July 11, 1896.
88 Bryan, *First Battle*, 218–219; *New York Times*, July 11, 1896; *New York Tribune*, July 10, 1896; Hollingsworth, *Whirligig of Politics*, 61–62.
89 *New York Times*, July 11, 1896.
90 *New York World*, July 11, 1896; "The Chicago Nominee," *Nation* 63 (July 16, 1896): 42.
91 *New York Times*, July 11, 1896.
92 Rosser, *Crusading Commoner*, 56–57.
93 *New York Times*, July 11, 1896; Abbot, *Watching the World Go By*, 162–165.
94 *Chicago Tribune*, July 11, 1896.
95 Harold Underwood Faulkner, *Politics, Reform and Expansion, 1890–1900* (New York: Harper, 1959), 197.
96 *St. Louis Post-Dispatch*, July 11, 1896.
97 Bryan, *First Battle*, 229.
98 Glad, *McKinley, Bryan, and the People*, 141.
99 *Raleigh (N.C.) Caucasian*, August 27, 1896; Glad, *McKinley, Bryan, and the People*, 140–141.
100 Bryan, *Memoirs of William Jennings Bryan*, 107; Koenig, *Bryan*, 211; Rosser, *Crusading Commoner*, 57–58.
101 Clark, *My Quarter Century of American Politics*, 2:403. Also, A. K. McClure, *Colonel Alexander K. McClure's Recollections of Half a Century* (Salem, Mass.: Salem Press, 1902), 427.
102 Edgar Lee Masters, *Across Spoon River: An Autobiography* (New York: Farrar and Rinehart, 1936), 209.
103 Daniels, *Editor in Politics*, 165. For Bryan's previous use of his themes, see *Nation* 63 (July 16, 1896): 40.
104 White, *Masks in a Pageant*, 249–250; William Allen White, *The Autobiography of William Allen White* (New York: Macmillan, 1946), 278.

CHAPTER 5 BRYAN TAKES THE STUMP

1 Richard Jensen, *The Winning of the Midwest: Social and Political Conflict, 1888–1896* (Chicago: University of Chicago Press, 1971), 275.
2 William Jennings Bryan, *The First Battle: A Story of the Campaign of 1896* (Chicago: W. B. Conkey, 1896), 450. For a similar opinion, see *Review of Reviews* 14 (August 1896): 132.
3 Dixon Wecter, *The Hero in America: A Chronicle of Hero-Worship* (New York: Charles Scribner's Sons, 1941), 368–371; William M. Curtin, ed., *The World and the Parish: Willa Cather's Articles and Reviews, 1893–1902*, 2 vols. (Lincoln: University of Nebraska Press, 1970), 2:788.

4   Debs to Bryan, July 27, 1896, in J. Robert Constantine, ed., *Letters of Eugene V. Debs*, 2 vols. (Urbana: University of Illinois Press, 1990), 1:120.

5   Wall to William F. Vilas, August 13, 1896, William F. Vilas Papers, Wisconsin State Historical Society, Madison, in Jensen, *Winning of the Midwest*, 271.

6   W. G. Comerford and wife et al., to Bryan, November 2, 1896, William Jennings Bryan Papers, Manuscript Division, Library of Congress, Washington, D.C., in Michael Kazin, *A Godly Hero: The Life of William Jennings Bryan* (New York: Knopf, 2006), xiii.

7   Bryan, *First Battle*, 299.

8   Ibid., 300; *New York World*, August 8, 1896.

9   Bryan, *First Battle*, 300–306.

10 William Vincent Byars, ed., *An American Commoner: The Life and Times of Richard Parks Bland* (Columbia, Mo.: E. W. Stephens, 1900), 298; Bryan, *First Battle*, 306.

11 Bryan, *First Battle*, 307–312; *New York Tribune*, August 13, 1896.

12 Bryan, *First Battle*, 314; *New York World*, August 12–13, 1896. For an analysis of the speech, see William D. Harpine, *From the Front Porch to the Front Page: McKinley and Bryan in the 1896 Presidential Campaign* (College Station: Texas A&M University Press, 2005), 69–89.

13 Bryan, *First Battle*, 316; *Official Proceedings of the Democratic National Convention* (Logansport, Ind.: Wilson, Humphries, 1896), 401; *Review of Reviews* 14 (September 1896): 261–262.

14 Bryan, *First Battle*, 319–320; *Review of Reviews* 14 (September 1896): 261–262.

15 *New York World*, August 13, 1896; Bryan, *First Battle*, 314–315; *Nation* 63 (August 20, 1896): 131–134; *New York Tribune*, August 14, 1896.

16 *Review of Reviews* 14 (August 1896): 141–142; *Chicago Chronicle*, July 11, 1896; Alexander K. McClure, *Our Presidents and How We Make Them* (New York: Harper & Bros., 1900), 393; Thomas Edward Felt, "Rise of Mark Hanna" (Ph.D. diss., Michigan State University, 1961), 341–342.

17 Paul W. Glad, *McKinley, Bryan, and the People* (Philadelphia: J. B. Lippincott, 1964), 171.

18 Bryan, *First Battle*, 292; statement of Senator J. K. Jones, Democratic national chairman, in Matthew Josephson, *The Politicos, 1865–1896* (New York: Harcourt, Brace, 1938), 664; Paolo E. Coletta, *William Jennings Bryan*, vol. 1, *Political Evangelist, 1860–1908* (Lincoln: University of Nebraska Press, 1964), 1:198n. Such charges die hard: e.g., Darcy G. Richardson, *Others: Third Parties during the Populist Period*, 2 vols. (n.p.: iUniverse, 2007), 2:241.

19 Teller to R. F. Pettigrew, September 3, 1896, Henry M. Teller Papers, State Historical Society of Colorado, Denver, in James E. Wright, *The Politics of Populism: Dissent in Colorado* (New Haven, Conn.: Yale University Press, 1974), 212.

20 Robert W. Cherny, *A Righteous Cause: The Life of William Jennings Bryan* (Norman: University of Oklahoma Press, 1994), 65.

21   Ibid., 66.

22   *Nation* 63 (August 6, 1896): 96.

23   R. Hal Williams, "'Dry Bones and Dead Language': The Democratic Party," in H. Wayne Morgan, ed., *The Gilded Age: Revised and Enlarged Edition* (Syracuse, N.Y.: Syracuse University Press, 1970), 129–148.

24   For Bryan, this assumption was confirmed immediately. During his trip to New York City to give his acceptance speech, more than thirty reporters accompanied him on the train, and at each station, they handed their dispatches to waiting telegraph agents who sent them on to their newspapers: Harpine, *From the Front Porch*, 75.

25   Ibid., 22–23.

26   Jensen, *Winning of the Midwest*, 274.

27   Bryan, *First Battle*, 534; Cherny, *Righteous Cause*, 67.

28   Bryan, *First Battle*, 619.

29   Robert Werner, *Bryan* (New York: Harcourt, Brace, 1929), 96; J. C. Long, *Bryan: The Great Commoner* (New York: D. Appleton, 1928), 123–124. The gin served only for rubdowns, of course. Bryan was a teetotaler.

30   Edward G. Lowry, *Washington Close-Ups: Intimate Views of Some Public Figures* (Boston: Houghton Mifflin, 1921), 34; Curtin, *World and the Parish*, 2:784; *Omaha World-Herald*, November 4, 1896, in Coletta, *William Jennings Bryan*, 1:174; Boyce House, "Bryan the Orator," *Illinois State Historical Society Journal* 53 (Autumn 1960): 278.

31   Jensen, *Winning of the Midwest*, 275.

32   Ibid., 275–276.

33   Daniel C. Roper, *Fifty Years of Public Life: A Collaboration with Frank H. Lovette* (Durham, N.C.: Duke University Press, 1941), 87–88.

34   Harpine, *From the Front Porch*, 57–59.

35   William D. Harpine, "Bryan's 'A Cross of Gold': The Rhetoric of Polarization at the 1896 Democratic Convention," *Quarterly Journal of Speech* 87 (August 2001): 296–298.

36   Bryan, *First Battle*, 235.

37   Ibid., 350.

38   Ibid., 531.

39   Ibid., 446.

40   Harpine, *From the Front Porch*, 1.

41   Jensen, *Winning of the Midwest*, 276–277.

42   Pam Epstein, "Religion, Bryan, and the Question of Silver," http://projects .vassar.edu/1896/bryanreligion.html, accessed through Rebecca Edwards and Sarah DeFeo, 1896, http://projects.vassar.edu/1896/1896home.html, accessed on October 1, 2008.

43   H. Wayne Morgan, *William McKinley and His America* (Syracuse, N.Y.: Syracuse University Press, 1963), 275; *Review of Reviews* 14 (November 1896): 519.

44   Harpine, *From the Front Porch*, 150.

45   Jensen, *Winning of the Midwest*, 277.

46   Harpine, *From the Front Porch*, 132, 178; Coletta, *William Jennings Bryan*, 1:176.

47 Coletta, *William Jennings Bryan*, 1:179; *Chicago Tribune*, September 23, 1896; Josephus Daniels, *Editor in Politics* (Chapel Hill: University of North Carolina Press, 1941), 190–99; Bryan, *First Battle*, 494.

48 Daniels, *Editor in Politics*, 197.

49 Jones, *Presidential Election of 1896*, 332–333.

50 See maps of Bryan's stops in Bryan, *First Battle*, 385, 601.

51 Harpine, *From the Front Porch*, 141.

52 Ibid., 31. Scorned by economists at the time, Bryan's emphasis on the quantity theory of money found later support in the work of Milton Friedman of the University of Chicago, who won a Nobel Prize in Economics.

53 Coletta, *William Jennings Bryan*, 1:164.

54 Bryan, *First Battle*, 320, 379, 410–413, 422–425; Coletta, *William Jennings Bryan*, 1:169–179, 186.

55 Bryan, *First Battle*, 378; Kazin, *Godly Hero*, 45–46.

56 Bryan, *First Battle*, 522.

57 Entry for September 4, 1896, in Charles G. Dawes, *A Journal of the McKinley Years* (Chicago: Lakeside Press, 1950), 96. For predictions of a Bryan victory, see Chairman Jones's statement: *St. Louis Post-Dispatch*, November 1, 1896.

58 Hay to Adams, October 20, 1896, in James Ford Rhodes, *The McKinley and Roosevelt Administrations, 1897–1909* (New York: Macmillan, 1922), 143; Bryan, *First Battle*, 602–603.

59 Bryan, *First Battle*, 205; Robert Kelley, "Ideology and Political Culture from Jefferson to Nixon," *American Historical Review* 82 (June 1977): 541.

60 Bryan, *First Battle*, 595.

61 Coletta, *William Jennings Bryan*, 1:188.

62 Bryan, *First Battle*, 603. There was one Republican, Bryan noted, who for some reason refused to remove his hat.

63 Coletta, *William Jennings Bryan*, 1:188–189.

64 Bryan, *First Battle*, 603.

CHAPTER 6 THE ALSO-RANS: THE PEOPLE'S PARTY AND THE GOLD DEMOCRATS IN THE CAMPAIGN OF 1896

1 C. Vann Woodward, *Tom Watson: Agrarian Rebel* (New York: Macmillan, 1938), 269.

2 William Jennings Bryan, *The First Battle: A Story of the Campaign of 1896* (Chicago: W. B. Conkey, 1896), 296.

3 Robert F. Durden, "The 'Cow-Bird' Grounded: The Populist Nomination of Bryan and Tom Watson in 1896," *Mississippi Valley Historical Review* 50 (December 1960): 403.

4 Fred E. Haynes, *James Baird Weaver* (Iowa City: Iowa State Historical Society, 1919), 468–469n.

5 B. K. Collier to Thomas V. Cator, July 13, 1896, Thomas Vincent Cator Papers, Stanford University Libraries, Stanford, Calif.; Durden, "'Cow-Bird' Grounded," 397–403; *People's Party Paper*, June 26, 1896.

6 Bryan, *First Battle*, 278; Haynes, *James Baird Weaver*, 379; Paul W. Glad,

McKinley, Bryan, and the People (Philadelphia: J. B. Lippincott, 1964), 156; Woodward, *Tom Watson*, 274–275.

7   Peter H. Argersinger, *Populism and Politics: William Alfred Peffer and the People's Party* (Lexington: University Press of Kentucky, 1974), 233–234; Stanley P. Jones, *The Presidential Election of 1896* (Madison: University of Wisconsin Press, 1964), 84.

8   *Topeka Daily Capital*, July 11, 1896, in Argersinger, *Populism and Politics*, 255.

9   Lawrence Goodwyn, *Democratic Promise: The Populist Moment in America* (New York: Oxford University Press, 1976), 472; Frederick Emory Haynes, *Third Party Movements since the Civil War, with a Special Reference to Iowa: A Study in Social Politics* (Iowa City: State Historical Society of Iowa, 1916), 349. Also, Weaver to Bryan, January 31, 1895, William Jennings Bryan Papers, Manuscript Division, Library of Congress, Washington, D.C.

10 Goodwyn, *Democratic Promise*, 459–463; Argersinger, *Populism and Politics*, 236–239; Marian Silveus, "Antecedents of the Campaign of 1896" (Ph.D. diss., University of Wisconsin, 1932), 110.

11 Caro Lloyd, *Henry Demarest Lloyd, 1847–1903: A Biography*, 2 vols. (New York: G. P. Putnam's Sons, 1912), 1:259; *Topeka Advocate*, in Argersinger, *Populism and Politics*, 244; *People's Party Paper*, February 14, March 20, July 17, 1896; *New York Tribune*, January 21–22, 1896.

12 Lloyd, *Henry Demarest Lloyd*, 1:259; R. Hal Williams, *Years of Decision: American Politics in the 1890s* (New York: John Wiley & Sons, 1978), 113.

13 Argersinger, *Populism and Politics*, 242–243; *St. Louis Post-Dispatch*, July 21, 1896; Lloyd, *Henry Demarest Lloyd*, 1:262; Jones, *Presidential Election of 1896*, 259–260.

14 Teller to Patterson, July 13, 1896, Henry M. Teller Papers, State Historical Society of Colorado, Denver, in Elmer Ellis, "The Silver Republicans and the Election of 1896," *Mississippi Valley Historical Review* 18 (March 1932): 531–532; Goodwyn, *Democratic Promise*, 473. For Taubeneck's strategy, see his letter in the *New York Tribune*, July 8, 1896.

15 Woodward, *Tom Watson*, 269.

16 John D. Hicks, *The Populist Revolt: A History of the Farmer's Alliance and the People's Party* (Lincoln: University of Nebraska Press, 1961), 358; Gregg Cantrell and D. Scott Barton, "Texas Populists and the Failure of Biracial Politics," *Journal of Southern History* 55 (November 1989): 675.

17 Barton C. Shaw, *The Wool-Hat Boys: Georgia's Populist Party* (Baton Rouge: Louisiana State University Press, 1984), 143.

18 Jones, *Presidential Election of 1896*, 254–255. For Norton and Burkitt, see Darcy G. Richardson, *Others: Third Parties during the Populist Period*, 2 vols. (New York: iUniverse, 2007), 2:25–30, 170–177; for Norton's thinking, S. F. Norton, *Ten Men of Money Island, or The Primer of Finance* (Chicago: F. J. Schulte, 1891).

19 Henry D. Lloyd, "The Populists at St-Louis," *Review of Reviews* 14 (September 1896): 298–303; Woodward, *Tom Watson*, 253–254; Jones, *Presidential Election of 1896*, 251. Robert Durden, *The Climax of Populism: The Election of 1896*

(Lexington: University Press of Kentucky, 1966), offers excellent coverage of the Populists in 1896.

20 *Chicago Tribune,* July 24, 1896; *New York World,* August 6, 1896.

21 Louis W. Koenig, *Bryan: A Political Biography of William Jennings Bryan* (New York: Putnam, 1971), 213; Arthur Wallace Dunn, *From Harrison to Harding: A Personal Narrative, Covering a Third of a Century, 1888–1921,* 2 vols. (New York: G. P. Putnam's Sons, 1932), 1:188; *National Economist,* July 16, 23, 1892, in Hicks, *Populist Revolt,* 232.

22 Bryan, *First Battle,* 261; James L. Hunt, *Marion Butler and American Populism* (Chapel Hill: University of North Carolina Press, 2003), 100–102.

23 Hicks, *Populist Revolt,* 362; Bryan, *First Battle,* 266.

24 Bryan, *First Battle,* 264–270.

25 Jones, *Presidential Election of 1896,* 257–258; Bryan, *First Battle,* 271–276.

26 Jones, *Presidential Election of 1896,* 255.

27 O. Gene Clanton, *Populism: The Humane Preference in America, 1890–1900* (Boston: Twayne Publishers, 1991), 154; M. A. Courtright to Allen, July 20, 1896, Allen Papers, in Hicks, *Populist Revolt,* 362; on this and other points, Connie L. Lester, *Up from the Mudsills of Hell: The Farmers' Alliance, Populism, and Progressive Agriculture in Tennessee, 1870–1915* (Athens: University of Georgia Press, 2006), 203–207.

28 Bryan, *First Battle,* 297.

29 Jones, *Presidential Election of 1896,* 259; Durden, "'Cow-Bird' Grounded," 419, 422.

30 Woodward, *Tom Watson,* 257–258; Durden, "'Cow-Bird' Grounded," 419.

31 Shaw, *Wool-Hat Boys,* 146–147; *New York Tribune,* July 25, 1896; Woodward, *Tom Watson,* 259; Richardson, *Others,* 2:179.

32 *People's Party Paper,* July 31, 1896.

33 *New York World,* August 3, 1896.

34 Lodge to Moreton Frewen, September 14, 1896, Moreton Frewen Papers, Manuscript Division, Library of Congress, Washington, D.C.; *New York Tribune,* July 26, 1896; *Chicago Chronicle,* July 12, 20, 1896.

35 Richard Franklin Bensel, *Passion and Preferences: William Jennings Bryan and the 1896 Democratic National Convention* (Cambridge: Cambridge University Press, 2008), 118; *New York World,* July 12, 1896.

36 *Canton Repository,* July 16, 1896.

37 Cleveland to Lamont, in Robert McElroy, *Grover Cleveland: The Man and the Statesman,* 2 vols. (New York: Harper & Bros., 1923), 2:226; Cleveland to Hoke Smith, July 15, 1896, in Allan Nevins, ed., *Letters of Grover Cleveland* (Boston: Houghton Mifflin, 1933), 447. Italics in the original.

38 Allan Nevins, *Grover Cleveland: A Study in Courage* (New York: Dodd, Mead, 1932), 498; Bryan, *First Battle,* 219; Bensel, *Passion and Preferences,* 281.

39 Smith to Cleveland, July 30, August 5 and 6, 1896, Cleveland to Smith, August 4, 1896, Grover Cleveland Papers, Manuscript Division, Library of Congress, Washington, D.C.; John R. Lambert, *Arthur Pue Gorman* (Baton Rouge: Louisiana State University Press, 1953), 253–256.

40   *New York Times*, July 12, 1896. As a Tammany leader told a *New York Tribune* reporter: "I believe in standing by the nominee of the Convention and standing by the platform. If I cannot talk in favor of the free coinage of silver, I can about something else which the platform supports. I am a Democrat, and intend to remain a Democrat." *New York Tribune*, July 9, 1896.

41   Richard Jensen, *The Winning of the Midwest: Social and Political Conflict, 1888–1896* (Chicago: University of Chicago Press, 1971), 299–300.

42   Wilson to W. C. P. Breckinridge, July 28, 1896, W. C. P. Breckinridge Papers, Manuscript Division, Library of Congress, Washington, D.C.; *Chicago Times-Herald*, July 10, 1896.

43   The New York City Democrat Bourke Cochran, in *Public Opinion: A Comprehensive Summary of the Press throughout the World on All Important Current Topics* 21 (July–December 1896): 200.

44   Olney to Cleveland, July 11, 1896, Cleveland Papers.

45   Bensel, *Passion and Preferences*, 117.

46   *New York Times*, September 4, 1896.

47   D. B. Griffin to Cleveland, September 2, 1896, Cleveland to Griffin, September 2, 1896, in Nevins, *Letters of Grover Cleveland*, 455–456; entry for July 28, 1896, Wilson Diary, William L. Wilson, *The Cabinet Diary of William L. Wilson: 1896–1897* (Chapel Hill: University of North Carolina Press, 1957), 126.

48   James A. Barnes, "The Gold-Standard Democrats and the Party Conflict," *Mississippi Valley Historical Review* 17 (December 1930): 438; *Boston Globe*, September 5, 1896, in Richardson, *Others*, 2:195.

49   Cleveland to William F. Vilas, September 5, 1896, William F. Vilas Papers, State Historical Society of Wisconsin, Madison, in Nevins, *Grover Cleveland*, 707; Arthur Krock, *The Editorials of Henry Watterson* (New York: George H. Doran, 1957), 75–87.

50   Cleveland to Vilas, September 5, 1896, Cleveland Papers; *Chicago Tribune*, August 7–8, September 3–4, 1896; "Proceedings of the Conference of the National Committee of the Sound Money Democracy," memorandum, William D. Bynum Papers, Manuscript Division, Library of Congress, Washington, D.C.; *Louisville Courier-Journal*, July 10, 1896; "A Notable Bolt of Newspapers," *Review of Reviews* 14 (August 1896): 142.

51   John M. Palmer, *Personal Recollections of John M. Palmer: The Story of an Earnest Life* (Cincinnati, Ohio: Robert Clarke, 1906), 617–619; George T. Palmer, *A Conscientious Turncoat: The Story of John M. Palmer, 1817–1900* (New Haven, Conn.: Yale University Press, 1941), 275–280; Paolo E. Coletta, *William Jennings Bryan*, vol. 1, *Political Evangelist, 1860–1908* (Lincoln: University of Nebraska Press, 1964), 1:192.

52   Silveus, "Antecedents of the Campaign of 1896," 116–117; Richardson, *Others*, 2:214.

53   Bryan, *First Battle*, 390–391. Bitterly hostile, the Bryan and Palmer camps were soon at war. Gold Democrats called the Bryanites the "Popocratic party" or the "Bryanarchy," and Bryan Democrats, in turn, labeled the Gold Democrats "The Republican Aid Society," "Boltocrats," "Cuckoos," "Yellowbellies," and

"Hannarchists." Coletta, *William Jennings Bryan* 1:171; Charles M. Rosser, *The Crusading Commoner: A Close-Up of William Jennings Bryan and His Times* (Dallas, Tex.: Mathis, Van Nort, 1937), 63.

54 Bryan, *First Battle*, 361.

55 *Nation* 63 (November 5, 1896): 337.

56 Barnes, "Gold-Standard Democrats," 441.

57 "The Populist campaign is somewhat of a guerrilla affair this year," the *Review of Reviews* commented, "and its headquarters are hard to find. Nominally they are at Washington." *Review of Reviews* 14 (September 1896): 267.

58 James L. Hunt, *Marion Butler and American Populism* (Chapel Hill: University of North Carolina Press, 2003), 112–118; Jones, *Presidential Election of 1896*, 320.

59 Peter H. Argersinger, "'A Place on the Ballot': Fusion Politics and Antifusion Laws," *American Historical Review* 85 (April 1980): 298–306; Roger L. Hart, *Redeemers, Bourbons & Populists: Tennessee, 1870–1896* (Baton Rouge: Louisiana State University Press, 1975), 220. For a detailed examination of the efforts at fusion, see Durden, *Climax of Populism*. For a recent account of Populist actions in North Carolina, see James M. Beeby, *Revolt of the Tarheels: The North Carolina Populist Movement, 1890–1901* (Oxford: University Press of Mississippi, 2008).

60 Goodwyn, *Democratic Promise*, 505, 509–510; Woodward, *Tom Watson*, 270.

61 *Dallas Morning News*, September 8, 1896, in Woodward, *Tom Watson*, 276; Goodwyn, *Democratic Promise*, 509–510. In a generous gesture, Sewall offered to withdraw from the ticket, but Bryan turned him down. Bryan wound up ignoring Watson throughout the campaign, one of the harshest insults ever paid to the vice-presidential candidate of a major party.

62 *Dallas Morning News*, September 8, 1896, in Woodward, *Tom Watson*, 276.

63 *Kansas City Star*, September 10, 1896, in O. Gene Clanton, *Kansas Populism: Ideas and Men* (Lawrence: University Press of Kansas, 1969), 195. The mention of Davis probably refers to John Davis, a prominent Populist politician in Kansas.

64 Richardson, *Others*, 2:235.

65 Woodward, *Tom Watson*, 282; Robert W. Cherny, *A Righteous Cause: The Life of William Jennings Bryan* (New York: Little, Brown, 1985), 67.

66 Durden, *Climax of Populism*, 162–163.

67 Rebecca Brooks Edwards, *Angels in the Machinery: Gender in American Party Politics from the Civil War to the Progressive Era* (New York: Oxford University Press, 1997), 142.

68 Walter T. K. Nugent, *The Tolerant Populists: Kansas, Populism and Nativism* (Chicago: University of Chicago Press, 1963), 204; Goodwyn, *Democratic Promise*, 557–558.

CHAPTER 7 THE FRONT PORCH CAMPAIGN: MCKINLEY AND THE REPUBLICANS IN THE 1896 ELECTION

1 Joseph P. Smith, ed., *McKinley's Speeches in September* (Canton, Ohio: Repository Press, 1896), 172.

2   James Ford Rhodes, *History of the United States from the Compromise of 1850,* 10 vols. (New York: Macmillan, 1893–1925), 9:18–19; Paul W. Glad, *McKinley, Bryan, and the People* (Philadelphia: J. B. Lippincott, 1964), 167. For an interview with Hanna about his plans for the campaign, see *Chicago Tribune,* June 20, 1896; for McKinley's, see *New York Tribune,* July 6, 1896. McKinley's reaction to Bryan's nomination is in *Canton Repository,* July 12, 1896.

3   Eugene Hale to William E. Chandler, July 16, 1896, William E. Chandler Papers, New Hampshire Historical Society, Concord.

4   H. G. McMillan to J. S. Clarkson, September 5, 1896, James S. Clarkson Papers, Iowa State Historical Society, Des Moines; G. B. Pray to Dodge, August 12, 1896, Grenville M. Dodge Papers, Iowa State Historical Society, Des Moines, in Robert D. Marcus, *Grand Old Party: Political Structure in the Gilded Age, 1880–1896* (New York: Oxford University Press, 1971), 235.

5   Roosevelt to "Darling Bye," July 26, 1896, Roosevelt to "Darling Bye," September 13, 1896, *Letters from Theodore Roosevelt to Anna Roosevelt Cowles, 1870–1918* (New York: Charles Scribner's Sons, 1924), 189, 192; *Nation* 63 (July 9, 1896): 19, 22; John P. Irish to George F. Parker, February 1, 1897, "Letters Written by John P. Irish to George F. Parker," *Iowa Journal of History and Politics* 31 (July 1933): 450; Stanley L. Jones, *The Presidential Election of 1896* (Madison: University of Wisconsin Press, 1964), 295–296.

6   Joseph Gilpin Pyle, *The Life of James J. Hill,* 2 vols. (New York: Doubleday, Page, 1917), 1:496–497. Italics in the original.

7   H. Wayne Morgan, "William McKinley," in Phillip Weeks, *Buckeye Presidents: Ohioans in the White House* (Kent, Ohio: Kent State University Press, 2003), 192.

8   Col. T. Bentley Mott, *Myron T. Herrick: Friend of France, an Autobiographical Biography* (Garden City, N.Y.: Doubleday, Doran, 1929), 64; Bascom N. Timmons, *Portrait of an American: Charles G. Dawes* (New York: Henry Holt, 1953), 56. Italics in the original.

9   Charles W. Calhoun, *Benjamin Harrison* (New York: Time Books, 2005), 52–53.

10 McKinley particularly feared repeating the experience of his Republican friend James G. Blaine, who lost the presidential election of 1884, many thought, because of an unfortunate last-minute remark by a minister at a rally. Also, Champ Clark, *My Quarter Century of American Politics,* 2 vols. (New York: Harper & Bros., 1920), 1:427–428.

11 Morrow interview with Charles Dick, Mark Hanna Papers, Manuscript Division, Library of Congress, Washington, D.C.

12 Reed to Platt, September 20, 1896, Thomas C. Platt Papers, Manuscript Division, Library of Congress, Washington, D.C.; Margaret Leech, *In the Days of McKinley* (New York: Harper, 1959), 88; Oscar Ameringer, *If You Don't Weaken: The Autobiography of Oscar Ameringer,* rev. ed. (Norman: University of Oklahoma Press, 1983), 153–155.

13 *Chicago Evening Post,* September 11, 1896; William D. Harpine, "'We Want Yer, McKinley': Epideictic Rhetoric in Songs from the 1896 Presidential Campaign," *Rhetoric Society Quarterly* 34, no. 1 (Winter 2004): 74; Smith, *McKinley's Speeches in September,* 177–178.

14 Ameringer, *If You Don't Weaken*, 153–155.

15 Leech, *In the Days of McKinley*, 88; Richard Jensen, *The Winning of the Midwest: Social and Political Conflict, 1888–1896* (Chicago: University of Chicago Press, 1971), 287.

16 *Review of Reviews* 14 (October 1896): 397.

17 Jensen, *Winning of the Midwest*, 2.

18 John E. Pixton Jr., "Charles G. Dawes and the McKinley Campaign," *Journal of the Illinois Historical Society* 48 (Autumn 1955): 283–306; McKinley to Dawes, April 30, 1896, in Charles G. Dawes, *A Journal of the McKinley Years* (Chicago: Lakeside Press, 1950), 81. Dawes went on after 1896 to a distinguished career that included service as vice-president from 1925 to 1929 and a Nobel Peace Prize in 1925. He was also a self-taught pianist and composer whose 1911 instrumental composition, recorded by Tommy Edwards in 1958, became a hit song, "It's All in the Game."

19 Entries for July 20, July 25, July 29, August 2, 1896, in Dawes, *Journal of the McKinley Years*, 90–93; Jones, *Presidential Election of 1896*, 278–281.

20 Jones, *Presidential Election of 1896*, 277–278.

21 *Cleveland Leader*, July 17, 1896, in H. Wayne Morgan, *William McKinley and His America* (Syracuse, N.Y.: Syracuse University Press, 1963), 224; Clarkson to H. G. McMillan, October 5, 1896, Clarkson Papers.

22 Dawes to McKinley, August 1, 1896, entry for August 2, 1896, in Dawes, *Journal of the McKinley Years*, 92. Also, entries for August 24 and August 28, 1896, ibid., 95–96.

23 Dawes to Hanna, December 19, 1896, Charles G. Dawes Papers, Northwestern University, in Thomas Edward Felt, "The Rise of Mark Hanna" (Ph.D. diss., Michigan State University, 1960), 348. On November 21, 1896, Dawes reported total expenditures in the campaign of $3,562,325.59: Dawes, *Journal of the McKinley Years*, 106.

24 Ron Chernow, *Titan: The Life of John D. Rockefeller* (New York: Random House, 1998), 388; Robert W. Cherny, *A Righteous Cause: The Life of William Jennings Bryan* (Boston: Little, Brown, 1985), 65.

25 Marcus, *Grand Old Party*, 248; John A. McCall, "Free Coinage and Life-Insurance Companies," *Forum* 22 (October 1896): 136–141. The president of a Philadelphia bank contributed $25,000 to the McKinley campaign, saying that he wanted to protect the funds of its depositors. "During the ten years I have been president of this institution, we have never before contributed a cent to politics, but the present crisis we believe to be as important as the war." Jones, *Presidential Election of 1896*, 282.

26 The Democrats in 1892, in key states such as Illinois, had pioneered the "merchandizing" style but not to the extent of the Republicans in 1896: Jensen, *Winning of the Midwest*, 154–177. Benjamin Harrison had used a smaller and effective version of a Front Porch Campaign in 1888: Charles W. Calhoun, *Minority Victory: Gilded Age Politics and the Front Porch Campaign of 1888* (Lawrence: University Press of Kansas, 2008), 132–134.

27 Jensen, *Winning of the Midwest*, 165, 173; Richard Jensen, "Armies, Admen,

and Crusaders," *History Teacher* 2, no. 2 (January 1969): 43; Michael McGerr, *The Decline of Popular Politics* (New York: Oxford University Press, 1986), 69–106.

28 Jensen, *Winning of the Midwest*, 174; McGerr, *Decline of Popular Politics*, 147.

29 McGerr, *Decline of Popular Politics*, 151.

30 Smith, *McKinley's Speeches in September*, 172.

31 *Canton Repository*, August 20, 1896.

32 W. B. Shaw, "Methods and Tactics of the Campaign," *Review of Reviews* 14 (November 1896): 550–559.

33 Jensen, *Winning of the Midwest*, 287–289; *New York Times*, October 4, 1896.

34 Herbert Croly, *Marcus Alonzo Hanna: His Life and Work* (New York: Macmillan, 1912), 218; Felt, "Rise of Mark Hanna," 341.

35 Lawrence Goodwyn, *Democratic Promise: The Populist Moment in America* (New York: Oxford University Press, 1976), 528–529; entry for November 22, 1896, in Dawes, *Journal of the McKinley Years*, 106; Henry Luther Stoddard, *As I Knew Them: Presidents and Politics from Grant to Coolidge* (New York: Harper & Bros., 1927), 241–242; Mary Rulkotter Dearing, *Veterans in Politics: The Story of the GAR* (Baton Rouge: Louisiana State University Press, 1952), 460; Frederick W. Holls to Hanna, June 27, 1896, Frederick W. Holls Papers, Columbia University, New York.

36 Charles S. Olcott, *The Life of William McKinley*, 2 vols. (Boston: Houghton Mifflin, 1916), 1:321; Julius Whitney to William C. Beer, July 18, 1896, William C. Beer Papers, Yale University Library, New Haven, Conn.

37 Leech, *In the Days of McKinley*, 90.

38 *Official Proceedings of the Eleventh Republican National Convention* (n.p.: C. W. Johnson, 1896), 151–159.

39 *Canton Repository*, August 2, 1896.

40 *Canton Repository*, August 20, 27, 1896. Also, McKinley to John N. Thurston, August 26, 1896, William McKinley Papers, Manuscript Division, Library of Congress, Washington, D.C.

41 *Official Proceedings of the Eleventh Republican National Convention*, 154.

42 Jensen, *Winning of the Midwest*, 291–292.

43 *Canton Repository*, September 20, 1896.

44 Joseph P. Smith, *McKinley, the People's Choice* (Canton, Ohio: Repository Press, 1896), 38.

45 Rosewell Miller to Lamont, September 21, 1896, Daniel S. Lamont Papers, Manuscript Division, Library of Congress, Washington, D.C.; Hay to Reid, September 23, 1896, Whitelaw Reid Papers, Manuscript Division, Library of Congress, Washington, D.C.; *Nation* 63 (August 13, 1896): 113.

46 McKinley to Wilbur F. Wakeman, August 7, 1896, McKinley Papers. Also, McKinley to Charles A. Boutelle, August 1, 1896, McKinley to Thomas N. Haskell, August 5, 1896, McKinley to L. D. Apsley, August 6, 1896, McKinley Papers.

47 *Review of Reviews* 14 (October 1896): 383–388; Paolo E. Coletta, *William Jennings Bryan*, vol. 1, *Political Evangelist, 1860–1908* (Lincoln: University of Nebraska

Press, 1964), 1:173; *Nation* 63 (September 10, 1896): 185, and (September 17, 1896): 203.

48 *Chicago Tribune*, October 3, 1896, in Gilbert C. Fite, "Republican Strategy and the Farm Vote in the Presidential Campaign of 1896," *American Historical Review* 65, no. 4 (July 1960): 797; *Review of Reviews* 14 (November 1896): 518; *Nation* 63 (October 22, 1896): 302.

49 *Orange Judd Farmer*, October 24, 1896, in Fite, "Republican Strategy and the Farm Vote," 800.

50 Untitled speech, 1896, Thomas Brackett Reed Papers, George J. Mitchell Department of Special Collections and Archives, Bowdoin College Library, Brunswick, Maine.

51 Thomas Richard Ross, *Jonathan Prentiss Dolliver: A Study in Political Integrity and Independence* (Iowa City: State Historical Society of Iowa, 1960), 128; Claudius O. Johnson, "The Story of Silver Politics in Idaho, 1892–1902," *Pacific Northwest Quarterly* 33 (July 1942): 286–288.

52 Hanna to Henry Adler, October 28, 1896, in Felt, "Rise of Mark Hanna," 361; Hanna to Harrison, October 23, 1896, Benjamin Harrison Papers, Manuscript Division, Library of Congress, Washington, D.C.

53 Coletta, *William Jennings Bryan*, 1:188.

54 *New York Tribune*, November 1, 1896; *New York Times*, November 1, 1896; *San Francisco Chronicle*, November 1, 1896; *Chicago Tribune*, November 1, 1896; *New York World*, November 1, 1896; Jensen, *Winning of the Midwest*, 290–291.

55 *New York Tribune*, November 1, 1896; *New York Times*, November 1, 1896.

56 Entry for October 1, 1896, in Dawes, *Journal of the McKinley Years*, 100.

57 Ibid; Smith, *McKinley, the People's Choice*, 38.

58 Entry for November 2, 1896, in Dawes, *Journal of the McKinley Years*, 104.

CHAPTER 8 "AN EXCITEMENT THAT WAS ALMOST TOO INTENSE FOR LIFE": ELECTION DAY, 1896

1 Diary of John A. Sanborn, Nebraska Historical Society, Lincoln, in Gilbert C. Fite, "Republican Strategy and the Farm Vote in the Presidential Campaign of 1896," *American Historical Review* 65 (July 1960): 805.

2 William Jennings Bryan, *The First Battle: A Story of the Campaign of 1896* (Chicago: W. B. Conkey, 1896), 603–604; Paolo E. Coletta, *William Jennings Bryan*, vol. 1, *Political Evangelist, 1860–1908* (Lincoln: University of Nebraska Press, 1964), 1:189; *New York World*, November 4, 1896.

3 *New York World*, November 4, 1896; *Canton Repository*, November 4, 1896.

4 G. W. Steevens, *Land of the Dollar* (Edinburgh: W. Blackwood, 1897), 274–295.

5 Sanborn Diary, in Fite, "Republican Strategy and the Farm Vote," 805.

6 *Chicago Tribune*, November 4, 1896.

7 James A. Barnes, "The Gold-Standard Democrats and the Party Conflict," *Mississippi Valley Historical Review* 17 (December 1930): 445–446. Bryan did win one electoral vote in both California and Kentucky.

8 Stanley L. Jones, *The Presidential Election of 1896* (Madison: University of Wisconsin Press, 1964), 332–350; Barnes, "Gold-Standard Democrats and the Party Conflict," 445–446; Lee Benson, "Research Problems in American Political Historiography," in Mirra Komarovsky, ed., *Common Frontiers of the Social Sciences* (Glencoe, Ill.: Free Press, 1957), 156–171.

9 *New York Times*, November 6, 1896; *New York Tribune*, November 6, 1896; *St. Louis Post-Dispatch*, November 6, 1896; William Jennings Bryan, *The Memoirs of William Jennings Bryan, by Himself and His Wife Mary Baird Bryan* (Philadelphia: United Publishers of America, 1925), 199–203; Coletta, *William Jennings Bryan*, 1:189–190.

10 Bryan, *First Battle*, 617–168; Thomas Edward Felt, "The Rise of Mark Hanna" (Ph.D. diss., Michigan State University, 1960), 358; LeRoy Ashby, *William Jennings Bryan: Champion of Democracy* (Boston: Twayne Publishers, 1987), 68.

11 Beer to Mrs. Beer, October 24, 1896, Henry W. Seney to W. C. Beer, October 29, 1896, Beer Family Papers, Yale University, New Haven, Conn.; William A. Dunning, "Record of Political Events," *Political Science Quarterly* 11 (December 1896): 766.

12 *Canton Repository*, October 22, 1896.

13 *Canton Repository*, October 25, 1896.

14 Richard Jensen, *The Winning of the Midwest: Social and Political Conflict, 1888–1896* (Chicago: University of Chicago Press, 1971), 49–57.

15 Gilbert C. Fite, "Election of 1896," in Arthur M. Schlesinger Jr., ed., *History of American Presidential Elections, 1789–1968*, 4 vols. (New York: Facts on File, 1971), 2:1822.

16 Jensen, *Winning of the Midwest*, 57; Geoffrey Blodgett, *The Gentle Reformers: Massachusetts Democrats in the Cleveland Era* (Boston: Harvard University Press, 1966), 220–240; Gilbert C. Fite, "Republican Strategy and the Farm Vote in the Presidential Campaign of 1896," *American Historical Review* 65 (July 1960): 787–806; *New York World*, November 4, 1896.

17 V. O. Key Jr., "A Theory of Critical Elections," *Journal of Politics* 17 (February 1955): 15.

18 Weaver to Bryan, November 7, 1896, William Jennings Bryan Papers, Manuscript Division, Library of Congress, Washington, D.C.; Edgar Eugene Robinson, *The Presidential Vote, 1896–1932* (Stanford, Calif.: Stanford University Press, 1934), 192–200. On farm results in other states, see *Nation* 63 (November 12, 1896): 356–358.

19 *Chicago Tribune*, November 4, 1896; Robinson, *Presidential Vote*, 200–208, 260–268; Fite, "Republican Strategy and the Farm Vote," 803–804.

20 Samuel T. McSeveney, *The Politics of Depression: Political Behavior in the Northeast, 1893–1896* (New York: Oxford University Press, 1972), 188–221; Paul Kleppner, *The Cross of Culture: A Social Analysis of Midwestern Politics, 1850–1900* (New York: Free Press, 1970), 316–368.

21 See, among other sources, Robert D. Marcus, *Grand Old Party: Political Structure in the Gilded Age, 1880–1896* (New York: Oxford University Press, 1971), 246–250, 254; Michael Rogin, "California Populism and the 'System of

1896,'" *Western Political Quarterly* 22 (March 1969): 179–196; Carl N. Degler, "American Political Parties and the Rise of the City: An Interpretation," *Journal of American History* 51 (June 1964): 41–49; H. Wayne Morgan, *From Hayes to McKinley: National Party Politics, 1877–1896* (Syracuse, N.Y.: Syracuse University Press), 524–527. David R. Mayhew, in *Electoral Realignments: A Critique of an American Genre* (New Haven, Conn.: Yale University Press, 2002), has argued against critical election or realignment theory, including the so-called System of 1896. Mayhew makes some telling points about certain parts of the theory, but the 1896 (and 1894) election brought changes in voter behavior and party and governmental policies that argue strongly for the continued usefulness of the theory.

22 *New York World*, November 4, 1896; Bryan, *First Battle*, 605.

23 Bryan to McKinley, November 5, 1896, in Bryan, *First Battle*, 605. McKinley wired back: "I acknowledge receipt of your courteous message of congratulations, with thanks, and beg you to receive my best wishes for your health and happiness." McKinley to Bryan, November 6, 1896, *Brooklyn Daily Eagle*, November 7, 1896.

24 Daniels to Bryan, telegram, November 4, 1896, Bryan Papers; *St. Louis Post-Dispatch*, November 6, 1896. Also, *Raleigh (N.C.) Caucasian*, November 12, 1896.

25 Robert McElroy, *Grover Cleveland: The Man and the Statesman*, 2 vols. (New York: Harper & Bros., 1923), 2:237; *New York World*, November 3, 6, 1896; Coletta, *William Jennings Bryan*, 1:197; Gilbert C. Fite, "William Jennings Bryan and the Campaign of 1896: Some Views and Problems," *Nebraska History* 47 (September 1966): 247–264; *San Francisco Examiner*, November 11, 1896. Arthur Wallace Dunn, a contemporary, put it well, noting how bleak the outlook for the Democrats had been before the election: "If any one had said in 1895 that the next Democratic candidate would receive 6,500,000 votes, a million more than had ever been given to any other Democratic candidate, that person would have been declared insane." Arthur Wallace Dunn, *From Harrison to Harding: A Personal Narrative, Covering a Third of a Century, 1888–1921*, 2 vols. (New York: G. P. Putnam's Sons, 1932), 1:151.

26 *People's Party Paper*, November 13, 1896; Paul W. Glad, *McKinley, Bryan, and the People* (Philadelphia: J. B. Lippincott, 1964), 197.

27 Entry for March 4, 1897, in Festus P. Summers, ed., *Cabinet Diary of William L. Wilson, 1896–1897* (Chapel Hill: University of North Carolina Press, 1957), 246–250; *Chicago Tribune*, March 3–5, 1897; *Raleigh News and Observer*, March 5, 1897; *San Francisco Examiner*, March 4, 1897.

28 Degler, "American Political Parties and the Rise of the City," 41–49.

29 Steevens, *Land of the Dollar*, 274–295.

CHAPTER 9 MCKINLEY'S AMERICA: THE ELECTION'S AFTERMATH

1 *San Francisco Examiner*, March 4, 1897.

2 George F. Parker, *Recollections of Grover Cleveland* (New York: Century, 1911), 250.

3   *Woman's Exponent*, December 15, 1896, mediacloisters.vassar.edu:9080/news-spirits/1896, accessed on July 15, 2008.

4   *San Francisco Examiner*, March 4, 1897; Margaret Leech, *In the Days of McKinley* (New York: Harper, 1959), 117.

5   Douglas W. Steeples and David O. Whitten, *Democracy in Desperation: The Depression of 1893* (Westport, Conn.: Greenwood Publishers, 1998), 188. The Dingley Act also provided, as the McKinley Act had, for reciprocity agreements with other countries that would lower rates where appropriate.

6   R. Hal Williams, *Years of Decision: American Politics in the 1890s* (New York: John Wiley & Sons, 1973), 130; H. Wayne Morgan, *William McKinley and His America* (Syracuse, N.Y.: Syracuse University Press, 1963), 303–325; William H. Crook, *Memories of the White House: The Home Life of Our Presidents from Lincoln to Roosevelt* (Boston: Little, Brown, 1911), 244–250.

7   *Review of Reviews* 23 (November 1900): 550; Lewis L. Gould, *The Presidency of William McKinley* (Lawrence: Regents Press of Kansas, 1980), 229.

8   Bryan to McKinley, November 8, 1900, William McKinley Papers, Manuscript Division, Library of Congress, Washington, D.C.; *New York Times*, November 7–9, 1900; William Jennings Bryan, "The Election of 1900," *North American Review* 71 (December 1900): 789; Walter LaFeber, "Election of 1900," in Arthur M. Schlesinger Jr., ed., *History of American Presidential Elections, 1789–1968*, 4 vols. (New York: Facts on File, 1971), 3:1877–1917.

9   Gould, *Presidency of William McKinley*, vii. Had he lived, McKinley planned in his second term to travel abroad—possibly to Haiti, Puerto Rico, and Cuba—which would have made him the first president to do so: ibid., 243.

10   Cleveland to Olney, January 16, 1898, in Allan Nevins, ed., *Letters of Grover Cleveland* (Boston: Houghton Mifflin, 1933), 491.

11   Allan Nevins, *Grover Cleveland: A Study in Courage* (New York: Dodd, Mead, 1932), 745–746.

12   Cleveland to Judson B. Harmon, July 17, 1900, in Nevins, *Letters of Grover Cleveland*, 532–533; Morton to Cleveland, November 2, 1900, Grover Cleveland Papers, Manuscript Division, Library of Congress, Washington, D.C.

13   Nevins, *Grover Cleveland*, 763.

14   R. Hal Williams, "'Dry Bones and Dead Language': The Democratic Party," in H. Wayne Morgan, ed., *The Gilded Age: Revised and Enlarged Edition* (Syracuse, N.Y.: Syracuse University Press, 1970), 129–148.

15   On Wilson, see Arthur S. Link, *Wilson: The New Freedom* (Princeton, N.J.: Princeton University Press, 1956). Michael Kazin, *A Godly Hero: The Life of William Jennings Bryan* (New York: Knopf, 2006), makes a persuasive case for Bryan's role in the change. For a broader statement of the meaning of the election for the Democrats, see Richard P. Bland, "The Duty of the Hour," *North American Review* 478 (September 1896): 370–371. David B. Hill, "The Future of the Democratic Organization," *Forum* 22 (February 1897): 641–658, argued forcefully for a return to older ways of thinking, an argument Hill did not win.

16   Robert W. Cherny, *A Righteous Cause: The Life of William Jennings Bryan* (Norman: University of Oklahoma Press, 1994), 71; Paxton Hibben, *The Peerless*

Leader: William Jennings Bryan (New York: Farrar and Rinehart, 1929), 207; *Raleigh (N.C.) Caucasian*, November 12, 1896.

17 John A. Garraty, *Henry Cabot Lodge: A Biography* (New York: Knopf, 1965), 176. Had Massachusetts allowed women to vote in 1896, Nannie Lodge undoubtedly would have voted for McKinley—and there were those words again: *crusader, fanatic, prophet.* For her husband's views, see Henry Cabot Lodge, "The Meaning of the Votes," *North American Review* 164 (January 1897): 1–11.

18 William Jennings Bryan, "Has the Election Settled the Money Question?" *North American Review* 481 (December 1896): 703–710; J. Rogers Hollingsworth, *The Whirligig of Politics: The Democracy of Cleveland and Bryan* (Chicago: University of Chicago Press, 1963), 109–112; Paolo E. Coletta, *William Jennings Bryan*, vol. 1, *Political Evangelist, 1860–1908* (Lincoln: University of Nebraska Press, 1964), 1:188.

19 *New York Times*, October 29, 1897, in Louis W. Koenig, *Bryan: A Political Biography of William Jennings Bryan* (New York: Putnam, 1971), 264; Richard Hofstadter, *The American Political Tradition and the Men Who Made It* (New York: Knopf, 1973), 194; William Jennings Bryan, *The Memoirs of William Jennings Bryan, by Himself and His Wife Mary Baird Bryan* (Philadelphia: United Publishers of America, 1925), 123–124.

20 During the 1960s and 1970s, opponents of the war in Vietnam found fresh respect for Bryan, using his example to urge members of the administration of Lyndon B. Johnson to resign in principle, as Bryan had, to protest against the war.

21 Henry Luther Stoddard, *As I Knew Them: Presidents and Politics from Grant to Coolidge* (New York: Harper & Bros., 1927), 273.

22 "Bryan, Bryan, Bryan, Bryan," Vachel Lindsay, *Collected Poems* (New York: Macmillan, 1925), 96–105.

23 Entry for August 21, 1897, Charles G. Dawes, *A Journal of the McKinley Years* (Chicago: Lakeside Press, 1950), 126.

24 Mark Sullivan, *Our Times: The United States, 1900–1925*, 2 vols. (New York: Charles Scribner's Sons, 1926), 1:156–157; Milton Friedman and Anna Jacobson Schwartz, *A Monetary History of the United States, 1867–1960* (Princeton, N.J.: Princeton University Press, 1963), 8; John D. Hicks, *The Populist Revolt: A History of the Farmer's Alliance and the People's Party* (Lincoln: University of Nebraska Press, 1961), 389. In 1890, the world's annual production of gold had amounted to $118,848,700; by 1899, it was $306,724,100.

25 Charles Postel, *The Populist Vision* (New York: Oxford University Press, 2007), 276; Steeples and Whitten, *Democracy in Desperation*, 5–6.

26 William McKinley, *Speeches and Addresses of William McKinley, March 1, 1897 to May 30, 1900* (New York: Doubleday & McClure, 1900), 237, 256, 331; Gretchen Ritter, *Goldbugs and Greenbacks: The Antimonopoly Tradition and the Politics of Finance in America, 1865–1896* (New York: Cambridge University Press, 1999), 61.

27 *Representative*, March 3, 1897, in Hicks, *Populist Revolt*, 388.

28 J. Q. White to Allen, July 8, 1897, Allen Papers, in Hicks, *Populist Revolt*, 387;

Ottawa Journal, April 14, 1898, in Walter T. K. Nugent, *The Tolerant Populists: Kansas Populism and Nativism* (Chicago: University of Chicago Press, 1963), 219.

29 C. Vann Woodward, *Tom Watson: Agrarian Rebel* (New York: Macmillan, 1938), 289.

30 Ibid., 309–310, 347.

31 Nugent, *Tolerant Populists,* 84.

32 O. Gene Clanton, *Kansas Populism: Ideas and Men* (Lawrence: University Press of Kansas, 1969), 238.

33 Richard Stiller, *Queen of Populists: The Story of Mary Elizabeth Lease* (New York: Thomas Y. Crowell, 1970), 212–221.

34 Woodward, *Watson,* 290–291; Barton C. Shaw, *The Wool-Hat Boys: Georgia's Populist Party* (Baton Rouge: Louisiana State University Press, 1984), 183, 212.

35 *Tom Watson's Magazine* 1 (June 1905), 298, in Woodward, *Watson,* 328–329; Shaw, *The Wool-Hat Boys,* 211, italics in the original.

36 Woodward, *Watson,* 420–421.

37 Morgan, *William McKinley and His America,* 516.

38 Ibid., 520–526; Stoddard, *As I Knew Them,* 230–231.

39 Eric Rauchway, *Murdering McKinley: The Making of Theodore Roosevelt's America* (New York: Hill & Wang, 2003), 3–11; "Medical Bulletins," http://www.eriebar .org, accessed on November 17, 2008.

40 According to the testimony in the trial of the assassin, a bystander thought McKinley actually said, "Be easy with him, boys." *Buffalo Commercial,* September 24, 1901, "Lights Out in the City of Light: Anarchy and Assassination at the Pan-American Exposition," http://www.eriebar.org, accessed on November 17, 2008.

41 H. Wayne Morgan, "William McKinley," in Phillip Weeks, *Buckeye Presidents: Ohioans in the White House* (Kent, Ohio: Kent State University Press, 2003), 209–210.

42 William Allen White, *Masks in a Pageant* (New York: Macmillan, 1930), 185–186.

43 Dawes, *Journal of the McKinley Years,* 275–281; Gould, *Presidency of William McKinley,* 251–252; Leech, *In the Days of McKinley,* 600–601.

44 Entries for September 13–21, 1901, Dawes, *Journal of the McKinley Years,* 281.

45 Gould, *Presidency of William McKinley,* 252. Hanna himself died from typhoid fever on February 15, 1904: *New York Times,* February 16, 1904.

46 Henry H. Kohlsaat, *From McKinley to Harding: Personal Recollections of Our Presidents* (New York: Charles Scribner's Sons, 1923), 157.

47 Michael McGerr, "Political Style and Women's Power, 1830–1930," *Journal of American History* 77 (December 1990): 869; Michael McGerr, *The Decline of Popular Politics* (New York, 1986), 184–210; Richard Jensen, "Armies, Admen, and Crusaders," *History Teacher* 2, no. 2 (January 1969): 33–50; Jensen, *The Winning of the Midwest: Social and Political Conflict, 1888–1896* (Chicago: University of Chicago Press, 1971), 175.

48   Robert H. Wiebe, *Self-Rule: A Cultural History of American Democracy* (Chicago: University of Chicago Press, 1995), 71.

49   Mark Lawrence Kornbluh, *Why America Stopped Voting: The Decline of Participatory Democracy and the Emergence of Modern American Politics* (New York: New York University Press, 2000), 89–90, 97–99; William E. Gienapp, "'Politics Seem to Enter into Everything': Political Culture in the North, 1840–1860," in Stephen E. Maizlish and John G. Kushma, eds., *Essays in American Antebellum Politics, 1840–1860* (College Station: Texas A&M University Press, 1982), 20–21.

50   LaFeber, "Election of 1900," in Schlesinger, *History of American Presidential Elections*, 3:1878; Paul Kleppner, *Who Voted? The Dynamics of Electoral Turnout, 1870–1980* (Westport, Conn.: Greenwood Publishing Group, 1981), 55.

51   Quoted in Kleppner, *Who Voted?* 55.

52   Lionel E. Fredman, *The Australian Ballot: The Story of an American Reform* (East Lansing: University of Michigan Press, 1968), 83–84.

53   McGerr, *Decline of Popular Politics*, 152, 177.

54   Kornbluh, *Why America Stopped Voting*, 111–115.

55   Francis Russell, *Shadow of Blooming Grove: Warren G. Harding in His Times* (New York: McGraw-Hill, 1968), 398–418; Samuel Hopkins Adams, *Incredible Era: The Life and Times of Warren Gamaliel Harding* (Boston: Houghton Mifflin, 1939), 170–178; Donald R. McCoy, "Election of 1920," in Schlesinger, *History of American Presidential Elections*, 3:2370–2385.

56   Joshua Green, "The Rove Presidency," *Atlantic*, September 2007, 52–72; James Traub, "The Submerging Republican Majority," *New York Times Magazine*, June 18, 2006; Dan Balz, "Karl Rove: The Strategist," *Washington Post*, July 23, 1999.

BIBLIOGRAPHIC ESSAY

The presidential election of 1896—and the people, issues, and parties involved in it—has long been a subject of fascination among historians and the general public. And no wonder: the election was important, it enlisted vivid personalities, it focused on intriguing issues, and its significance was long-lasting. What follows are some of the sources I found most useful in writing this book, selected to guide those interested in further reading on the election and the events surrounding it.

The personal papers of both major presidential candidates, William McKinley and William Jennings Bryan, have been indexed and microfilmed, and they are quite easy to use. So, too, are the papers of Grover Cleveland, essential for an understanding of the challenges he and the Democratic party faced during the decade of the 1890s. The papers of other figures prominent in the decade's events, including Benjamin Harrison, Daniel S. Lamont, Richard Olney, John Sherman, Matthew S. Quay, William C. Whitney, James S. Clarkson, and Donald M. Dickinson, are in the Manuscript Division of the Library of Congress, in Washington, D.C.

Fortunately, the published sources on the 1896 election are numerous, including Allan Nevins, ed., *The Letters of Grover Cleveland* (Boston: Houghton Mifflin, 1933), which offers Cleveland's thoughts on the events of his presidency and the growing discontent in his own party. William Jennings Bryan, *The First Battle: A Story of the Campaign of 1896* (Chicago: W. B. Conkey, 1896), covers in detail Bryan's campaign travels and speeches in 1896. William McKinley's letters have not yet been published, though it is to be hoped that they soon will be.

In a presidential year, decisions at the parties' national conventions are important, and for this year, we have official accounts of two of them: *The Official Proceedings of the Eleventh Republican National Convention, Held in the City of St. Louis, Mo., June 16, 17, and 18, 1896* (n.p.: C. W. Johnson, 1896), details the adoption of the gold platform, the dramatic walkout of the silver Republicans, and the nomination of McKinley; *The Official Proceedings of the Democratic National Convention* (Logansport, Ind.: Wilson, Humphreys, 1896), follows the fight in Chicago between the supporters of gold and silver and Bryan's famous speech. The People's party chose not to issue its own official proceedings, so events at that convention require careful scrutiny of contemporary newspapers, memoirs, and other sources.

There are several helpful accounts of the 1896 election. The most detailed is Stanley L. Jones, *The Presidential Election of 1896* (Madison: University of Wisconsin Press, 1964), which has long been the standard work on the election. Paul W. Glad, *McKinley, Bryan, and the People* (Philadelphia: J. B. Lippincott, 1964), is balanced and thoughtful; Gilbert C. Fite, "Election of 1896," in Arthur M. Schlesinger Jr., ed., *History of American Presidential Elections, 1789–1968*, 4 vols. (New York: Chelsea House Publishers, 1971), 2:1787–1873, is a helpful brief overview; Richard Franklin Bensel, *Passion and Preferences: William Jennings Bryan and the 1896 Democratic National Convention* (Cambridge: Cambridge University Press, 2008), a recent account, offers a great deal of detail on events and personalities at the convention; and Robert F.

Durden, *The Climax of Populism: The Election of 1896* (Lexington: University Press of Kentucky, 1965), is superb on the Populist-Democratic efforts at fusion.

Among the studies that set the elections of the 1890s in a larger context, the best include H. Wayne Morgan, *From Hayes to McKinley: National Party Politics, 1877–1896* (Syracuse, N.Y.: Syracuse University Press, 1969), which is both perceptive and a pleasure to read; Richard Jensen, *The Winning of the Midwest: Social and Political Conflict, 1888–1896* (Chicago: University of Chicago Press, 1971), an important book that traces political developments in that crucial region; Robert D. Marcus, *Grand Old Party: Political Structure in the Gilded Age, 1880–1896* (New York: Oxford University Press, 1971), which looks at Republican party organization over several decades; Paul Kleppner, *Continuity and Change in Electoral Politics, 1893–1928* (Westport, Conn.: Greenwood Press, 1987), and Kleppner, *The Cross of Culture: A Social Analysis of Midwestern Politics, 1850–1900* (New York: Free Press, 1970), which both analyze underlying patterns in American politics; and Samuel T. McSeveney, *The Politics of Depression: Political Behavior in the Northeast, 1893–1896* (New York: Oxford University Press, 1972), which skillfully uses quantitative data to probe deeply into political trends.

Michael E. McGerr, *The Decline of Popular Politics: The American North, 1865–1928* (New York: Oxford University Press, 1986), and Mark Lawrence Kornbluh, *Why America Stopped Voting: The Decline of Participatory Democracy and the Emergence of Modern American Politics* (New York: New York University Press, 2000), look at the dramatic falloff in voting. Morton Keller, *America's Three Regimes: A New Political History* (Oxford: Oxford University Press, 2007), is a new and stimulating interpretation. Charles W. Calhoun's masterful *Conceiving a New Republic: The Republican Party and the Southern Question, 1869–1900* (Lawrence: University Press of Kansas, 2006), places Republican doctrines in the context of the party's defining issues.

Biographies are useful in learning more about the individuals involved in the 1896 election. Allan Nevins, *Grover Cleveland: A Study in Courage* (New York: Dodd, Mead, 1932), is biased in favor of Cleveland but remains the best biography. Richard E. Welch Jr., *The Presidencies of Grover Cleveland* (Lawrence: University Press of Kansas, 1988), is a balanced study by a master historian of Cleveland's two administrations. More critical is Horace Samuel Merrill, *Bourbon Leader: Grover Cleveland and the Democratic Party* (Boston: Little, Brown, 1957). Robert McElroy, *Grover Cleveland: The Man and the Statesman*, 2 vols. (New York: Harper & Bros., 1937), offers considerable detail. George Parker, *Recollections of Grover Cleveland* (New York: Century, 1911), is a helpful memoir from someone who knew him.

William McKinley, one of the nation's most important presidents, has received superb attention in H. Wayne Morgan, *William McKinley and His America* (Syracuse, N.Y.: Syracuse University Press, 1963; reissued in a revised edition by Kent State University Press, 2004), a full-scale biography, and Lewis L. Gould, *The Presidency of William McKinley* (Lawrence: University Press of Kansas, 1980), which examines in rewarding fashion the presidential years. An older study, Margaret Leech, *In the Days of McKinley* (New York: Harper & Bros., 1959), is useful for lively and anecdotal material on the Major's life. William McKinley, *Speeches and Addresses of William McKinley from March 1, 1897 to May 30, 1900* (New York: Appleton, 1900), provides a sense of his presidential authority and style.

William Jennings Bryan was a central figure in American political life from his campaigns in the 1890s to his death in 1925. The best multivolume biography of him remains Paolo E. Coletta, *William Jennings Bryan*, 3 vols. (Lincoln: University of Nebraska Press, 1964–1969), which, however, is now dated. Michael Kazin, *A Godly Hero: The Life of William Jennings Bryan* (New York: Knopf, 2006), the most recent study, is superb and suggestive. Louis William Koenig, *Bryan: A Political Biography of William Jennings Bryan* (New York: G. P. Putnam's Sons, 1971), is a good one-volume treatment, though readers must look elsewhere for analysis of the Republican opposition and the workings of politics in the decade. Paul W. Glad, *The Trumpet Soundeth: William Jennings Bryan and His Democracy, 1896–1912* (Lincoln: University of Nebraska Press, 1960), is helpful. Lawrence W. Levine, *Defender of the Faith: William Jennings Bryan—The Last Decade, 1915–1925* (New York: Oxford University Press, 1965), is an eloquent look at Bryan's final years. Robert W. Cherny, *A Righteous Cause: The Life of William Jennings Bryan* (Boston: Little, Brown, 1985), is an excellent account. Bryan offered his own interpretations, with his wife Mary Bryan, in *Memoirs of William Jennings Bryan* (Philadelphia: John C. Winston, 1925), which, like Bryan himself, does not probe deeply but provides some important insights.

The literature on the Farmers' Alliance and People's party is vast, though uneven. John D. Hicks, *The Populist Revolt: A History of the Farmers' Alliance and the People's Party* (Minneapolis: University of Minnesota Press, 1931), one of the first accounts, is dated but still has value. Lawrence Goodwyn, *Democratic Promise: The Populist Moment in America* (New York: Oxford University Press, 1976), is a provocative account whose findings, though questioned by other scholars, still reward examination. Steven Hahn, *The Roots of Southern Populism: Yeoman Farmers and the Transformation of the Georgia Upcountry, 1850–1890* (New York: Oxford University Press, 1983), treats the effect on southern farmers of the movement from diversified crops to cotton. Also useful are Robert C. McMath Jr., *American Populism: A Social History, 1877–1898* (New York: Hill & Wang, 1993); McMath, *The Populist Vanguard: A History of the Southern Farmers' Alliance* (Chapel Hill: University of North Carolina Press, 1975); and Walter T. K. Nugent, *The Tolerant Populists: Kansas Populism and Nativism* (Chicago: University of Chicago Press, 1963), which is a careful response to Richard Hofstedter's *The Age of Reform: From Bryan to FDR* (New York: Random House, 1955). Charles Postel, *The Populist Vision* (New York: Oxford University Press, 2007), is a recent and helpful addition to the literature. Rebecca Edwards, *Angels in the Machinery: Gender in American Party Politics from the Civil War to the Progressive Era* (New York: Oxford University Press, 1997), points to the importance of women in the Populist movement.

There are numerous studies of Populism in specific states and regions, some of the best of which include Sheldon Hackney, *Populism to Progressivism in Alabama* (Princeton, N.J.: Princeton University Press, 1969); James E. Wright, *The Politics of Populism: Dissent in Colorado* (New Haven, Conn.: Yale University Press, 1974); and O. Gene Clanton, *Kansas Populism: Ideas and Men* (Lawrence: University Press of Kansas, 1969). One of the best of the historians of Populism, Clanton has also published *A Common Humanity: Kansas Populism and the Battle for Justice and Equality, 1854–1903* (Manhattan, Kans.: Sunflower University Press, 2004, an updated version of his book on Kansas Populism); *Populism: The Humane Preference in America, 1890–1900* (Boston: Twayne Publishers, 1991); and *Congressional Populism and the Crisis of the 1890s* (Lawrence: University Press of Kansas, 1999). Jeffrey Ostler, *Prairie Populism: The Fate of Agrarian Radicalism in Kansas, Nebraska, and Iowa, 1880–1892*

(Lawrence: University Press of Kansas, 1993); Peter H. Argersinger, *The Limits of Agrarian Radicalism: Western Populism and American Politics* (Lawrence: University Press of Kansas, 1995); and Stanley B. Parsons, *The Populist Context: Rural versus Urban Power on a Great Plains Frontier* (Westport, Conn.: Greenwood Press, 1973), are also helpful.

Biographies of important Populist figures include C. Vann Woodward's classic *Tom Watson: Agrarian Rebel* (New York: Macmillan, 1938), a model of the way a biography can be written. Martin Ridge, *Ignatius Donnelly: The Portrait of a Politician* (Chicago: University of Chicago Press, 1962), covers that eccentric figure. Peter H. Argersinger, *Populism and Politics: William Alfred Peffer and the People's Party* (Lexington: University Press of Kentucky, 1974), is superb on Peffer, one of the party's most important leaders, an editor and U.S. senator. James L. Hunt, *Marion Butler and American Populism* (Chapel Hill: University of North Carolina Press, 2003), is a recent biography of that up-and-coming figure.

There are good, though dated, biographies of leading Democrats and Republicans who played prominent roles in the 1896 election. On the Democratic side, they include Mark D. Hirsch, *William C. Whitney: Modern Warwick* (New York: Dodd, Mead, 1948); James Anderson Barnes, *John G. Carlisle, Financial Statesman* (New York: Dodd, Mead, 1931); John R. Lambert, *Arthur Pue Gorman* (Baton Rouge: Louisiana State University Press, 1953); Herbert J. Bass, *"I Am a Democrat": The Political Career of David Bennett Hill* (Syracuse, N.Y.: Syracuse University Press, 1961); and Festus P. Summers, *William L. Wilson and Tariff Reform: A Biography* (New Brunswick, N.J.: Rutgers University Press, 1953).

Leading Republicans receive treatment in James A. Kehl, *Boss Rule in the Gilded Age: Matt Quay of Pennsylvania* (Pittsburgh, Pa.: University of Pittsburgh Press, 1981); Leland L. Sage, *William Boyd Allison: A Study in Practical Politics* (Iowa City: State Historical Society of Iowa, 1956); Samuel W. McCall, *The Life of Thomas Brackett Reed* (Boston: Houghton Mifflin, 1914); and William A. Robinson, *Thomas B. Reed, Parliamentarian* (New York: Dodd, Mead, 1930). Reed, an important figure in the period, deserves a fresh biography, as does McKinley's friend and campaign manager, Mark Hanna. Herbert David Croly, *Marcus Alonzo Hanna: His Life and Work* (New York: Macmillan, 1912), and Thomas Beer, *Hanna* (New York: Knopf, 1929), remain the standard works.

There are already helpful Internet sources on the election, which will of course grow in number. A Web site containing political cartoons and songs, as well as biographies of the major players, can be found at http://projects.vassar.edu/1896/1896home .html. The text of Bryan's famous "Cross of Gold" speech, along with a recording he made of the speech in 1921, is at http://historymatters.gmu.edu/d/5354/. The homepage of the McKinley Museum, a wealth of information on McKinley, his life, and his presidency, is at http://www.mckinley.lib.oh.us/McKinley/biography.htm, along with a link to Ohio Memory (http://www.ohiomemory.org/). A recording of a McKinley speech in Canton during the famed Front Porch Campaign is at http://www.youtube.com/watch?v=m6ZUneyU7Vo. For an overview of the People's party and its role in the 1896 campaign, see the detailed site at Missouri State University: http://history.missouristate.edu/wrmiller/Populism/Texts/populism.htm.

INDEX

National Silver party, 98, 110, 125
Naturalization laws, 192–193
Navy, upbuilding, 193
New Deal, 108, 166
New Orleans Picayune, 97
New York City, returns for, 147, 149
New York City Board of Education, 165
New York Evening Post, 59, 97
New York Herald, 97
New York Journal, 53, 88, 90, 97
New York Life Insurance Company, 137
New York Sun, 97, 119
New York Times, 77, 86, 138
New York Tribune, 56, 72, 145, 147
New York World, 83, 88, 96, 97, 147, 165
North American Review, 162
Northern Pacific Railroad, 28, 33, 130
Norton, Seymour F., 114, 117

Olney, Richard, 27, 40–41, 122, 160
Orcutt, Susan, 67–68
Osborne, William McKinley, 49, 136

Palmer, John M., 123, 124, 150
Pan-American Exposition, 67
Panic of 1893, xii, 27–29, 31, 51
  photo of, 30
Parades, 145
  photo of, 135
  torchlight, 4, 9–10, 137, 138
Partisan competition, 21, 169
Partisan loyalty, 4, 5, 68, 168
  ruptured, 15, 103, 169
Party system, 8, 10
  change in, xi, 169, 170, 199n23
Patriotism, 105, 138, 139, 189, 192, 193
Pattison, Robert E., 72, 121, 217n83
Peffer, William A., 18, 113, 126, 127, 164
  on Populists, 112
  silver and, 111
Pennoyer, Robert E., 217n83
People's party, 19, 98, 118, 128, 204n4
  Bryan Democrats and, 116
  challenge of, 22
  decline of, 23, 164–165

defeat of, 23, 46
reforms by, 116
Republican party and, 17
rise of, 44
success for, 155
See also Populists
People's Party Paper, 117
Philadelphia and Reading Railroad, 27
Philadelphia Centennial Exposition
  (1876), 25
Philadelphia Record, 97
Philadelphia Times, 97
Platt, Thomas Collier, 49, 55, 56, 57
  gold and, 60
  McKinley and, 59, 61, 136
  politics and, 47, 48
Politics, 4, 5, 8, 69, 99, 192
  changes in, xi, 168, 169, 170
  educational style and, 168
  language of, 9
  military-style, 4, 9–10, 102, 137, 143, 145
  power and, 153
Polk, James, 19
Polk, Leonidas L., 16, 22, 113
Populism, xiii, 89, 126
  cartoon about, 120 (fig.)
Populist national convention, 110, 112,
  114–115, 117, 165
Populists, 42, 63, 74, 75, 79, 82, 90, 98,
  119, 166, 204n4, 225n59
  Bryan and, 81, 112, 113–114, 116
  Bryan Democrats and, 116, 117
  campaign by, 22, 225n57
  criticism of, 32
  decline of, 39, 164–165
  defeat of, 23, 43–44
  Democratic party and, 71, 111, 125
  Far West and, 22–23
  foreign policy and, 165
  party system and, 170
  reforms and, 115–116
  Republican party and, 29, 110–111
  rise of, 44, 154–155
  silver and, 111
  silver Democrats and, 113